The system of GULAG (Main Camp Administration) was subdivided in ten regions. In each of the regions the numbering of hard labour prison camps began with 1. Jānis Dreifelds and Aleksandrs Kalnietis were imprisoned in the following camps:

Jānis Dreifelds:
II—42 Yukhnovo; IV—24 Vyatlag (area of Vyatka/Kirov).

Aleksandrs Kalnietis:
I—22 Sevdvinlag (area of Velsk); IV—3 Ustvymlag (Komi Autonomous Republic); IV—5 Pechorlag (area of Pechora River).

With Dance Shoes in Siberian Snows

By Sandra Kalniete

With Dance Shoes in Siberian Snows

By Sandra Kalniete

Translated by
Margita Gailītis

Rīga 2006
Latvijas Okupācijas muzeja biedrība

SANDRA KALNIETE

WITH DANCE SHOES IN SIBERIAN SNOWS

Translated by Margita Gailītis
Foreword by Valters Nollendorfs

Rīga: Latvijas Okupācijas muzeja biedrība 2006
367 pages

Original publication in Latvian:
Ar balles kurpēm Sibīrijas sniegos
(Rīga: Atēna, 2001)

The English version includes subsequent changes and additions by the author.

All illustrations from the private archive of the author.
GULAG map by Ļevs Domburs and Ruta Ozoliņa (Rīga: Memorial, 1993)

Financial assistance:
Latvijas Kultūrkapitāla Fonds
Latviešu Nacionālā Apvienība Kanādā (LNAK)

Text Editor: Valters Nollendorfs
Cover and Book Design: Juris Petraškevičs
Computer Layout: Oskars Stalidzans
Historical Consultant: Ainars Bambals

Museum of the Occupation of Latvia,
Strēlnieku laukums 1, Rīga, LV-1050, Latvia
www.occupationmuseum.lv

ISBN 9984-9613-7-0

Contents

Foreword

I think that I am here, on this earth,
To present a report on it, but to whom I don't know.
As if I were sent so that whatever takes place
Has meaning because it changes into memory.

– Czeslaw Milosz, "Consciousness"

In my childhood, the past was only mentioned in connection with household incidents and family events, but almost never in its political or historical significance. I grew up under the influence of Soviet propaganda, knowing almost nothing about the real history of Latvia. The latter was totally buried in silence. This self-imposed censorship mirrors the desire of my parents not to complicate the life of their child with unanswerable questions and dangerous doubts. Above all, they wanted to protect me from a repetition of their own tragic fate.

– Sandra Kalniete, "With Dance Shoes in Siberian Snows"

"Constructing memory" could very well be the subtitle of this book. When I first read it, that is what struck me about it: the meticulous, even merciless, construction of memory that never was. Its style, introspective, involuted, at times willful, that the translator has attempted to emulate, betrays the labours of the mind. Imagine – at the age of thirty-five you suddenly discover that your memory is badly flawed: its private building blocks do not fit together with the public ones. The mortar is crumbling. There are gaping holes all over. At first you are afraid to make the slightest move, lest it collapse. Then you move, and it collapses, but the very collapse allows you to start constructing anew.

That is what Sandra Kalniete discovered in 1987, when a small group of Latvian dissidents held the first public demonstrations protesting Soviet deportations by placing flowers at the Freedom Monument in Rīga. She says: "I did not have enough courage to leave the silent crowd of sympathisers and cross the street while the Soviet militiamen and Chekists watched. I hate myself for it, but that's what I was like – having soaked up the invisible fear of my deported family. It is precisely in these days at the Freedom Monument that my sense of freedom was reborn."

Kalniete's reborn sense of freedom enabled her not only to commemorate, but to become one of the leaders in the Latvian struggle to renew their independence. She has described her work in the Latvian Popular Front during the heady days of the non-violent Singing Revolution in her first book *Es lauzu, tu lauzi, mēs lauzām, viņi lūza* (*I Broke Them, You Broke Them, We Broke Them, They Broke Apart*). Overcoming intimidation and inculcated fear, a critical mass numbering hundreds of thousands joined the Singing Revolution, and the Soviet Communist order with its ideological constructs and the Soviet Union itself fell apart. The wave carried Sandra Kalniete, educated as an Art Historian, to diplomatic service of the renewed state. She became Ambassador, Foreign Minister, lastly – European Commissioner when Latvia joined the European Union.

Deconstructing the distorted and deceitful Soviet history and reconstructing the hidden and forbidden history of the Latvian state and people was relatively easy. The gaping discrepancy between the official version and the remembered one was too obvious. Soviet complicity with Nazi Germany in the occupation before the war was too perfidious. It was the history-building task of the entire nation, which would not have been possible without the building blocks in the collective memory ready to be put back in place. For Sandra Kalniete, however, a much more difficult task lay ahead: constructing her own family's past. Why was she born in Siberia? Who were her ancestors? Parts of the past were not there. And she set about finding them.

In an interview she admitted: "When I began writing this book, I had only general knowledge of what it was all about. I carried the idea for a long time without deciding whether I would actually write it. Then one day, absolutely spontaneously, the introductory paragraph, as it were, appeared on paper. … When I saw it finished, I understood that I was mentally ready for the book. Then I began to do the research." There were memoirs about Siberia and the newest historical research in Latvia and in the West, all carefully documented in the book. "When I had agonized through it all – a kind of Kafkaesque labyrinth – I knew what to search for and went to the archive."

Thus began the piecing together of a complex construction – her family's story as part of the nation's history. For Kalniete's family indeed is a microcosm of the nation and its history in the twentieth century. The Latvian lands as parts of the Russian Empire; World War I; battling for and building independent Latvia; Soviet occupation; arrests and deportations; Nazi German occupation; the Holocaust; refugees to the West as the second Soviet occupation threatens; partisan war against the Soviet occupants; more arrests and deportations; finally liberation and independence once more. One look at the family tree says it all just by looking at the place names: many Latvian ones, but Russian ones as well, then – Belgium, Canada, England, Germany, denoting births, deaths and dislocations. A family and a nation – scattered between the East and the West and, miraculously, even still in Latvia. Cryptic notations denoting violence and tragedy: "Missing without trace," "Missing without trace in Russia, "Deported to Siberia," "Deported to Siberia," "Deported to Siberia," "Deported to Siberia," "Deported to Siberia," "Arrested," "Death in Vyatlag," "Death in Tomsk region," "Death in Pechorlag."

Soviet criminal records, no matter how bizarre the contents, allow constructing the past of some of those who were caught in the machinery of the Cheka, as it is still called in Latvia, or KGB, as it is known in the West. Errors abound. Preordained results of interrogations and court cases. A shocking discovery: "... my mother and grandmother do not have their personal records. Their cases are bound in my grandfather's case file. My father and his mother, too, are not treated as individuals but as family members of a 'bandit' – classified according to group." The dehumanising nature of the system is revealed page, by page, by page of documents on matters of life and death written in stilted, emotionless Soviet bureaucratese. In Russian, of course.

Constructing the past as a nation's history is difficult. Constructing personal memory is a torturous task. Each discovery is more shocking and painful than the previous one. It is so painful that there is a great temptation to hide behind a mere recounting of facts: "I had the problem to prevent the dry, rational aspects from stifling the subjective ones," Kalniete says. Yet she admits at the same time: "It was most difficult to distance myself." Indeed there is a creative tension between the documentation – the objective recording of facts – and the subjective need to re-experience lives: "I re-created for myself, as it were, both of my dead grandfathers and grandmother, whom I had never seen." That re-creation forced Kalniete to delve into the world of empathy, where no records exist. She dies with her grandfather Jānis in Vyatlag; she dies with her grandmother Emilija in a cow barn in the Siberian village of Togur; and she dies with her grandfather Aleksandrs in Pechorlag. She suffers deprivation and starvation with her mother and grandmother in Siberia. Is it just imagination? Can we trust subjectively recreated existential conditions? Kalniete answers by quoting her mother's words after reading the chapter "Forced Settlement and Starvation": "How could you know how I felt at that time?" Kalniete concludes: "After I heard those words, I no longer cared what anyone else says." How could anyone dare?

What makes reconstructed events and emotions communicable to the reader? What makes us accept as believable events and emotions so far removed from our everyday reality? As I read and later edited the book, I asked this question time and again. I think the answer lies in the fact that Kalniete leads us by hand, Dante-like, as it were, into the labyrinthine abyss of the Siberian and GULAG experience and then out of it again. It is her time travel of discovery that leads her and us from the objective distance of our time and documented history to the subjective re-experience of past time beyond documents and the safety of our own protected lives. The ancient Greeks called it catharsis, the experience of common humanity in tragedy that makes sense of suffering through empathy and allows life to continue.

Yet it is not all about suffering and death. The book's ultimate message is rather the other side of our common humanity, the more enduring one – resilience, survival and revival. That is the mortar that holds the memory blocks together lest they collapse again. As she constructs her personal and her family's memory, Kalniete achieves much more: she also helps to construct parts of her nation's, Europe's and the world's memory that, too, was for a long time hidden away in concocted case files and deceitful histories. Sandra Kalniete's book is one of the rare instances where the one-syllable difference between "story" and "history" has almost vanished. One corrects, defines and refines the other, reaching out and achieving a fine balance between personal experience and common human experience; between family story and a small nation's history; and between the nation's history and the momentous world events that engulf it and threaten it with extinction.

There is, however, a warning in all of this. Despite the book's hopeful ending, memory's recesses remind us that behind the freedom that Sandra Kalniete, her family and Latvia attained after the long years of Soviet occupation still lurks what Czeslaw Milosz in his most famous book called the "captive mind" of the Soviet Communist system: the blind, unconditional submission to doctrine. That system's toll in human lives destroyed and ruined runs into tens of millions. Its toll in deformed human minds is inestimably larger. It encompassed not only the ruling elites but the masses as well. Kalniete shows this captive, controlled mind at work interrogating her grandfather Jānis, obviously close to death in the Vyatlag prison camp. She shows it during the interrogation and court proceedings against her other grandfather Aleksandrs. Guilt in this system was preordained, human emotion precluded. But Kalniete's family also meets the dulled, listless minds among the Siberian population, most of whom themselves were victims of earlier persecutions and deportations. Though they meet many people who extend a helping hand and share what little of their poverty they can, the years of cruel deprivation have left others devoid of human civility and compassion. Isolation and captivity have made them submissive without any sense of initiative or freedom. It almost seems that the newly arrived captives are the freest among the deprived. News of Stalin's death is received with tears and wailing even among his victims. In the meanwhile, the image of Kalniete's father sitting on the electrical pole to insure the functioning of the sound system transmitting his funeral is the very image of freedom: "... he had the luxury of not having to make a sanctimoniously sombre face, or worry about people reading his thoughts." Looking back and looking in, there is something absurd about it all. Yet it happened. It happened in Nazi Germany; it happened in the Soviet Union. If it happened, it can happen again.

It is only a matter of time. The Latvian mind did not submit to captivity, as the Singing Revolution and its successful re-entry into the free world so amply have demonstrated. But how about the minds of those who were held captive much longer? How about the minds of the emotionless interrogators; the blind executioners of orders; the mindless masses of followers? Is it indeed all past? The book ends with a final word from the author, describing a recurrent nightmare of her mother, with whose deportation in dance shoes to the Siberian snows it all began: "Again it is night and someone is knocking at the door. Strange men enter and order her to get ready. The deportation nightmare begins, and my mother in despair thinks: 'The last time it was a dream. Now it's real.' On waking she gazes long into the empty night until she calms down and understands: she is home again. In Latvia." Was it a dream? Is it a dream? The rest is memory.

– *Valters Nollendorfs*

For my mother's mother, Emilija Dreifelds, née Gāliņa,
my mother's father Jānis Dreifelds,
my father's father Aleksandrs Kalnietis,
who never returned

For my father's mother, Milda Kalniete, née Kaimiņa,
who survived and returned

We are sitting at a beautiful and richly clad table. Candles are burning. My father always lights them when the three of us are together. In the crystal glasses sparkles the French wine I have brought for the occasion. We are eating beef ragout prepared by my mother. We talk of my life and work in Paris, the day-to-day life of my parents and the most important events that have taken place since I was last in Rīga. With what now has become a customary action, my mother takes a slice of bread, breaks it in half and gives a half to my father. Then both of them carefully start to clean their plates. So not a drop of sauce or a crumb of bread remains. Already forty-four years have passed since they have returned from Siberia, but the starvation my parents had experienced there has marked them for life. No matter where or to what grand events we are invited, when the hostess clears the dishes from the table, my mother's eyes, full of worry, follow her, as the dish with remnant specks of food or traces of sauce leaves the table. At such times, however, the norms of politeness accepted by society are stronger than the Siberian experience – my mother does not dare to disregard them and take a piece of bread.

My mother, Ligita Dreifelde, was fourteen and a half years old when on the 14th of June, 1941 she, together with my grandfather and grandmother, was deported to Siberia by the Soviet regime. My grandfather Jānis was separated from his family in Babinino, Russia. Since then, both my mother and my grandmother have had no further news of him. In April 1990, my mother received a notice from the State Security Committee of the Latvian SSR that grandfather had died on December 31, 1941, six days before his sixty-third birthday. Grandmother Emilija died on the 5th of February 1950 in Togur. Mother's three brothers, Voldemārs, Arnolds and Viktors, were able to escape deportation. Voldemārs and Arnolds were not at home at the time the arrests were made, while Viktors succeeded in hiding in a storage closet and, numb with fear and despair, heard as his parents and sister were led away. Toward the end of the war, together with 240,000 other refugees from Latvia, the brothers, together with their families, fled the red terror to the West. After a long desultory stay in displaced persons camps in Germany, they found shelter in Canada and Great Britain.

My father Aivars Kalnietis, a seventeen-year-old young man, together with my grandmother Milda, was deported on the 25th of March 1949. They were considered members of a family of "bandits," because my grandfather Aleksandrs continued to resist the Soviet occupiers after the war and belonged to the "forest brethren" – the partisans. Father's younger brother Arnis had the fortune to escape deportation because he was in the country with his grandmother at the time of the arrests. Grandmother died shortly thereafter, and the boy became an orphan of parents who still were alive. In the fall of 1945, the Peoples Commissariat of State Security had arrested grandfather Aleksandrs and after protracted torture in the cellars of the Cheka and fabricated legal proceedings, was deported to Siberia. He died on February 18, 1953, in one of the prison camps. Grandmother Milda survived and, together with us, returned to Latvia. She died on November 5, 1975, in Rīga.

My parents met in Siberia and were married on May 25, 1951. I was born in the village of Togur, Tomsk region, Kolpashevo district on December 22, 1952. Every month my parents had to register twice at the commandant's office – this is how the Soviet security agencies made certain that the deportees had not arbitrarily left their designated places of residence. A month after my birth, my father had to register me for the first time – thus also I was destined not to be free. Father and mother did not wish to give any more slaves to the Soviet regime. I have no brothers or sisters.

We returned to Latvia on May 30, 1957.

Family Ties

Jānis Dreifelds

Ilze Emilija Dreifelde

Ligita Dreifelde

Aleksandrs Kalnietis

Milda Kalniete

Aivars Kalnietis

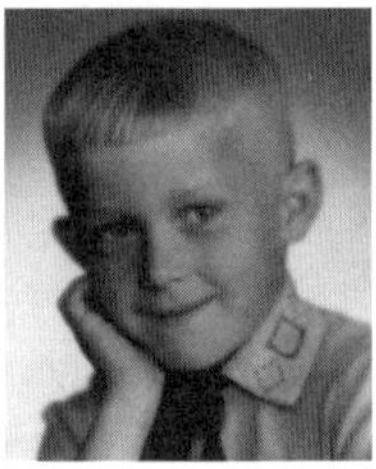

Arnis Kalnietis

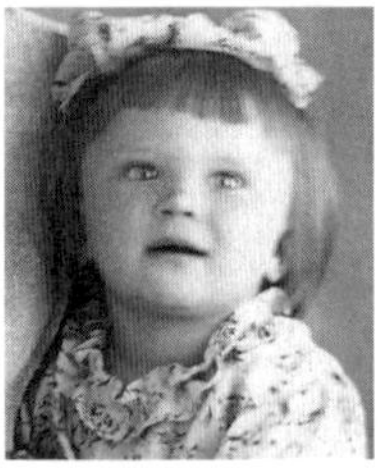

Sandra Kalniete

Jānis Dreifelds
1878.06.01.
St. Petersburg
1941.14.06.
Deported to Siberia
1941.31.12. Vyatlag
7 prison camp

Ilze Emilija Gāliņa
1892.02.01. Saraiķi
1941.14.06.
Deported to Siberia
1950.05.02.
Tomsk region
Kolpashevo district,
Togur village

- **Voldemārs**
  1914.01.04.
  St. Petersburg

  Zenta Bergmane
  1926.26.01.

  - **Juris**
    1942.17.04. Jelgava
  - **Jānis**
    1943.24.09. Jelgava
  - **Pēteris**
    1949.21.02. Beļgium
    1992.07.06. Canada
  - **Rūta**
    1949.21.02. Beļgium

- **Arnolds**
  1916.09.01.
  St. Petersburg
  1989.04.09. England

  Nellija Biteniece
  1912.23.09.
  2001.08.05.

  - **Mārīte**
    1941.03.11. Jūrmala
  - **Andris**
    1944.01.03. Jūrmala

  Marta Dobele
  1925.16.02.

  - **Ligita**
    1958.05.08. England
  - **Marta**
    1960.05.01. England
  - **Zīle**
    1963.17.11. England

- **Viktors**
  1919.08.06.
  St. Petersburg

  Anita Purnis
  1918.15.11.
  1997.20.04.

  - **Dace**
    1945.05.04.
    Germany

  Austra Lilija Šīre
  1920.05.09.

  - **Daina**
    1952.15.09. Canada
  - **Gunta**
    1952.15.09. Canada
  - **Viktors**
    1957.01.03. Canada

- **Ligita Dreifelde**
  1926.09.12.
  Jūrmala
  1941.14.06.
  Deported to Siberia

Pēteris Augusts Kaimiņš
1875.24.09.
Valmiera district
1930.28.12. Rīga

Berta Matilde Eglīte
1878.20.10.
Valmiera district
1952. Bērze

- **Voldemārs Pēteris Kaimiņš**
  1903.–1976.
- **Milda Kaimiņa**
  1908.07.05. Rīga
  1949.25.03.
  Deported to Siberia
  1975.05.11 Rīga

Aleksandrs Kalnietis
1907.05.03.
1945.13.11.
Arrested by the KGB
1953.18.02. Pechorlag
AA-274 prison camp

- **Aivars Kalnietis**
  1931.10.05. Rīga
  1949.25.03.
  Deported to
  Siberia

  Ligita Dreifelde + **Aivars Kalnietis**:
  - **Sandra Kalniete**
    1952.22.12.
    Tomsk region
    Kolpashevo district,
    Togur village

    - **Jānis Aivars Kalnietis**
      1974.07.09. Rīga

      Gita Malvesa
      1975.21.01. Rīga

      - **Armands Kalnietis**
        1993.21.09. Rīga

- **Arnis**
  1938.22.06. Rīga
  1986.17.01. Jelgava

  Dzidra Tarvida
  1933.07.01.

Prelude

It is said that in August 1939, the sun sank into the Baltic Sea as if into blood-soaked sheets. The old women looked at the red sunsets with dreadful premonition. How much truth is in these stories, how much fantasy, it is hard to say today. It also is not of particular significance, because the memory of a nation sifts out and supplements events and phenomena, organising them in meaningful cause and effect sequences. Europe found itself on the edge of war, and later, looking back at history, people saw this remembered image as an ominous sign that foretold the bloodiest war in the history of the world.

I would like to believe that on the 23rd of August, 1939, the sunset was also bloody. People had spent the day peacefully. For the end of August the day was unseasonably warm. The sun and the southeast wind had warmed the air to 23 degrees centigrade. The spring crops and rye had almost all been gathered in Latvia, and farmers were content because the harvest had been good. The water in the Baltic Sea was as warm as milk, and people were eagerly taking advantage of this last flare-up of summer. Some went for swims in the sea; others worked their fields or picked mushrooms in the woods. The previous day, news had appeared in the newspapers that the USSR and Germany were getting ready to sign a non-aggression pact,[1] but the dreadful significance of this event was beyond the understanding of ordinary people. The press, however, was full of agitated voices about the change in balance of power in Europe and threats to the security of the Baltic States, but immediately adjacent to these were calming comments proffered by the USSR and Germany that "the non-aggression pact could only be of benefit to the independence and security of the Baltic States."[2] Through diplomatic channels, rumours reached Rīga that supplementary protocols were secretly appended to the Ribbentrop–Molotov Pact, but there was no formal confirmation of this. Later, after the war, when the U.S. found the secret protocols in the archives of the German Foreign Ministry and when they were read as testimony at the Nuremberg trial,[3] the world found out that the two Super Powers had agreed on the division of Europe into their spheres of influence. Latvia, Lithuania and Estonia were left under the control of the USSR. In addition, Germany invaded Poland a few days later. While the Allies soothed their conscience with the words "Why die for Danzig,"[4] the Soviet Union readied to stretch out its armed hand for Latvia, Estonia, Lithuania, and the Eastern territories of Poland, Bessarabia and Finland.

Neither in my mother's nor my father's conscious memory does the 23rd of August register with any significance. My mother was twelve years and nine months old; my father was eight. What did my grandparents think? Did they understand the inevitability of war, or did they, like many other people not associated with politics, allow themselves to be lulled by the hope that all would be settled and the horror or the First World War would not be repeated in their lives?

Latvians had experienced this horror to the point of despair, because Latvia had for four years been the theatre of war, wherein the Russian Czar fought with the German Kaiser. The people, the land and the animals suffered. Thousands and thousands of Latvians fled as refugees to the interior of Russia and further into Siberia and the Altai. The family of my father's mother Milda already lived in St. Petersburg when war came, because my grandfather, Pēteris Kaimiņš, given his stately build and upright bearing, had earned the privilege of serving in the Semyonovsk Guard Regiment, which had the honour of guarding the family of the Czar.

Pēteris Kaimiņš at the Austro-Hungarian front. 1914.

My grandfather had already taken part in the military action in the Japanese–Russian War. Now, for the second time, he had to go into battle on behalf of the Russian Czar Nicholas, leaving his six-year-old daughter Milda and his ten-year-old son Voldemārs in the care of his wife Berta Matilde. Already in the first days of war, Pēteris Kaimiņš was sent to the Austro-Hungarian border. In the family archives a touching photograph has been saved, which Pēteris had sent to his small daughter Milda, my grandmother. "Cherish and keep this until you are grown-up, then you will always remember that your papa was a soldier, who fought against a monstrous enemy. I kiss you a hundred times." Unlike for thousands of other children in the rest of Europe, this photograph did not become the only memento my grandmother Milda had of her father. Pēteris had the good fortune to go also through this war untouched and to return to his family. The only thing known about my father's father, Aleksandrs, is that he was an orphan. It is probable that he had lost his parents during the war. Since their wedding in 1912, my mother's parents, Emilija and Jānis, had been living in Russia, not far from St. Petersburg, where my grandfather owned his own store. Thus, both branches of my family, unaware of each other's existence, found themselves in the same distant corner of Russian Empire during the First World War. After the Bolshevik Coup d'Etat in 1917, and the subsequent nationalisation of property, the Dreifelds family returned to Latvia in 1919. The Kaimiņš family, also safe and sound, settled down for life in war-ravaged Rīga.

The Kaimiņš family in the 1930s
(Pēteris, Matilde, Voldemārs and Milda).

My mother's parents could not have foreseen the fearful signs and symptoms that foretold a full repeat of history. Most certainly, their bitter experiences and the insane and confused images of the First World War once imprinted on their subconscious were again revived, but they warded off these troubling thoughts. The Indian summer of 1939 was so beautiful. It was too difficult to think dark thoughts. In the evenings, Emilija, her arm hooked in the elbow of her husband,

Jānis, went for staid strolls along the seashore. Their sons, Voldemārs, Arnolds and Viktors, already were living their own separate lives. On occasion, their daughter Ligita still accompanied them, but signs of the developing beauty of young womanhood had already touched the girl's face and body. Their daughter's – my mother's – thoughts were preoccupied with a life that offered so much variety and promise to intoxicate, excite and captivate her. Seeing how their daughter was changing, Jānis and Emilija tried not to think about the war that had just started nearby, in Poland. Oh, it won't touch Latvia, they comforted each other, it won't touch our daughter!

In 1939, my father, Aivars, was a lively eight-year old boy, who spent that summer, as he had every previous summer, at his grandmother Berta Matilde Kaimiņa's farm. After the death of her husband, she had continued to rent land from the Manor of Jumprava near Rīga and earned her living by growing sugar beets. The boy battled the neighbour's malicious geese, played brash war games with his friends, and, on occasion, if he could find an adult to accompany him, went for a dip in the River Daugava. Aivars' true passion, however, was reading. Having got hold of the most current "gangster" novel, he hid behind the barn and lost himself in fantastic adventures. Grandmother Matilde could call or grumble as loudly as she could, but the boy would not heed her calls for help.

In contrast to my mother Ligita, my father's childhood was very poor. His real father had died of pneumonia before his son was born, and his mother Milda was raising the boy alone. Milda was an independent and modern-thinking woman, who had acquired a good education in comparison to her generation. I remember with what pride my grandmother used to recount to me that she had been the only student in school whose parents had asked to have her released from religious studies. The courage of Pēteris Kaimiņš, the father of this grandmother, to go against the tide, always delighted me. His stance was even more surprising because he earned his living as a shoemaker. But he was a very intelligent man, who refused to buckle under the limitations imposed by life, and spiritually he was able to lift himself above the shoemaker's mould. After finishing his township school, Pēteris continued to learn on his own, because he firmly believed that humanity could be saved through education. He wanted his children to be educated. When Milda finished high school, however, the material circumstances of the family had deteriorated and, despite the hard work of the parents, the daughter could not to be sent to university like the son. The girl reconciled herself to her fate without grumbling and became a nurse instead. Milda never regretted her choice, because she had found her true calling and fulfilment. At the hospital, my grandmother met her second husband, Aleksandrs.

It was the classical story, the story of a patient, depressed by the idleness and monotony of a hospital, falling in love with his nurse. It is still a mystery to me, how Aleksandrs could fall in love with Milda, my grandmother, while she was dressed in the light blue uniform of a nurse and wore a white kerchief so like the head covering of a nun. Because she was of such slight build, she looked more like an adolescent girl than a thirty-year-old woman in her uniform. Aleksandrs needed a very vivid imagination to guess what values were hidden under the formless nurse's uniform and apron. The dress concealed Milda's womanly round hips and her greatest asset – her enticing legs. And my grandmother knew how to use them. Her head thrown back slightly, her legs crossed, she would pull up her skirt inconspicuously, so the dimples on her knees would show. Then it only remained for her to gently swing her small foot in its lovely shoe and to enjoy the result of her manoeuvres. The response was not long in coming. Even though my grandmother was not beautiful, she had sex appeal that, invariably, attracted men. Of course, the hospital was not the place where one could practice coquetry. She was aware of this and was primarily and foremost a nurse there – kind and talkative, with gentle hands. Perhaps Aleksandrs was attracted to my grandmother's eyes, the beauty of which could not be concealed by the nurse's cap. They were large and clear blue, with a special shine, which was immediately felt by everyone who came within her eyesight. The shine in my grandmother's eyes was retained until the very last moments of her life filled with suffering. In any case, Aleksandrs was enraptured.

Aleksandrs and Milda Kalnietis on their wedding day 1937.

Initially, Milda remained cool to his advances, but my grandfather did not give up and was very persistent. In order not to seem too forward, he carefully hid behind a newspaper, but in reality, through a small gap, was attentive to every move of his intended. Little by little, the talkative Aleksandrs conquered Milda. And, at the end of 1937, they were married. In particular, her heart was melted by her husband's readiness to adopt her son, which he did right after their wedding. Thus my father became Aivars Kalnietis and immediately started to call Aleksandrs his father, for he had never known another. Even though I am not the direct descendant of Aleksandrs, I consider him my grandfather, because I have inherited his lovely last name – Kalniete – meaning "woman of the mountain." The name is carried on by my son Jānis and my grandson, Armands. But, returning to the story of my grandparents – a son, named Arnis, was soon born to the newlyweds, and my father's sovereignty over my mother's heart had ended.

In August 1939, politics was the furthest thing from my father's parents' minds. Aleksandrs had an uncontrollable temper. Also Milda did not lack in stubbornness. Her husband was pathologically jealous, which was unacceptable to my sociable grandmother. Like the majority of people, who in their childhood have enjoyed parental love, my grandmother did not understand that behind Aleksandrs' self-confident and brash exterior hid an insecure little boy, whose heart would never recover from the feelings of fear and abandonment, which set in after he lost his parents as a child. He wanted to have Milda exclusively for himself, and whenever his wife was not near him, Aleksandrs was overtaken by feelings of panic. He calmed his fear with the help of a shot glass, which, in turn, displeased Milda. For imagined transgressions, Aleksandrs made Milda pay dearly, accusing her unjustly of almost all the world's sins. With passion uncharacteristic of the calm-tempered Latvians, they engaged in pitched verbal battles, each trying to prove their own truth to the other. The torrid scenes took place in front of Aivars, and his child's heart overflowed with sadness and love for his mother, whom his father was so undeservedly hurting.

My grandparents, the same as many, who had been lulled by the calm flow and the intense social whirl of the patriarchal regime of President Ulmanis, wanted to pretend that they did not see the major and minor events that, after the signing of the August Pact and invasion of Poland by Germany, signalled the irreversible approach of disaster. Intellectuals and army personnel were angered by President Ulmanis' pathos-filled cult of leadership and speeches about what it meant to be genuine Latvian, the Latvian work ethic and neutrality of the State. Precisely in neutrality hid the greatest danger to State independence. Latvia had to choose allies, and on this issue there were differences of opinion among the governing elite. Some believed that it was necessary to forge closer links with Germany; others hoped for support from Great Britain and France, while a third faction speculated about a closer relationship with the Soviet Union. The latter position, however, did not gain much support, because fear of the Soviet Union had become deeply ingrained in people: so non-erasable were the memories of the monstrosities worked by the Bolsheviks in Latvia in 1919. Along with the signing of the Ribbentrop–Molotov Pact, the time for choosing allies had passed, and on the 1st of September 1939, Latvia had no recourse but to declare its neutrality.

In September 1939, Estonia was forced to acquiesce to a USSR demand to locate Soviet military bases on its territory. On October 2, a similar demand was issued to Latvia, and after several days of talks, the Minister of Foreign Affairs Vilhelms Munters gave in to the pressure of Stalin and Molotov and signed the Mutual Assistance Pact between Latvia and the USSR. Assistance, as interpreted by the Soviets, meant that the "Soviet Union had the right to keep, at its expense, a strictly limited number of land and air force personnel in areas specifically designated for bases and airfields."[5] Very shortly thereafter, 21,000 soldiers crossed into Latvia – slightly fewer than all of the armed forces in Latvia.[6] My mother remembers that, after the signing of the Pact, her high school principal Mr. Urpēns had called together the senior class students and in a long, protracted speech had explained why the Soviet soldiers were permitted to stay in Latvia, and had reiterated, again and again, why the students needed to act in a friendly fashion to them. Poor principal, who like other principals had to find the words to explain the inexplicable! Initially the Soviet soldiers behaved discreetly and were almost unnoticeable outside their designated territory. The initial excitement about what had happened abated after a while, and people again resumed their everyday lives. Was Latvia, after all, the only country that had military bases of a super power on its territory? This surely would not be sufficient reason for war to start immediately. Maybe there was still time to manoeuvre. Some restrictions on the sale of food products were introduced. Manufacturers started to run short of raw materials. Travelling passports were annulled. But otherwise the calm magic of life had not disappeared. Only the more perceptive understood that the country's independence was literally lost and that Latvia had become a Soviet protectorate.

The second ominous sign was the mass repatriation of Baltic Germans that started in November.[7] From the Reichstag platform, on the 6th of October, the Führer had invited ethnic Germans living in Latvia and Estonia to return to their historical fatherland. The Baltic Germans had lived for generation upon generation in this country and, until recently, had also governed it. Some, with dislike, had accepted the new Latvian state policies, which rescinded their privileges and stripped them of economic power by nationalising their large landed properties.[8] At the time, it had been one of the most radical agrarian reforms in the world. Also the brothers of my mother's mother Emilija, Einis, Jānis and Kārlis Gāliņi were granted ownership of land from the nearby Kapsēde manor, to whose "hereditary property" the ancestors of Gāliņi family had belonged until 1817 – the time when serfdom was abolished in Kurzeme. It must have been with feelings of triumph and joy that the brothers ploughed their first furrow in these fields, which their ancestors had worked for centuries as serfs without any rights, later as hired farm labourers or leaseholders. Now the Führer was calling, and the Germans had to leave the land with which they had deep personal ties. In reality, they felt that their homeland was Latvia, while Hitler's Third Reich for them was as distant as any mythical primal homeland. But no one, of course, is able to love a myth. Only admire it. Though with a heavy heart, they did, nonetheless, leave. By the 12th of December already forty-five thousand had left Latvia.[9] Feelings differed concerning the repatriation of the Germans. There were those who wished them a good voyage and never to return. Others understood that it was an escape from a sinking ship. Also in Dubulti high school, where Ligita was studying, several Baltic Germans were students. Gunnar Kreisler left from my mother's class. In parting, the boy had said tellingly – we shall return! Was it

Ligita Dreifelde as a secondary school student 1938.

simply a brash phrase or did the boy repeat what he had heard from his parents? In fact, some of the Baltic Germans did return in the summer of 1941, when the victorious Nazi armed forces invaded and the second occupation of Latvia began. Ligita was not to experience this, because she was already on her way to Siberia.

The Soviet military bases and the German repatriation were the visible signs of danger. However, not even in their worst nightmares could anyone in Latvia imagine that in the back offices in the Kremlin almost everything had been prepared – not only staging the socialist revolution with the objective of subsequently establishing a Soviet regime, but also for the first wave of repressions in Latvia. In principle, the fate of my family and also of others who were to suffer repression, had already been decided on October 11, 1939, only five days after the signing of the Assistance Pact with Moscow, when the Peoples Deputy Commissar of the USSR State Security, Ivan Serov, signed Order No. 001223 regarding deportation procedures of anti-Soviet elements from Lithuania, Latvia and Estonia.[10] The instructions contained nothing new or original, because since its founding the Peoples Commissariat of the Interior[11] had been perfecting this genre. It only remained to follow the previous examples, supplement them with local "specifics," and the implementation rules for another wave of repression were ready.

Even I, so accustomed to the Soviet bureaucratic and ideological jargon, am devastated by the inhuman terminology in the instructions – weapons ready-to-fire, contingents, collection points, convoys, separation of the head of the family, loading, unloading, transport. These instructions are terrifying: their content so convincingly unmasks the inhuman and criminal essence of the Soviet regime.

How many other instructions of similar content were worked out in the fall of 1939 in Moscow will probably never be known fully. It is likely that the occupation of the Baltic States would have occurred a half year earlier, if Moscow did not have to face the unexpected resistance of Finland. At the beginning of October, the same sort of demands were issued to Finland as had been given to Latvia. Finland refused to lease its territory for military bases and to allow Soviet soldiers entry. Such insubordination surprised the Kremlin. The small state had to be taught a lesson as an example to others! The USSR started to get ready for armed intervention. The Russians were convinced that it would suffice just to shoot a few rounds and the Finns would surrender. They miscalculated, and the blitzkrieg did not work. The Red Army was ill prepared for extended resistance, because it had lost the majority of its best commanders after the waves of Stalinist repression. The world looked on in awe and sympathy, as for a solitary 105 days, supported by no one, Finland defended itself against overwhelming odds until March 13, 1940, when it was forced to capitulate. Though the Winter War ended with the defeat of Finland, in fact the Soviet Union had suffered a defeat. It was not able to realise its hoped-for Socialist revolution in Finland, followed by the mandatory people's request to be included in the USSR. Finland preserved its independence for a very high price – twenty-three thousand Fins were slain in battle and 10% of their territory had to be handed over to the Soviet Union.[12] The large number of victims and the outcome of the Winter War reconfirmed the conviction in Latvia that the right choice had been made and that, by yielding to USSR demands, the country would succeed in saving its nation from annihilation. This consolation turned out to be deceptive, but at that moment no one could imagine that Latvia would have to experience three consecutive occupations – Soviet, German and, again, Soviet – and the blood money postponed for a brief period, would nonetheless have to be paid. On the eve of war, Finland and Latvia were on equal footing in their standard of living, however, in terms of welfare, Latvia was, if anything, ahead. When, in 1991, Latvia again regained independence, Finland had moved ahead of us by exactly the fifty years of occupation we had experienced.

Occupation

On Monday, June 17, 1940, my father Aivars together with his brother and mother Milda were at the Jumprava Manor. While his mother and grandmother were raking sugar beets, Aivars was playing without a care in the world on the shore of River Daugava. His brother Arnis, in infantile innocence, was rolling around on a blanket laid out on the grass. It was a day like any other at the Jumprava Manor. Nothing pointed to the fact that the inevitable had already happened and that Soviet armed forces had invaded Latvia.[13] Milda's mother did not have a radio in the house. Nor did the immediate neighbours have one, thus the only operative source of information about current events was not accessible. In the evening the family went to bed as usual. The shocking news became known only the next day. Aivars had noticed several Latvian army aircraft land in the Jumprava Manor fields and with boyish curiosity had run to look at the planes. From the agitated talk of the pilots and the nearest neighbouring men, he learned for the first time that Russians had entered Rīga, that there were tanks in the station square, that in the Moscowite suburb people were walking around with red flags… Today, in an era of information overload, it is hard to understand that on June 17 many of the country people in Latvia were in a similar situation as the Kalnietis family, and knew nothing of the tragic events in Rīga. Even listening to the radio would not have helped much, because the medium was already controlled by the Soviet armed forces. Reliable information about what was happening could also not be obtained from newspapers.

How events unfolded on the 16th and the 17th in fact, is known with relative precision today from carefully collected and collated documents that had been dispersed in several foreign archives and have become available in Latvia after the renewal of independence, as well as the recollections and mementoes of Latvians scattered across the world. Latvian historians still do not have access to the archival collections of the USSR Interior People's Commissariat and USSR State Security Committee that could provide complete insight into the documents preparing the occupation of Latvia.[14] Now it is known what happened on the afternoon of the 16th of June in the President's palace and what the government members, the military high command, as well as the border guards did after they received a coded telegram with the USSR ultimatum from the Latvian envoy in Moscow, Fricis Kociņš. Testimonies have been preserved regarding the discussions and the difficult decision reached by the members of the government to hand Latvia over without resistance in order to save the nation from unnecessary sacrifices. People on the street at that moment knew almost none of the specifics of this imminent historic turn of events. Newspapers were not issued on Sunday, hence nothing appeared in the press about the ultimatum. Similarly, there was no press coverage of the Soviet attack on Masļenki border crossing point that occurred on the 15th of June. Three border guards were shot and ten border guards and twenty-seven civilians were taken captive.[15] There were dreadful premonitions in the air, because rumours were circulating about Red Army incursions into Lithuania, but the radioed news from the Song Festival in Latgale somewhat calmed people. Would there be such celebration if the situation were so life threatening?

O, the Latgale song celebration! The last regional Song Festival of independent Latvia, which had bee planned to celebrate the beauty of this very Latvian land of blue lakes, was fated to take place under the sombre shadow of fearful premonition and go down in history as a festival of grief. This song celebration was forever etched in each participant's memory and eventually became transformed into a painful legend. In the memory of many of the singers as well as the audience, the tragic events of the next few days have been so intertwined, that more than a few are convinced that it was precisely during the Festival that President Ulmanis had announced that the Soviet armed forces had crossed the border into Latvia. My mother's brother Viktors, who took part in the Latgale Song Festival singing with the Military School Cadet Choir, has retained exactly this sort of impression in his memory.

The President could not have announced the incursion of the Red Army, because the Latvian government had not yet accepted the Soviet ultimatum. In his speech to the Festival participants, made at approximately five in the afternoon on the radio, the President did not reveal how dangerous the situation was. Only in the words "the swift progress of international events in this week has exceeded anything we have experienced up to this time,"[16] can be heard a significant allusion to the approaching danger. Rumours of Soviet tank and infantry unit concentration near the border, as well as the incursion of the Soviet armed forces into Lithuania, had already reached both the audience and the singers in the choirs. The President's failure to talk about the events seemed like the greatest indication. In despair and hope, the choirs and the public sang the nation's prayer, the Latvian anthem "God bless Latvia" three times. The same as everyone else, also my mother's brother Viktors prayed to God three times to save our sacred land of Mary. When the Latvian hymn was finished, the cadets received a secret order to return to barracks forthwith and to depart for the Latvian border. By sunset, the Latgale Song Festival came to an end and the participants dispersed, each in his own direction.

The next day – Monday, 17th of June, the people woke, as they had every workday, to start their normal daily activities and discovered that Soviet bombers were circling over Rīga. A few hours later, tanks drove into the city centre.[17] The shock was the greater because everything seemed to happen at the same time – the ultimatum, the resignation of the government and the invasion by armed forces. It was only after the fact that people read about the resignation of the government and the demands issued in the June 16 ultimatum by the USSR:

(1) to form without delay a government in Latvia that will be ready and able to ensure reliable implementation of the Soviet-Latvian mutual assistance pact;
(2) to ensure without delay the admission without restrictions of Soviet army units in the territory of Latvia, in order that they may be located in the most important Latvian centres in such numbers as are necessary to ensure the implementation of the mutual assistance pact between the USSR and Latvia and to avert probable provocative actions against the Soviet garrison in Latvia.[18]

In the same newspaper, at the bottom, in bolder letters, it was announced that the Latvian government agrees to the Soviet conditions, that "the Soviet Army divisions crossed the border of Latvia in the early morning hours of June 17" and that the President has accepted the resignation of the government.[19] Given this announcement, it was strange and out of context to read on the first page of the newspaper *Jaunākās Ziņas* a quote of the calmly delivered President's speech at the Song Festival the previous day. The speech sounded as if it had originated in a different world and a different era. What was fated to happen, had come to pass. There was neither spontaneous resistance, nor screams of dismay. With the exception of a small crowd organised by the communists in the railway station square, the rest of the Rīgans, as if struck dumb, stared at the tanks and the poorly dressed Red Army soldiers in city squares and on the streets.

The afternoon passed in anxious uncertainty. Rumours spread that the President and the government had been arrested, however at four in the afternoon, Ulmanis rode through Rīga streets in an open car to the President's palace. He, it appeared, was safe and sound. That somewhat calmed everyone. On the evening of June 17, at 10:15, the State President made his last speech to the people. A month later, he was arrested and deported to Russia, where he died in unknown circumstances in a place unknown.[20] This context, as well as subsequent events, assigns a tragic significance to the speech. With the passage of time, each word and each sentence has been subjectively interpreted and explained in various ways, creating a manifold mythology. Almost no Latvian can hear the most significant and most often quoted words "I will stay in my place, you stay in yours," with which the President finished his speech, without feeling deeply touched. I too, on reading or hearing these words, get tears in my eyes, however, when I try to imagine how they sounded on the day of the occupation, I am overcome with confusion.

On June 17, after the incomprehensible events of the day, people were waiting for explanations and assurance from the President, but he did not respond to these expectations. The speech was full of indirect allusions and pathetic appeals, which did not calm, but, on the contrary, increased the agitation and confusion. How dangerous the situation was, could be sensed from Ulmanis' plea to countenance the incoming Soviet army units with friendship, to curb excessive curiosity and refrain from actions that would disturb law and order. The President invited all "to stay in their place with the same solidarity and will to work as in the past and to serve what, for all of us, is uppermost and sacred – the interests of Latvia and our nation."[21] Pathetically, he begged the people: "Show by your thoughts, deeds and demeanour, the spiritual strength of the nation released during the years of flower of renewed Latvia. Then I will be certain that everything that is happening now and will happen further will be for the good of the future of our nation and our people and for our good and friendly relationship with our large Eastern neighbour – the Soviet Union."[22] Also the explanation about the future actions of the government is just as non-specific and puzzling:

"I am convinced that you will understand the decrees that the government has issued and will issue, even though, in some instances, they will be stringent and even harsh. Follow them conscientiously, for they have no other objective than your peace and well-being."[23] The next day the speech was published in the newspapers.

It was not a coincidence that, in issuing its ultimatum and occupying the Baltic States,[24] the Soviet Union chose the same June days in which the world with bated breath was following the irreversible approach of the capitulation of France. On the 17th of June, the hero of the First World War, Marshall Petain, asked the army to cease resistance and, within a few days, the Germans ceremoniously marched across the Champs Élysées. Hitler enjoyed his retaliation: in Bois de Compiègne: France's humiliating cease-fire with Third Reich was signed in the same railway carriage, where in 1918 Germany had agreed to its capitulation. What did the fate of the small Baltic States matter in comparison to this drama, which staggered Europe and the world? Thus we were left alone with our despair.

Latvia officially was still an independent state. To stage the Socialist "revolution" Moscow chose as its chief director Andrei Vyshinsky, the Vice-chairman of the USSR Peoples Council of Commissars, who had proven himself to be a particularly avid implementer of Stalin's repressions. He needed only 34 days to complete the assignment, and on August 5, 1940, Latvia became the fifteenth Soviet Republic. As one of his first gestures, Vyshinsky handed a list of personnel for the new government to Ulmanis, explaining that the President did not have a right to change anything. In silence, Ulmanis signed it, as he had also signed other documents, thus destroying all that he had tirelessly built as a statesman since 1918. Did he really not understand that by "staying in his place" he was legalising what was transpiring and that he had become a perfect instrument of Soviet will and an accomplice in the liquidation of the statehood of Latvia?

It is easy to ask this question today, but then everything seemed inexplicable and confused. From the eyewitness accounts of his contemporaries, it is known that until the end the President believed that his presence was his greatest obligation and that with his presence he would be able to save Latvia for the future, limit the repressions and the bloodshed.[25] Not everyone understood or accepted this position of the President. In particular, the army rank and file could not reconcile themselves with what was happening. In spite of the overpowering numbers of the enemy, officers and the rank and file had been preparing to defend their homeland and die with honour since the border attack on June 15th. Contrary to what was expected, an order arrived to let the Soviet army divisions in without resistance. This humiliation could only be washed away with blood. On the morning of the 21st of June, having lost hope, in protest, General Ludvigs Bolšteins shot himself. Several other Latvian army officers followed his example.

The uncertainty that ruled in society in those June days was staggering. The most unlikely rumours were circulating. Almost nothing of what was happening with the political elite was known, since the press and the radio were totally under the control of the occupiers. Most of the newspapers still were being issued, but within the space of a few days their content changed in substance and they started to sing to the tune of the Soviets – of the mass support of the working people for the new government; the friendship of Latvian and Soviet soldiers; the great and peaceful Soviet nation; about the Great Stalin, etc. Touching stories could be read in the press about the enthusiasm and love with which the friendly Soviet armed forces had been welcomed.

In reality "the welcome" was bitter. With each new day, the feeling of humiliation grew stronger. The sharp pain could not be silenced, as in the streets and squares the Soviet army personnel were seen filing by. Their presence was a harsh reminder of what had happened. Every day people laid flowers at the Freedom Monument. On occasion, my father's mother, Milda, too, went to the Monument after work, so that, together with other men and women, they could mourn their lost independence. Some sank to their knees at the foot of the monument and prayed to Mother Latvia to take pity on her children and not to turn away from them. Others went to church with the same prayer and turned to God, their Heavenly Father. Thus, in this critical moment for our nation, the Latvian spirit manifested itself inseparably both in its reliance on a Mother, inherited from paganism dating back many centuries, and its Christian faith in a Heavenly Father introduced at a later date.

The Freedom Monument has always held a special place in our history. After many years of occupation, it is precisely at its foot that the Third Awakening of the Latvian nation began and ended with the renewal of independence. On June 14, 1987, after many years of silence, the dissident group Helsinki-86 was brave enough to extend the invitation to place flowers at the Freedom Monument in remembrance of those who had died in Siberia. On the appointed day and hour the brave were not many, but, for several days running, singly or in pairs, people headed for the Monument. I had something to commemorate as well. Several times each day, I stood in the crowd and cried as I watched. The same as in the summer of 1940, people again sank to their knees and prayed to Mother Latvia. I did not have enough courage to leave the silent crowd of sympathisers and cross the street while the Soviet militiamen and Chekists watched. I hate myself for it, but that's what I was like – having soaked up the invisible fear of my deported family. It is precisely in these days at the Freedom Monument that my sense of freedom was reborn.

My mother does not remember the first year of occupation as being bleak and dreadful. More likely, it was grotesque. The comment repeated again and again in the reminiscences of other people surprised me: what was happening then seemed to them so stupid and unreal that the anecdotal took precedence over the dramatic and the tragic. Seemingly, life continued at its customary rhythm and the day-to-day level was not immediately touched by what was happening beyond it. Shops, factories and movie theatres continued to function. The season in Jūrmala – the Baltic Sea resort – was in full swing. Līgo Night – Midsummer's Eve – was celebrated with many bonfires. Concerts and garden parties were scheduled. But a new, strange public had materialised at the seashore – Russian vacationers in striped pyjamas. Emilija and Jānis no longer wanted to go for their nightly strolls. The Soviet uniforms were unpleasantly bothersome to the eye. There was no reprieve from them anywhere. Especially on Sundays, when the Red Army orchestras, obsessively fulfilling their mission of forging closer cultural ties, thundered in the sand dunes and open-air stages with jaunty Soviet marches. Their artificial and infantile enthusiasm was foreign to the lyrical world view of the Latvians. The situation was unpleasant, but because of it, feelings of threat still did not arise, and people slowly calmed down.

With resignation, Jānis Dreifelds accepted the new reality, comforting the agitated Emilija: "We'll manage to survive the Russians. I know the Russians. They're all right, though somewhat stupid. I'll know how to deal with them." He was basing this on the experiences of his youth. Could my grandfather imagine that in twenty years the Bolsheviks had brainwashed people so much that they had totally lost a sense of good and evil and that they would take on as a necessary norm the extermination of innocent people. When, at a later date, my grandfather had experienced the brutality of the GULAG, and had became aware of his error in judgement, he surely must have chastised himself about his naiveté and shortsightedness, and God knows what else. In vain. It was not within the powers of a mortal – to foresee the unforeseeable and to be more adept than the perverse extinction machine of the Soviet regime. Sooner or later it found its victim. In those June days my grandfather still believed in his ability to survive and, planning ahead, began to stockpile food and kerosene. Like many others, he tried to get rid of paper money, to change it in for the more secure silver coins.

Neighbours and friends recounted to each other funny incidents, which revealed the lack of civilisation, gullibility, or stupidity of the Soviet occupiers. By ridiculing their "liberators," Latvians were compensating for the profound humiliation that the occupation had created. It was a psychologically based, defensive reaction that helped maintain self-respect and, at the least, internally, allow people to feel superior to their occupiers. In truth, laughter was an escape from reality and a means of finding shelter in an illusory world, where the intelligent one always turns out to be stronger than the strong one. When I was a child, I also laughed, listening to my grandmother Milda's stories about the wives of Russian officers who had gone to the theatre dressed in silk night gowns trimmed with lace, or about the Red Army soldiers, who had again and again asked a salesgirl if you really can buy white bread and butter in a shop each day and without limitation. These legends persisted throughout the Soviet occupation years, and I retold my grandmother Milda's stories to my son Jānis. Other families did the same.

In leafing through the newspapers from the first months of occupation, it is totally obvious why people could not take seriously the exaggerated language of Soviet propaganda, when the same slogans and images that were considered effective in the Soviet Union were circulated in Latvian without any modification. How ludicrous such expressions as "Lenin, the mountain eagle" or "Soviet Union – the greatest country in the world. Moscow – the most beautiful city in the world." must have sounded to the Latvian ear. Only someone living in the Soviet Union, who had not been anywhere and who had barely conquered illiteracy, could be convinced by this. Not Latvians, who at that time ranked among the first in Europe in terms of the number of people per capita who were university students or graduates.[26] Left-wing intellectuals attempted to write articles lampooning Ulmanis' autocratic regime or the corruption of some other higher government official, but the effect of these minor articles was exactly the opposite of what was intended. The tragic events had assigned martyrs' haloes to the President and members of the government, and every one such instance of slander only reinforced this halo. Also, the demonstrations by the working people extolled in Soviet history books from which I had to learn at a later date looked like organised theatrical events in the eyes of the Rīgans of the time and were the cause of smirks. Who were these people who had crawled out from nowhere with their frozen faces, who, led by strangers, as if by command, marched in disciplined columns, carrying gigantic portraits of Lenin, Stalin and others not recognised by Rīgans? They marched along the virtually empty streets with a purpose known only to themselves. How could one believe that they expressed the will of all the Latvian people, if each knew within himself what that will was. It looked like the theatre of the absurd that had a director, actors playing main roles, and mass scene participants. But the nation was assigned the role of an audience.

Fear developed slowly. Together with the first rumours about the arrests. With increasingly aggressive language in the press. With the prohibition of the paramilitary Home Guard and other public organisations. The first painful blow was the arrests of the Democratic Block of activists that started on July 9. Elections for the Saeima – the Latvian parliament – had been announced for July 14 and 15. Despite the ludicrously short campaign period of ten days, the most enterprising Latvian political activists had managed to unite in a Democratic Block, but their list was not accepted for registration. In Vyshinsky's scenario, only the Working Peoples Block of Latvia was to have a role in the socialist revolution. The brave democrats did not capitulate but continued their campaign. Campaign materials, printed in secret, were passed from hand to hand. From mouth to mouth spread the news: "Vote for the second list!" Seeing that a national wave of protest was gathering momentum, and in order to prevent any unwanted incidents during the "democratic" election, by stages, several hundred of the Democratic block activists were imprisoned.[27]

The frightening news about what had happened spread quickly. This cooled the greatest hotheads. Also my great grandparents understood that they could not risk failing to vote, because all who participated in the voting got their passports stamped, and the absence of a stamp would bring misfortune down on the family. When I familiarised myself with the case file of my father's father in the State Archive of Latvia, among the things taken away from him, I found the passport of my great grandmother Berta Matilde Kaimiņa. In it was a stamp confirming her participation in the July 14, 1940, elections. Such stamps also had to have been in the passports of my grandparents Jānis, Emilija, Aleksandrs, and Milda. According to official Soviet statistics, 94.8% of Latvians voted, and 97.8% of these voted for the Working Peoples' Block.[28] No one believed it then, did not believe it during the time Latvia was part of the Soviet Union, and no one believes it now. As a result of a slip-up, the Soviet news agency TASS announced the election results in the Baltic States already on the 14th of July, even though the elections in Estonia and Latvia still continued on the 15th, while in Lithuania voting continued until the 17th of July.[29] The published numbers agree precisely with the election results officially announced three days later.

Now that the hardest part of the socialist "revolution" was over for the Soviet emissary, Andrei Vyshinsky, there only remained the supervision of the first session of Saeima. He was convinced that there would not be any more surprises, because the members of the parliament had been chosen carefully. Just as carefully, "correct" deputy speeches and "correct" draft laws were written and translated into Latvian at the Soviet Embassy. Vyshinsky had read them over and polished up some rough spots. The Saeima session took place without incident, and the newly elected deputies obediently fulfilled the task assigned to them – unanimously deciding "to request [...] that the Soviet Socialist Republic of Latvia be accepted as a constituent republic into the Union of Soviet Socialist Republics."[30] On July 30, the Saeima delegation led by marionette Prime Minister Augusts Kirchenšteins, headed for Moscow and begged the USSR Supreme Council to satisfy "the fervent hope of the working people." Thus Latvia became a constituent part of the USSR, and on August 5, 1940, the State of Latvia *de facto* ceased to exist. My mother and father have registered this tragic fact in their memory with the following funny quatrain:

> Beside Stalin's door pale Kirchenšteins stands,
> a petition for bread and salt in his hands,
> He begs and begs, as his tears flow,
> But Stalin laughs and tells him to f... off!

From August 5 onward, fear became a part of everyone's life in Latvia. Acquaintances and people previously well known by the public started to disappear. Caution and stress started to engrave the faces of people. Laughter was stilled, and the poison of mutual distrust, like cobwebs, started to spread over society. As it usually happens in moments of great trial, this unhealthy atmosphere released the basest instincts and, encouraged by envy, sloth and malice, the weakest turned to exploitation and the writing of denunciations. These local traitors helped Soviet officials to point out enemies of the people and to fulfil the plan created by Moscow to isolate "socially subversive elements."[31]

Fear reached its apogee on the 14th of June, 1941. In one night 15,424 Latvian residents were deported.[32] Among the deported were 290 infants and 55 elderly people 60 years of age and over.[33] The oldest of the deportees was born in 1857. Many infants were born and also died in the cattle cars en route to Siberia. In the last days of June, the number of arrested and deported was increased by 13,077 people. To this number must be added the rest of the victims of the first year of Soviet Occupation – the murdered and those gone missing, which increased the total number to 34 250.[34] The information about the arrested and the deported is not quite accurate. These numbers range within a few hundred in different sources. According to approximate calculations, Latvia had lost 18 people for every 1000 residents – Latvians, Jews, Russians and people of other national origin during the first year of occupation.[35]

Deportation

I have always wondered how so large a mass campaign as the June 14, 1941, deportation could be organised in total secrecy. There was so much preliminary work: creation of lists of people to be deported, preparation of the railway cattle cars and their assembly into trains, ensuring automotive transport for the transport of the arrested people to the railway station and staffing of the brigades for arresting people, etc. How could so much preparatory work go on without notice? There had to be rumours circulating, half-whispered conversations and dreadful premonitions, but there were none. Also from the reminiscences of other deportees, it is obvious, that the deportation caught almost everyone by surprise and unprepared, like my mother's family. There was some talk, but were rumours uncommon?

In my comprehension, ruined as it is by my Soviet life experiences, it seems totally self-explanatory that people, on hearing something like this, had to be afraid – whether they were guilty or innocent. I forget that people had been accustomed to living in a state of justice, where an innocent person could not, like a criminal, be pulled from his or her house at night and put in a cattle car to be sent into unknown exile. In Latvia, nothing of the sort had ever been experienced in peacetime. Also, in other free countries of the world nothing of the sort has been experienced, and that is why someone living in France, United States or Great Britain would probably have acted the same – would not have been afraid and, convinced of the safety of an innocent person, would not have taken precautions.

Jānis and Emilija also did not pay any attention to the warnings they received from their tenant, the railwayman Šveheimers. On seeing cattle cars being converted for transport of people and being linked up in very long trains, he had come to see my grandfather Jānis on the 12th of June, to tell him anxiously about what he had seen. However, Jānis and Emilija did not understand the warning. They were simple people who were far removed from politics and hence felt safe. Some days earlier, Jānis had been invited to the militia, where a friendly Soviet militiaman had questioned him in detail about his family, relatives and property. In parting, the Russian officer had praised my grandfather – if all people were as honest as Jānis Kristapovičs, using the familiar Russian patronymic, then the world would be a better place. Relieved, on arriving back home, Jānis, had said to his wife: "Now finally they'll leave us alone! Now we'll be able to live in peace." The only one in the family who was in real danger was the youngest son Viktors, who was an officer in the Latvian army. Rumours had been circulating about repression of army personnel and the Home Guard. But the rest of the family members – what crime could they have committed? No, these things could not apply to us, decided Jānis and Emilija. Why would Jānis otherwise leave his family and on June 13 head for the family's farmstead, to remain there until Sunday, June 15.

How could my great grandparents know that on the 9th of June, Captain Shustin of the State Security People's Commissariat of the Latvian SSR had confirmed with the notation "Top Secret" the decision prepared by Sergeant Mutin regarding the arrest of J.K. Dreifelds.[36] The word "arrested" is used in the past tense in the decision, as if it were a confirmation of an action already implemented, but four more days remained until the actual arrest. As basis for the arrest, Comrade Mutin had accused Jānis Dreifelds of allegedly having been a past member of the radical organisation "Thunder Cross,"[37] and for his anti-Soviet activity. This was a fabrication because grandfather kept as far away from politics as possible. He had never been a member of any political organisation, much less of "Thunder Cross," whom my grandfather considered to be rabble-rousers. His only social activity was associated with the local Landlords Association. Based on this invented accusation, the Chekist Mutin wrote on a pre-printed form his judgment: "The family of the *prisoner* Dreifelds, Jānis Kristapovičs, *consisting of the following*, son Dreifelds, Viktors, born 1919, is to be deported *outside the boundaries of Latvian SSR.*"[38] Mutin's decision was approved by

Voldemārs Dreifelds.

Viktors Dreifelds.

Arnolds Dreifelds.

the State Security People's Commissariat's Secret Political Division Chief Gavars with the notation "Agreed." In the first decision, my grandmother and mother are not mentioned. Then, as if realising their omission, the Chekists wrote a new deportation decision, wherein, in addition to the son, Viktors Dreifelds, also Jānis' wife, Emilija Dreifelde, and his daughter, Ligita Dreifelde, were included.[39] According to the strange logic of the Cheka, the sons, Voldemārs and Arnolds, were not considered "socially subversive elements" and were not intended for deportation. It is probable, however, that a decision also existed regarding the sons and can be found in the Ventspils and Skrunda branches of the Security Commissariat where the brothers lived and worked.

Not sensing the dreadful turn life was about to take, Ligita, the same as her other classmates, already for the third day had been working in a workers' cafeteria, one of several now installed in nationalised private houses in Jūrmala. Ligita had no objections against the Soviet principle "Those who do not work, will not eat." As long as she could remember, everyone in the family had always worked. The girl had successfully passed the nine exams needed for her to finish the first form of high school. Now the summer was hers. Her parents had promised to have a party for each of the successfully completed exams, and the following day, on June 14, the first of the dance evenings was scheduled. For several days, Ligita's thoughts were excitedly preoccupied with questions essential to a young girl: what to wear and how to fix her hair. Some days earlier,

Ligita with her secondary school classmates in Dubulti 1940.

she had gone with Emilija to a seamstress for the last fitting of new outfits sewn for this summer. The green silk suit was so beautiful! In it, Ligita looked so grown up! She and her mother debated that a hat with a rounded rim, fashioned of the same material, would go with the suit wonderfully. "Liguci," Emilija said, "it should be made from the same green silk, let's have the seamstress make one." "Yes, mamma," Ligita happily agreed. In the evening Viktors came home from work. He also had a gift for his little sister – a wonderful pair of high-heeled suede shoes with a cork sole. "Well, do you like them? Will you wear them?" Ligita, totally delighted, hugged her brother and right then and there tried on the shoes. They fitted as if made especially for her. At that moment she still did not know that the shoes would become the only shoes she would wear during the first winter of deportation.

With dance shoes in Siberian snows!

That night Ligita slept in her parents' bedroom. She enjoyed this privilege each time her father left on business or went to the family farmstead. On these occasions, she crawled in beside her mother under the satin coverlet and fell into deep sleep. In warmth and comfort. This time her sleep was disturbed by sharp knocks at the door. Sleepily, she heard Emilija get up and head for the door. Later, during the long, hopeless Siberian nights, they would recall these events again and again.

It had happened around three in the morning. Before opening the door, Emilija had managed to run to the stairs that led to the second story, to scream at her son Viktors that the police had arrived. It seems that Viktors had not allowed himself the carefree peace of mind his parents had felt and, as if expecting something, had screwed out the fuses that night. While Emilija took care of the electricity a good while passed. The knocks became louder and louder. Now and again, an angry shout could be heard. Her heart trembling with dreadful premonition, Emilija went to open the door. In her fear it had seemed to my grandmother that there had been six or seven men there. In fact there had been five, as was confirmed by the report of Rūdolfs Briedis, the senior officer of the operative group, regarding the "execution of the campaign."[40] From Briedis' report I also learned the surnames of the rest of the members of the arresting group – Dumbergs, Bogorad, Šteinbaums and Sozonov. The men executing the arrests had stationed armed guards at each corner and at the door of the house. The men inside had quickly searched the rooms on the first floor and then had gone to the foot of the stairs. Briedis had asked: "What's up there?" Emilija in a calm voice had replied: "The tenants live up there." The Chekists, however, did go up to make certain themselves. Emilija heard how they knocked at the door of her son's room and then opened it. After a while, the Chekists returned without Viktors. Emilija never found out what Viktors had said to the Chekists, but, miraculously, his lies of despair were believed. Perhaps they did not want to create needless noise, because they had been warned to take the "guilty persons" into custody discreetly, as much as possible without attracting the attention of the neighbours.[41] That is how Emilija saved her son Viktors from deportation and certain death.[42] All night Viktors had lain there and listened how his parents and sister were taken away.

Having drawn the blanket up to her chin in fear, Ligita listened to the dreadful noises and strange, rude voices. The uncertainty was unbearable. Finally, Emilija came in. With her, a soldier in uniform also broke into the bedroom. Emilija said to her daughter in a loving voice: "Liguci, you have to get up." The stranger interrupted her and harshly ordered them to get dressed and pack their belongings. They were being sent to another place to live. Not far, right here in Latvia – in Ogre. He asked where Jānis Dreifelds and Viktors Dreifelds were. Emilija responded that she did not know where her son was, but that her husband was on their farmstead and that without the head of the family they would not go anywhere. Having left some guards, the rest of the Chekists drove off to get my grandfather at farmstead." Perhaps if my grandmother had not revealed the location of her husband he would have been spared the suffering and death in Siberia. There were instances when, having not found the person they were looking for, the Chekists dropped the case. Thus quite a few people were saved on June 14. At that moment Emilija did not know the *via dolorosa* that was awaiting them – they were only being forced to move to nearby Ogre, some 70 kilometres from Dubulti. How could they leave without Jānis? While some of the Chekists went looking for the head of the family, the remaining ones continued a careful search of the Dreifelds home.

While waiting for her husband, Emilija and Ligita helplessly tried to gather together some belongings. What to take? What not to take? Why leave? Unanswerable questions ran through their heads, and in their consternation, they kept dropping things. Emilija fervently wished that her husband would arrive as quickly as possible. He would know what to do. Finally the roar of a lorry could be heard. It stopped by the house. Her husband was here – now everything would be all right! Nothing evil would happen to them now. Jānis would again take care of everything this time. As he had always. As that time when Russia was ravaged by civil war, when he was able to bring his family home safely to Latvia.

Energetic and practical, he immediately started to act. Everyone now had an assigned task. Blankets, pillows, sheets, clothing and shoes had to be packed. They also had to take along some necessary household items. In hearing unusual noises from the first floor and seeing the lorry parked at the gate, the neighbour, Mrs. Mačans, arrived to see what was happening to the Dreifelds. She opened the door and, frightened, drew back. On seeing the unknown woman, a Chekist abruptly ordered her to enter, then questioned her to find out who she was. On learning that she was not related to the Dreifelds, he ordered her to wait until the "operation would be finished."[43] Recovering from shock, Mrs. Mačans, as best she could, attempted to help packing. She insisted that they should take along all the butter that was in the house and filled up a five-litre pot with it. From the larder, a piece of smoked bacon and a loaf of rye bread were brought – surely more food would not be needed to get to Ogre. Jānis secretly managed to take some money from the table drawer and press it into his wife's hand. Emilija slipped the money inside her vest. After the famine and devastation that they had experienced in Russia during the First World War, Jānis had become far-sighted. He only relied on himself. Soon after the Russian incursion in 1940, food reserves were buried in the barn – flour, sugar, smoked bacon. An order of the Soviet regime foresaw harsh punishment for the creation of such reserves. So, at least for now, let them stay where they are – no need to show the Chekists the hiding place. Close by, in the woodshed, in a corner, were buried Emilija's jewellery and silver. Surely, they would be able to come back from Ogre at a later date. Also Viktors' service revolver was hidden in the shed.

The Chekists did find the barn key and confiscated it, but, as can be seen in Briedis' report, the buried belongings were not found. After a search of the Dreifelds' home the following "things" were taken away: a typewriter, gunpowder, gunshot, various documents, the key to the barn with various building materials, cement, lime, kerosene can, etc.[44] The loot was meagre indeed – no weapons, no counterrevolutionary literature, no foreign currency. None of the confiscated goods could be used to support the charges in the case. Later the sons tried to dig up the family valuables in the barn, but they did not find anything. Obviously someone had been there before them and removed the hidden belongings. Thus the valuables have been scattered to the four winds, and who knows which family's third generation by now wonders at the ancient-looking silver tableware with the unknown monogram ED – Emilija Dreifelde – that does not belong to their family.

In the meantime, Ligita had started to fill her own small blue suitcase. She too had to take along what was most needed. Some cream, perfume, nail polish – surely there would be the same dances and girls making themselves pretty. And why would she have a bad time in Ogre? It was a beautiful place. Ogre was also in Latvia. With childish naiveté, my mother consoled herself. "Ligita, stop fooling around," Emilija snapped at her daughter with unusual abruptness, and in one fell swoop shook out the collected valuables on the satin bed coverlet, throwing the suitcase in the corner. Ligita let out a sob. The world had become harsh. The time for dreams and games had ended.

The Chekists hurried the Dreifelds – by now much unplanned for time had passed driving to the farmstead. "Faster! Faster! Finish packing!" they barked. Finally they had to leave. On the doorstep Ligita turned and looked toward the yard. She ran toward her beloved dog to say good-by. The Chekists stopped her, pushing her in the direction of the gate. The girl pressed against the corner of the house and cried plaintively. Emilija put her arm around the girl's shoulders and said quietly and sadly: "It'll be alright, Liguci. Let's go!" But her voice broke tearfully. Jānis, sounding bitter, loud enough for the men detaining them to be sure to hear, called to the women: "Get in, your crying doesn't help with these scoundrels!" – and they clambered into the back of the lorry, where, already ahead of them, waited other unfortunates – the local policeman Anškins with his wife and daughter Nellija. These were the last words of his father my mother's brother Viktors heard from his second-story hiding place. The lorry did not stop anywhere else.

They were first driven to the railway station at Torņakalns, but all the cattle cars were already full and the men driving the convoy were ordered to drive the "transport" on to another "loading point." It was already sunrise when the Dreifelds and the Anškins arrived at the Šķirotava Station. There they were told to disembark. More and more lorries arrived, bringing more and more unfortunates. Women, children, old people crowded near the black, gaping mouths of the cattle cars. All around could be heard wailing and crying. Confused, the Dreifelds looked around, not comprehending why they should have to go to Ogre in a cattle car. But where then?! In the crowd they saw faces of acquaintances. Jānis Dreifelds managed to greet the factory owner Muška. Then they were ordered to get into one of the cattle cars. It was almost full but, again and again, the doors were opened and new families were squeezed into the already overcrowded car. The Soviet regime had "furnished it well." At both ends, two wide bunk beds had been hastily nailed together. Above the sleeping places, there were small barred windows. Between the plank beds an empty space had been left in the centre of the car. On the outside wall there was a hole created for taking care of nature's needs. Immediately beside the hole was a stack of brick-like loaves of rye bread. In the Dreifelds' car there were about forty people. And small children…

The train stood in the Šķirotava Station for three nights and three days – the 14th, 15th and 16th of June. The people herded into the car were not allowed to get out. Even their natural functions had to be taken care of right there in the car, in front of everyone. Although the rest did turn their eyes away in embarrassment, it was still humiliating. Especially for the girls and women, who, from modesty, could not force themselves to go to the dark, repulsively smelling hole. Finally someone handed over a sheet and the hole was somewhat closed off, providing some privacy, but not improving the sanitary conditions. Twice a day, two pails of water were brought into the car. The daily ration for each person was a half-litre of water for drinking. Washing was out of the question. Those who had some kind of vessel loaned it to those who, in shock at being arrested, had not recovered enough to take along with them the most elementary of household goods. The prisoners sat hunched on their bunk beds or on their belongings in the middle of the car. Their despondency was interrupted by wailing and weeping. From time to time, someone climbed up to a barred little window to see what was happening outside. During all this time, more lorries kept arriving and new people were herded into the cars. No food was given, nor did anyone want to eat.[45] Jānis Dreifelds, however, in a stern voice ordered Emilija and Ligita to eat something of the food they had brought with them, but the dry morsels could not be swallowed. As it was, they had a constant lump in their throat. They were terribly thirsty, but there was not enough drinking water, and they, as "criminals," did not deserve more.

On June 16, around lunchtime, the Chekists walked through the railway cars, called out the names of people to be deported and made them sign some kind of paper. Finally, on the night from the 16th to the 17th of June, the train headed out. People tried to throw out small notes to let their relatives know about their fate. In the wind created by the speeding train these notes again and again fluttered up into the air and like white butterflies swarmed around the railway tracks. Later, the residents in the houses near the railroad tracks carefully picked them up and sent them to the relatives. The Dreifelds were too depressed to write.

At dawn, the train crossed the border of Latvia at Zilupe. In a tear-choked voice Jānis, Emilija and Ligita sang a folksong: "Fare thee well, my midland country, I will walk your paths no more ..." . Eight years later, in March, 1949, my grandmother Milda and my father Aivars sang the same song when they crossed the border of Latvia and began their own *via dolorosa* to Siberia. Many of the memoirs of the deported mention the last song sung on leaving Latvia. Some sang "God bless Latvia" others sang "Blow, wind ...," others – "I'll sing of you, my fatherland." Thus, on the first anniversary of the occupation, on June 17, 1941, my mother's family, together with more than fifteen thousand other unfortunates, left Latvia. Many never to return, others for many long years.

How the landscape changed beyond the border of Latvia! Lopsided huts. Unkempt fields. Run-down, emaciated farm animals. So this is what the Soviet Union looked like! How very much it differed from what they had heard in the first year of the Soviet regime about the joyous and free Soviet people, who lived happily in a prosperous land of plenty under the wise leadership of Stalin.

The train headed farther into the interior of Russia. Now and then it stopped for a short while in some station, but no one was allowed to disembark. Once a day, the doors, rattling and squeaking, opened, in order to allow two persons to bring in water. Along the railway cars ran ragged, thin children begging for bread. The deportees occasionally threw a piece of bread to the hungry children. Some, from compassion. Others, because the bread stacked in the railway car was starting to grow mouldy. Almost no one ate it, because the majority still had some food left from home. Also, the bread seemed so unpalatable. Bleak women attempted to sell a boiled potato or two or a drop of milk to the deportees. They were happy to exchange potatoes and milk for the bricks of bread so despised by the Latvians. Jānis Dreifelds tried to get into the good graces of one of the sentries by offering him money, asking if he could buy something to eat. The soldiers refused. Such "kind-heartedness" toward the "criminals" was severely punished. However, someone did give in to temptation, and thus the family obtained a packet of dry, tasteless biscuits – nothing else could be bought at the station counter. Jānis tried to find out where they were being taken, but the rank-and-file soldiers did not respond to questions. Most probably, they themselves did not know anything. Their superiors did the thinking for them. Uncertainty about their fate was so tormenting for the prisoners. The deportees speculated anxiously about the probable final destination of the journey. At the time it seemed dreadful that they might be left to settle in such poor places as the villages they saw through the barred small window. How could the unfortunates imagine that, in comparison to the starvation and cold of Siberia, which was to be their fate, settlement in these impoverished villages would have been salvation.

After five days, the train reached the Babinino station. There it stopped for a while. Could it be that they had arrived at their destination? Finally the cattle car door was opened and the women and children were told to get out. Protesting and screaming, the women did not comply. They refused to leave their husbands and sons, their brothers and fathers. Seeing that force would not accomplish anything, the Chekists tried cunning. They attempted to calm the deportees by saying that the families would be reunited at the final destination ... That such separation was dictated by humane considerations of the Soviets ... That it was immoral for women and men to be together for an extended periods in such close quarters ... That this did not comply with Soviet rules of order.[46]

There was nothing else to do but to comply, and Emilija and Ligita, together with other women, children and old people, hesitantly climbed from the car. They both believed that they were to be parted from their husband and father for just a few days, so they did not even say good-byes properly. Jānis was also convinced of this: why else would he have let his wife and daughter leave dressed so lightly and only carrying a small suitcase? Even though the Chekists did not allow any time to transfer and divide the belongings, my capable grandfather certainly would have managed to throw out some bags. But he did not wish that his wife and daughter should exert themselves by carrying so heavy a load. As always, he was ready to take on the hardest burden himself, in order to spare the women in his family. Thus Emilija and Ligita parted from Jānis Dreifelds at the Babinino station, not being aware that this was a parting for life. Until spring 1990, our family had no news of the subsequent fate of Jānis Dreifelds ...

My Grandfather Jānis

I know little about my grandfather Jānis. When I was a very little girl I pored with great interest through the family photographs reclaimed from relatives. In them, grandfather appears as a corpulent man with a decisive, even stern face. I would have been afraid to approach him and to play in his presence – these were my thoughts as I closely examined his face. But I did not talk to my mother about my fears, because she always remembered her father with affection. Ligita was a child of elderly parents – longed-for and eagerly awaited, because after three sons Emilija and Jānis very much wanted a little girl. When, in 1926, the stork finally brought them a daughter, my grandfather was nearly forty-eight years old. Tiny Ligita wound the stern Jānis Dreifelds around her little finger whenever she wished – the father only smiled at his daughter's pranks, while the sons received proper scolding.

Later, when I was older, in place of the strict family patriarch I discovered Jānis Dreifelds, the man. The seeming and perhaps somewhat assumed sternness now slipped into the background, and I saw how attractive my grandfather was – how handsome, self-confident, energetic, with an impish sparkle in his eyes. Jānis was born in Russia, where his father Krišs or Kristaps Dreifelds worked as a forester in a manor not far from St. Petersburg. Fast-tempered and decisive, he started to work right after finishing primary school. Since he was a good worker and quick to catch on, soon he had worked himself up to owning a shop and a restaurant. Now it was time to form a family, so in 1912 he headed for Skrunda, where his father and father's father were born and which he considered to be his ancestral home, to look for a wife. En route, he visited his aunt

Wedding of Jānis and Emilija Dreifelds 1912.

in Liepāja, who owned a department store there. This is how he met the young and beautiful Ilze Emilija Gāliņa, who worked as a salesgirl in the aunt's store. It was love at first glance for Jānis. He had found his wife and future mother of his children. They started to exchange letters, reverently observing the very stringent forms of etiquette of the time: Most respectable Miss Gāliņa. Highly honourable Mr. Dreifelds ...This correspondence lasted for about six months, and then Jānis headed for Liepāja again. He invited Emilija for a stroll in the Rose Square, well known to all residents of Liepāja. Here he asked my grandmother to marry him. Emilija accepted the proposal. They were now engaged. Jānis kissed his fiancée's hand. He did lean in the direction of her lips but was shyly refused. He then gave Emilija a gold engagement ring and a bracelet as a gift. It was the second meeting for both of them.

The fact that Emilija accepted the proposal without hesitation confirms that it did not come as a surprise to her. Someone had obviously prepared the girl for it, and she was aware of Mr. Dreifelds' intentions. To whom else but his aunt would Jānis have entrusted his future plans and begged to know Emilija's possible frame of mind? He also did not want to be refused. Therefore, his aunt started to talk to Emilija about Jānis' good character and his prosperity, until the girl abandoned her flighty dreams of a great, romantic love and started to listen more closely to what Jānis' relative was telling her. It is very likely that my great grandmother Lība and other female relatives also added their share of praise of Jānis. According to the standards of the era he was a good prospect – able to support a family and ensure a well-to-do-life for his wife. Emilija knew what poverty was. She had watched how hard, to the point of exhaustion, her parents Lība and Indriķis had worked to feed their six children. My grandmother appreciated the opportunity to leave her modest circumstances and let it be known that she would not turn down Jānis' proposal. Excitedly the girl started to wait for Jānis' second appearance in Liepāja. Did Emilija love Jānis? Not yet at that moment, but she was happy about the upcoming wedding and the prospect of a good life in the future. At the turn of the century many unions were contracted in such fashion, because marriage was not looked upon frivolously. It was primarily viewed as an obligation, and if one was lucky, then this obligation was enhanced by love. Emilija was lucky. She fell in love with Jānis.

Emilija's and Jānis' third meeting was at their wedding. This took place on Martinmas, in autumn, in Liepāja. Before the wedding, Jānis had not kissed Emilija, not even once. A splendid hotel room had been rented for the newlyweds. There, on their wedding night, they were alone together for the first time. It is almost impossible to imagine the feelings of the newlyweds standing by the wedding bed. My grandparents were virtual strangers to each other. Emilija had been raised in a Victorian fashion and had been prepared for her obligation as a woman "to tolerate this side of things" to ensure a happy marriage. My grandmother's enterprising spirit and willpower were to be admired. One can just imagine how difficult it must have been for the never-kissed Emilija to overcome her shyness and give herself physically to her new husband – a stranger. She was determined to be happy, but between "deciding" and "being" a thousand steps had to be taken, and for this, my grandfather Jānis is also to be admired, for he had enough tact and patience to win his wife's devotion. From what my grandmother's sister Anna has said, it is known that Emilija soon loved Jānis very deeply, and that, in my opinion, is the greatest proof of the goodness of my grandfather's personality. Both were happy in their marriage.

A week after the wedding, Emilija wrapped herself in the fur coat her husband had given her as a gift, and they both headed for Russia, where, not far from St. Petersburg, in Kikerino, the next chapter in her life unfolded. Having spent most of his life in Russia, Jānis had come to love the country and the largesse and sincerity of its people. On the other hand, to Emilija Russia was foreign and unfamiliar. There were other Latvians in Kikerino, including Jānis' sister, Aleksandrina Vilnīte, with her husband Jēkabs and their three children. But, in the initial period, Emilija desperately longed for Latvia. The vast flatlands of Russia depressed her. Also, the people in Russia lived in greater poverty than in Latvia and elsewhere in Europe. Emilija was able to make this comparison, because before her marriage, she had had the opportunity to travel abroad. Captain Nevigers and his wife had been happy to take their young relative along on sea voyages because they did not have children of their own. Thus the young girl saw Amsterdam, Rotterdam, Hamburg and other large European ports, where the standard of living was the same as it was in Rīga and Liepāja. In Kikerino, Emilija quickly learned to speak Russian fluently. The language was not unknown to her, because in compliance with the 1885 decree by Czar Alexander III, Russian became the only permitted language of instruction in schools of non-Russian provinces throughout the

Russian Empire.[47] With this restriction, the Czar hoped to keep in check the freethinking secondary school and university students, as well as other revolutionaries who more and more threatened his absolute power. It was assumed that people speaking one language were easier to control.

Emilija helped her mother-in-law Pauline in the restaurant. That gave Jānis the opportunity to devote more time to selling timber. Expecting her first-born dispelled Emilija's longing for her homeland. The thoughts of the future mother were totally preoccupied with the expected child. Jānis felt proud and happy. He tried to spare his wife as much as he could. On April 1, 1914, their son Voldemārs was born. Now Emilija's and Jānis' life took on totally different meaning and content. With love-filled eyes Jānis looked on at an unfolding miracle – after the birth of her son, the timid, shy Emilija blossomed into womanly self-assurance. Emilija, too, discovered in herself powerful emotions she had previously not known. She became aware of the beauty of her body and the power it had over her and her husband. Both were intoxicated by the sensual discovery of how exhilarating and satisfying it was to give and receive. They did not know then that this harmonious period in their life and work was soon to end.

Across Europe clouds of war were already gathering. In Serbia, on June 28, the Crown Prince, heir to the throne of the Austro-Hungarian Empire, was murdered, and on August 1, Germany declared war on Russia. The waves of horror of the First World War shattered the existing world order. The Austro-Hungarian and Russian Empires collapsed. In February 1917, Czar Nicholas II was forced to step down from the throne, and, for the first time in the history of Russia, there was hope of creating a democracy. In order to weaken and divide Russia even further, Kaiser Wilhelm allowed the leaders of the Russian Bolshevik Party to return to Russia via Germany. The Communist Party had great ambitions to seize power, and found it easy to incite a people exhausted by poor governance, war and disorders. Thus, on October 25, 1917, the Bolsheviks succeeded in a coup d'état, imprisoned the interim government and for seventy long years stopped democratic development in Russia. Early hopes for a Just State, as promised by the Bolsheviks, soon turned into the opposite – into a bloody dictatorship of the proletariat. Europe was flooded with Russian aristocrats, intellectuals, civil servants, entrepreneurs and tradesmen – all those who were enterprising enough and succeeded in fleeing.

Reverberations of what was happening in Latvia reached Jānis and Emilija through letters from their relatives. But they could not envisage the extent of the devastation, because they still remembered Latvia as the land of peace and plenty that they had left at Martinmas time in 1912, a week after their wedding. The Russian army retreated from the region of Kurzeme, leaving behind burned-down houses and crops. In addition, all adult men were conscripted into the army. On May 8, 1915, the Germans took Liepāja. Emilija worried about her parents, because she did not know if they, together with the 400,000 other people from Kurzeme, had become refugees or if they had remained in the city.[48] Lība and Indriķis had decided to stay in the city. They did not have any property to lose, and they also reasoned that every regime would need diligent workers. A year later, as many as 850,000 Latvians had left their homeland, heading for Estonia and onward to Russia.[49]

For three years, the front cut across Latvian territory. The newspapers wrote about the heroic battles of the newly formed units of Latvian Riflemen against the German Army on Death Island, a bridgehead on the river Daugava. In the newspapers, however, nothing was said of the huge losses suffered by the Riflemen and civilians. Later, after the war, when information about the fallen, slain and the missing had been collected, it was noted in the annals of Latvian history that, besides civilian victims, the First World

War had extinguished the lives of 30,000 soldiers.[50] Among the missing was also Jānis' brother Juris, for whom the family unsuccessfully continued to search for many years after the war. After the 1917 Bolshevik coup d'état, the news they received about events in Latvia were very fragmentary and contradictory, and my grandparents vacillated in uncertainty about what would be safer – to remain in Russia and to wait until the disorders would end, or to leave everything and flee to Latvia.

After the war, events in Latvia developed just as dramatically as they did in Russia. A week after the 1918 cease-fire on November 11, when Germany signed the unconditional surrender to the allies in the Bois de Compiègne, on the 18th of November in Rīga, the Latvian National Council met and proclaimed the founding of an independent State of Latvia.[51] It was a fragile independence, which already in December was threatened by Bolshevik intervention. After the senseless losses that the Latvian Riflemen had suffered during the war due to bumbling by the high command of the Czar, a portion of the Riflemen had split off, becoming supporters of the Bolsheviks. The Riflemen were to pay dearly for their unfortunate choice. During the 1934 and 1937 waves of Stalinist repression approximately 70,000 Latvians, who had remained in the Soviet Union, were subjected to repression or exterminated, among them a significant number of veterans of the Bolshevik revolution – the Riflemen.[52] It is precisely the bayonets of the Latvian Riflemen that had allowed Russia to realise their intervention in Latvia in 1919, and as in a similar scenario in Petrograd, establish a Soviet state of workers and peasants. The Communists, however, quickly lost the support of the poor, because the residents, initially supportive, very soon became familiar with the Red Terror. Fearing the expansion of Bolshevism, the Western Allies decided to support the new government of Latvia. In long, drawn-out and self-sacrificing battles the loyal Latvian Riflemen and the Home Guard took care of both factions hostile to independence – the Bolsheviks and the military formations of German general von der Goltz and Russian adventurer Bermondt-Avalov. Emilija's brothers Einis, Jānis and Kārlis Gāliņš also fought for the independence of Latvia. By February 1920, the territory of Latvia was totally freed of all foreign militia. Soviet Russia was forced to admit its defeat, and on August 11, 1920, in Rīga, a Latvia–Soviet Russia Peace Accord was signed, wherein

> Russia unreservedly recognises the independence, self-subsistence and sovereignty of the Latvian State and voluntarily and forever renounces all sovereign rights over the Latvian people and territory which formerly belonged to Russia under the then existing constitutional law, as well under international Treaties, which, in the sense here indicated, shall in the future cease to be valid.[53]

This disclaimer did not, however, stop the Soviet Union from breaking this accord in 1940, as well as five other bilateral agreements.[54] On January 26, 1921, at a conference of the Allies, a decision was made "regarding the *de jure* recognition of the Republic of Latvia as a state."[55]

Seeing Russia rocked by this change in fortunes, my grandfather Jānis arrived at the harsh realisation that a new and different Russia was born, which no longer bore any resemblance to the country that he loved and knew, where he had spent most of his life. A Bolshevik victory was irreversibly in the offing, and he could no longer delay the decision to remain or to leave. It was hard for Jānis to abandon his life's work, leaving behind the fruit of his labour in Russia. Given hyperinflation, his savings no longer had any real value, and the family would have to return to Latvia almost empty-handed. But Emilija calmed her husband: "Let's go. Let's save ourselves. We'll surely be able to start again. Just as long as we can get to Latvia safe and sound." And so, Grandfather Jānis decided to return to Latvia – he had to save his family: his wife, mother and three sons. Grandfather's sister, Aleksandrina Vilnīte, remained in Russia with her husband and children. In 1937, Jānis received the last letter from his sister.[56] The subsequent fate of Aleksandrina is not known, but it is thought that both she and her husband were killed during the wave of Stalinist repression in 1937.

My Grandfather Jānis, his mother Pauline, and his family headed for their native land. Their journey was fraught with danger, because in both Russia and Latvia civil war was still raging. How the Dreifelds reached Latvia – by rail or by horse carriage – is not known. In any case, at the end of 1919, the family had already arrived in Latvia.[57] Their return coincided with the final freedom battles of Latvia. Jānis and Emilija did not grieve long about what they had lost. The most important thing was that their sons were safe and sound. They themselves were young and full of energy, and a person who was willing to work hard could earn his daily bread anywhere. Their start was even better than for most of the other refugees who returned to their homeland after the devastation and horror experienced in Russia. From his uncle Jānis had inherited a house and some land in Jūrmala. There the family settled. To help them start again, Emilija's brother, loaned them a small amount of money, for which Jānis could get what was necessary in order to begin selling firewood.

The Dreifelds were saved the hardships that many other Latvian refugees were forced to experience who were still in Russia at the time of the signing of the Peace Treaty in 1920. Latvia now was a sovereign state, and for this reason they had to obtain exit permits by proving that prior to settling in Russia they had been registered in their civil parishes in Latvia and therefore were Latvian citizens. Although in the Latvian–Soviet Russian Peace Treaty there were specific provisions covering the return of refugees and an agreement had been reached that official Russian agencies would not interfere with the return of Latvian citizens, the treaty and its execution,

Emilija and Ligita on the front porch of their family home.

however, were two different things.[58] Soviet Russian officialdom often maliciously delayed the issue of necessary documents or tried to conceal information from Latvians concerning their right to return to Latvia. During the war years in Russia, Latvian refugee committees had started up, but they too had to deal with all sorts of obstacles and interference in communication with Latvian nationals scattered across the wide expanse of Russia. Thus about 150,000 Latvians were forced to remain in Russia for life.[59] For the majority it was not a voluntary choice.

Twenty years after returning to Latvia, Emilija's conviction that what they had lost could be regained through work, was fully realised. The Dreifelds were, if not wealthy, then, according to Latvian standards, a well-to-do family. In 1938, the loan taken from the Hypothecary Bank to build a new two-story, four-apartment building had been paid off. The Sloka sawmill and lumber store were operating successfully. They had money saved in the bank. Jānis and Emilija could allow themselves to envisage a peaceful old age. They both had been born in the country, and they longed to return to the land; therefore, in 1936, Jānis acquired 7 hectares of land and built a farmhouse there. A small river flowed past the property; hence, the place was named "Upītes" (River Farm). The

The Dreifelds family relaxing.

sons had already finished school. The eldest, Voldemārs, had obtained a degree in agriculture. The youngest, Viktors, had graduated from the Military Academy and had begun his career as an officer. Arnolds did not lean to studying, but he had golden hands and was working as a blacksmith. The much-loved baby sister Ligita was enrolled in secondary school and dreaming of going to university. The girl knew nothing of the hardships and poverty of the first years after the family's return from Russia. The brothers had lived through this. She was born in the new house and prosperity. Such was the life of the Dreifelds family when, on June 17, 1940, the Soviet army invaded Latvia. According to Soviet terminology, Jānis Dreifelds was a class enemy, who "had become rich by exploiting the worker and peasant class" and was therefore classifiable as a "socially subversive element," who in compliance with the October 11 order of the Deputy Peoples Commissar of the USSR State Security, was to be deported from Latvia.[60]

ХРАНИТЬ ВЕЧНО

Ansons

секретно

СССР

НАРОДНЫЙ КОМИССАРИАТ ВНУТРЕННИХ ДЕЛ

Rīga

ДЕЛО № 13207

По обвинению Дрейфельдс Янисa Кристаповича

Начато „14 июня 1941 г.

Окончено „26 3 1942 г.

В 1 томах

Том №

После судебного рассмотрения и вступления приговора в силу, настоящее дело подлежит немедленному возвращению в

указать название органа НКВД

К делу должна быть приобщена копия приговора.

Основание: приказ НКВД, Прокуратуры и НКЮ Союза СССР № 00359 от 10 апреля 1939 года.

Передача находящихся в производстве следственных дел, а также взятых из архива дел в другие отделы или органы НКВД, хотя бы и временно, производится исключительно через

название учетного аппарата

Передача следственного дела оформляется постановлением, утверждаемым начальником соответствующего управления НКВД или его заместителем.

20293 1030

Арх. №

Сдано в архив „ “ 1941 г.

УЧТЕНО В 1962 г.

RANCĀNS

Т. им. Воровского. Н. 10429 ст

Cover of Jānis Dreifelds' deportation case file.

Vyatlag

It is July, 2000. I am sitting in the Latvian State Archive, and I am holding in my hands a thin, brown cardboard folder. On it, in Russian, is written "*Delo Nr.13 207 po obvineniyu Dreifeld(s) Yanisa Kristapovicha*".[61] The case was begun on June 14, 1941, and terminated on March 3, 1942. It contains 39 sheets of paper.

Jānis Dreifelds.

I can't bring myself to open my grandfather's case file. My hands have gone limp. I am breathing heavily. I realise that I am the first close person who is going to touch these documents that bear witness to what happened after June 1941, when my grandmother and mother were taken off the train and my grandfather was left alone. How unbelievably thin is this case file! How can my grandfather's suffering and death, my grandmother's and mother's sixteen years of deportation fit in such a thin folder! Finally I gather enough courage to open it. The first document in the file is the decision written on December 17, 1941, regarding arrest. I'm dumbfounded. How could the decision regarding arrest be made on December 17, six months after the actual imprisonment? I quickly turn over the other pages – the personal questionnaire of the prisoner, the record of the interrogation, the decision to bring charges, the conclusions regarding the charges etc. Everything is dated on the same

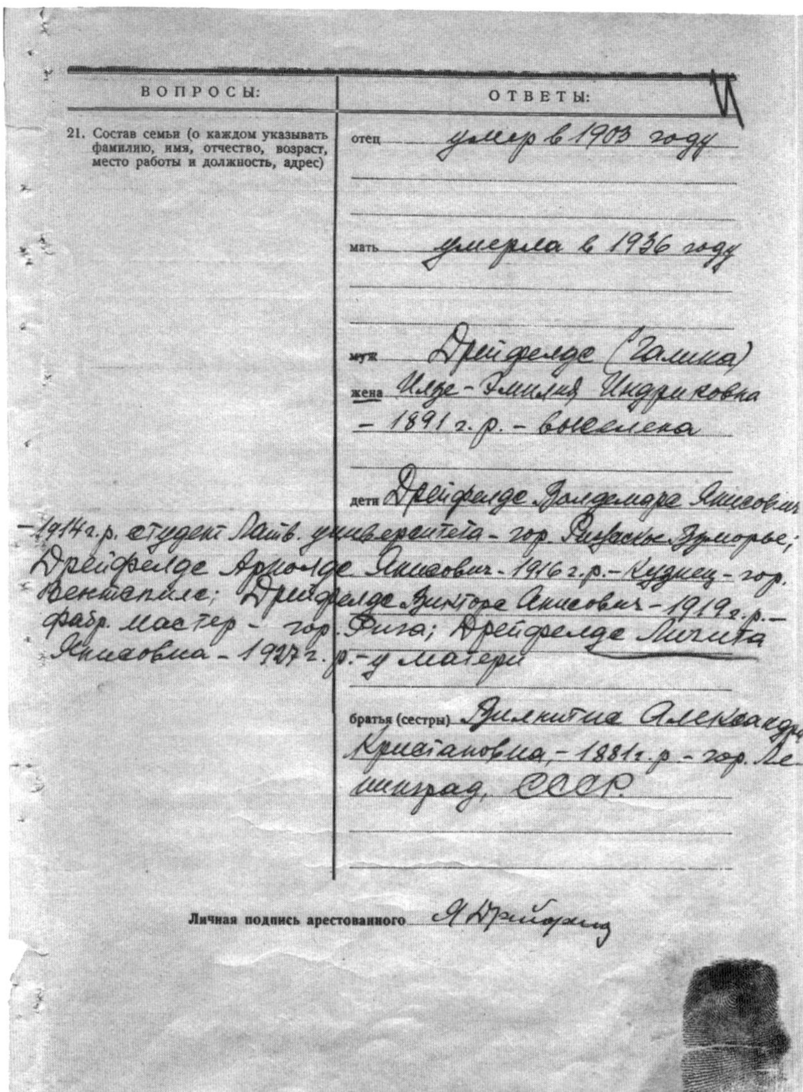

ВОПРОСЫ:	ОТВЕТЫ:
21. Состав семьи (о каждом указывать фамилию, имя, отчество, возраст, место работы и должность, адрес)	отец умер в 1903 году мать умерла в 1936 году муж Дрейфелде (Гамина) жена Илзе-Эмилия Индриковна – 1891 г.р. – выселена дети Дрейфелде Волдемарс Янисович – 1914 г.р. студент Латв. университета – гор. Рига; Дрейфелде Арнолде Янисович – 1916 г.р. – кузнец – гор. Вентспилс; Дрейфелде Викторс Янисович – 1919 г.р. – фабр. мастер – гор. Рига; Дрейфелде Лигита Янисовна – 1927 г.р. – у матери братья (сестры) Эмилтина Александра Кристиановна, – 1881 г.р. – гор. Ленинград, СССР.

Личная подпись арестованного Я. Дрейфелдс

Prisoner's form with the signature and fingerprint of Jānis Dreifelds.

17th of December. And then the next item is a 9 x 12 centimetres small grey piece of paper, on which some sort of a scrawled notation has been made. In my agitation, I can only make out a few words and the date – 31./XII/41. I understand that it is a notification of my grandfather's death! This insignificant small piece of paper, a torn-off piece of some ruled form, is a document, stating my grandfather's death … I gather courage and try to make out the writing, letter by letter, but I am unable to decipher the almost illegible handwriting. I ask the historian Ainārs Bambals to help me. The notice has been issued in Vyatlag,[62] at the Camp 7 hospital, and in it is written that Dreifelds Jānis Kristapovičs has died as a result of croupous pneumonia and chronic myocarditis on December 31, 1941.

When I have recovered from my contact with the barbarity of the prison camp death machine, I once again turn to the first page of the case file and start to read systematically and carefully. I don't allow myself to feel emotional. I must get to the end of my grandfather's case file, because nine volumes of the file of my father's father, Aleksandrs Kalnietis, still lie ahead of me, as well as the case file of my father's mother Milda and my father Aivars. However, on the fourth page a new emotional shock is in store for me. On the prisoner's form, beside his signature, is my grandfather's fingerprint. I dissolve into tears. I put my hand on my grandfather's fingerprint and allow myself the illusion, that our hands touch …

The Chekist Vids, an interrogator with the expeditionary group sent out by the Peoples Commissariat for State Security (PCSS) of the Latvian SSR, was the one who occupied himself with the invention of charges against my grandfather. Headed by the infamous Captain Jānis Vēveris of the PCSS, this group had been working since the middle of August in Vyatlag and Usollag and at great speed had rubber stamped indictment cases so they could be transferred for examination by the Kirov Regional Court or by the

Special Commission of the People's Commissariat of the Interior of the USSR. On December 17, after Comrade Vids had "acquainted himself with the materials at his disposal regarding Jānis Dreifelds' criminal activities" (proof of criminal activities was based on my grandfather having a house with four apartments, a 12,000 lats annual income and a farm), the investigator had found it expedient, as a means of security, to imprison Dreifelds, Jānis Kristapovičs in the Vyatlag prison camp until a trial could be held. The "upstanding" KGB official Vids was not at all confused by the obvious fact that the accused had already been imprisoned since the 9th of July. After the security measures had been written down on paper, it was possible to look over a recently filled-out personal questionnaire and begin the interrogation.

The interrogation lasted only an hour and a half, which gives us the hope that Grandfather was not beaten or tortured. Comrade Vids wanted to know what organisations Grandfather had belonged to, which of these he had supported financially, if there were any relatives who had been subject to repression – but nothing of value to support such charges was to be found in the answers. There was nothing else to be done but to tackle the standard question regarding anti-Soviet activities, which Grandfather denied. Vids, in indignation, screamed: "You're not telling the truth! Tell us, how you expressed your dissatisfaction with the Soviet power in Latvia!"[63] Grandfather calmly maintained that he had been satisfied with the Soviet regime. The emaciated old man was starting to bore Comrade Vids. What a tough job a KGB official had! For months on end he had to live in uncivilised conditions in some stinking prison camp and day after day interrogate all kind of riffraff infected with contagious diseases and infested with lice. Besides that, he also had to fabricate evidence of guilt. Later when, as a matter of routine, he had asked more questions about Jānis' property and income, he noticed something of more interest in the prisoner's form – the prisoner had a sister, who lived in Russia. Could some vestiges of counterrevolutionary activity perhaps be found here? No, it appeared as if not, because the communication between the brother and the sister had ceased in 1937. Obviously Aleksandrina Vilnīte had already been unmasked and sentenced. That would have to be checked at a later date. Lunchtime was approaching, and Vids decided to stop. Therefore, on December 17 at 12:00 the interrogation of my grandfather was terminated. In the afternoon, Vids wrote up the rest of the documents, and so the investigation file had been created in accordance with Soviet procedural requirements and was now ready to be handed in to the Special Commission of the USSR Interior People's Commissariat. In the written charges "Dreifelds Jānis Krisapovičs is accused of having owned a four-apartment building with an annual turnover of 1200 lats, a farm with 7 hektares of land, a shop with a 12,000 lats annual turnover, with one exploited worker."[64] For this crime, it is recommended that a sentence of deportation for five years to distant regions of the USSR be applied. In comparison to the majority of the deported people who had received a sentence of twenty years or death, Vids had been unusually merciful. Perhaps my grandfather had looked so emaciated that the very experienced Chekist had concluded – he will soon die anyway, why ask for more. He was not mistaken. My grandfather died fourteen days later.

Once more, I leaf through the results of Chekist Vids' efforts and wonder why the Soviet judicial system had to preoccupy itself so extensively with creating this illusion of legality, concealing behind it the mass extermination of people. This took time and unnecessary expenditures; moreover, it unnecessarily employed a gigantic army of Chekists and judicial system officials. It would have been simpler not to pretend and to murder without these mountains of paper. However, for some unknown reason the edicts of the Soviet Procedural Code were observed scrupulously. This assigns a tragic surrealism to what was happening. Illegally pulled from their homes, separated from their families, and emaciated from hunger, these prisoners were forced to play this game of legality. For the "correct" completion of the case file, six signatures by the accused were required.

First of all, my grandfather Jānis had to put his signature on the decision regarding the imposition of security measures. Then, with his signature, he had approved the prisoner's personal form filled out in Russian. The third signature on the minutes of the interrogation testifies to the fact that what was said during the interrogation "confirms in writing what I have said and has been read to me in Latvian." Even that seems odd: why would the protocol, written in Russian, have been read in Latvian, given that Jānis Dreifelds understood Russian. He would have been able to read it himself, or he would have been able to listen as it was read and would have understood the Russian. Obviously this was the prescribed investigative procedure or perhaps it was more practical, because, without undue objection, it was thus possible to force a person to sign anything: the majority of the interrogated did not understand Russian, and as my grandfather's case reveals, it did not make any difference. By hook or crook, the required signature was obtained anyway. They did not even need to expend much energy. The prisoners were emaciated and apathetic. Only few had the strength to object, much less resist. Those who did not want to sign immediately were beaten until they complied. The really obstreperous ones, as a warning to others, were left outside overnight to freeze in –50 degrees Celsius. After this, there was no need to continue the case, because even the Soviet judicial process had not perfected its absurdity to the level of accusing corpses.

The next stage in the judicial process game was to prove the charges, which ended with an obligatory rhetorical question to the accused himself, if "according to the substance of the charges, did he consider himself to be guilty."[65] As if he had any choice! Of course, my grandfather, the same as many people before him and after him, admitted that he was guilty. The last response from my grandfather in this theatre of the absurd was his signature at the bottom of the protocol about the termination of the investigation. The text is printed and in a space left for this purpose, the investigator had scribbled "Dreifelds Jānis Kristapovičs does not wish to add anything to the investigation and confirms the previously submitted testimony."[66] My grandfather was spared further games by the judicial process. He died before the review of the case by the Special Commission of the USSR Internal Peoples Commissariat (IPC),[67] and, by a decision made March 25, 1942, the investigation was suspended and the case file transferred to the archives.

Since Jānis Dreifelds did not get to the stage of having a criminal case established against him, the investigative case invented by Vids was combined with the initial action – the file of the family of the deported Jānis Dreifelds, started on June 14, 1941. There, without being identified, were included also the "administratively" deported, Emilija and Ligita Dreifelde. Their first names and surnames do not even appear on the cover of the case file. In my mind, it is incomprehensible, that for their sixteen years of deportation, my grandmother and mother had not even merited their own case files! Like adjuncts, objects or furniture, they are written into Jānis Dreifelds' case file, and Jānis Dreifelds, who had died long ago, continued to influence the fate of our family until 1957 and even beyond. The very last time was on December 29, 1988, when the Deputy Minister of the Interior of the Latvian SSR, Zenons Indrikovs reviewed this file in order to ascertain, if the Latvian Popular Front[68] activist Sandra Kalniete had some connection with the deported Jānis Dreifelds.[69]

The "correctly" composed charges in the case do not say anything about what happened between the Babinino railway station and December 17, when the first entry appeared in the file. Nothing is to be found there about my grandfather's life: how did he get to Vyatlag? What happened to the family belongings that remained with my grandfather when my grandmother and mother were taken off the train? What he did he eat, if he ate at all? What was he wearing? What illnesses did he have? Did he suffer from dystrophy? How did he die? Where was he buried? The surreal Soviet judicial process did not care about such factual details. It preoccupied itself with the class struggle and was disinterested in the object of this struggle – the human being. I have no other option but to try to imagine what my grandfather's *via dolorosa* was like from the crumbs of recollections of those who survived Vyatlag and from historical research.[70] I am aware, that this reconstruction is only an assumption, because my grandfather could not have been in the same place at the same time as other martyrs. What he experienced could have differed from what others experienced, but basically the path of the prisoners was the same – from Babinino to Yukhnovo transfer camp, from Yukhnovo through Babinino to Vyatlag 7 prison camp.

In the Occupation Museum archives a new blow is in store for me. In the list of the imprisoned and deceased Latvians that, at the moment, is the most complete compilation of the people who were deported and names of the camps where Latvian residents died, I don't find the name of Jānis Dreifelds. I feel bitter. He has even been robbed of the honour of a place in the list of victims. Yes, a woman working at the museum comforts me – also the names of members of her family are not to be found on any list for the moment. Therefore, there are many like Jānis Dreifelds, whose death is confirmed by a notation in his personal file, but in the administrative chaos of the camps a surname has vanished from the operative list in the file or, through a slipup or carelessness, has been placed in the section of a different administrative territory. According to SSPC data, Jānis Dreifelds is considered to have been born in Russia. Perhaps because of this, his surname has been omitted from the list of Latvians who died in Vyatlag. Only when, on

June 14, 2001, the book of commemoration *Aizvestie* (The Deported) compiled by the Latvian National Archive is issued, finally, on page 560, I find my grandfather's name.[71] However, even this book is probably not complete, because Latvian historians still don't have access to the case files of the highest statesmen, diplomats and the army high command. The facts about the circumstances and places of their death are still unclear.

Shortly after Emilija and Ligita were transferred to another cattle car, and as it headed out, the men who had remained on the train were told to get off. This is how Dr. Jānis Šneiders describes the preparation of the convoy: "… all of us, one after the other, were searched, all writing instruments were taken away, as well as knives and even a nail file." At the station there were individual tables where officers sat, and all the gold and silver jewellery, watches etc. had to be handed over. The belongings and suitcases were put in a pile, and all of us were lined up in rows six people deep. We were surrounded by guards – on foot and on horses, and finally, there were also dogs."[72] It is very probable that my grandfather also walked in such a column the kilometres that separated Babinino from Yukhnovo. In the memory of the prisoners the estimated distance differs. Some recall 15 kilometres, others – 30 or 40 kilometres. This difference is of significance, because it mirrors the level of exhaustion and the psychological condition of the people walking. In reality Babinino is located about fifty kilometres from Yukhnovo.

The convoy of prisoners stumbled along the much-trod trail that in places was trampled into mud. The men still had some strength built up in Latvia in their bones. Only thirst tormented them, because they were not given anything to drink. To step to the side or to lag behind was also not allowed. The guards had warned that they would shoot immediately. The slower ones were urged on with the help of hits with a gun barrel. Some had teeth knocked out or earned a large, blue bruise. Would that my grandfather had missed these hits, because he no longer was a strong man!

After many hours of dragging along, the attention of the deported men was drawn to the cawing of crows. Like a black cloud they were circling over some buildings that appeared in the distance. The column was approaching the Yukhnovo transfer camp, which had been installed in an erstwhile manor. Before this transport of Latvians, Polish officers from the regions of Poland occupied by the USSR had lived there. The prisoners were herded into a vegetable garden littered with refuse and glass shards, where they were again registered and searched. The agitated crows, cawing without cease, circled over the heads of the condemned. The earth had been dug up. An unpleasant odour could be discerned in the air. It seemed to the agitated people that the smell was that of corpses, and they asked themselves and each other if this was the end. Was death waiting for them here? Someone's nerves did not hold out: he pulled out a knife he had hidden in his clothes, brandished it and then hacked at his temple. Blood spurted. The Chekists and guards started to scream in panic: "Lie down! Or I'll shoot!" Blood flowing copiously, the unfortunate man stumbled a few steps and then collapsed. Yukhnovo had now been consecrated with Latvian blood…

Having recovered from this unfortunate incident, the guards continued the registration of the prisoners, placing them into groups of hundreds. As soon as a hundred had been organised, the group was herded off to the prison camp. The captives felt somewhat reassured – they probably will not shoot us right away! In total, 80 groups of a hundred each were created.[73] In an adjacent, separately fenced-off area, approximately 300 Latvian Army officers were imprisoned, and in another – a group of women.

Jāņi – Midsummer's Eve – arrived at Camp Yukhnovo, and in spite of everything, the men were preparing to celebrate it. Among the litter in the camp, a metal barrel was found. In it, the traditional Midsummer's fire was lit. Everyone gathered in a circle around it. Looking at his brothers in misfortune, Jānis Dreifelds tried to suppress the lump that had risen in his throat. He so much longed for his wife and children! He remembered the last Midsummer's Eve, when his little sweetheart, Ligita, had been the cause of so much worry. Jānis and Emilija had been celebrating with their neighbours at Doctor Ozoliņš' house. When they had sung and celebrated their fill, they both returned home, only to discover that Ligita was missing. What an uproar! The girl had sneaked out of the house, not saying a word to the maid. After a few hours, when the sinner, flushed and happy, returned, Jānis shook her vigorously – how could she leave without permission! Where had she been? Emilija tried gently to stand up for her daughter, but this time her husband was not to be swayed. The worry and anger the family patriarch had felt about the girl's wilfulness made him unreachable. He thundered his decision: she would be housebound next week! Ligita, offended, let out a sob – she had not done anything bad. Together with her friend Aina, she had only wanted to look at the Midsummer bonfires at the seashore. After having walked a little after having a mock fight with their gathered bunches of sweet flags and flowers, they had gone to sleep in the hayloft of Aina's mother. After screaming out her truth, the girl had run off to her room upstairs. Emilija looked reproachfully at her husband and went to follow the girl … Soon Jānis' anger subsided – she was only a stupid child. Suddenly a congratulatory song sounded outside the window. As they did every year, musicians had come to honour Jānis on his name day. Hearing the sound of music, Emilija and Ligita forgot the incident as well. Emilija silently snuck up to the window and lifted the edge of the curtain. Then she whispered to her husband – there are six of them. Now Jānis knew how much money he would have to prepare for the musicians. Ligita understood that the right moment had arrived to make peace with her father, and, having thrown her arms around her father's neck, she whispered: "Forgive me, dear papa!"… Oh,

Emilija and Ligita! Where were the both of them now? His eyes filled with tears. Jānis quickly took a deep breath and stood up straight. He could not allow himself to sink into reminiscences and despair. This madness could not continue forever, and surely life would return to its accustomed path. It was just necessary to have faith and be patient.

During Midsummer's Eve, rumours spread that war had started. One of the prisoners had succeeded in buying a newspaper from a chauffeur. From mouth to mouth the news spread that Germany had attacked the Soviet Union on June 22. The prisoners were agitated; the war created hopes of being freed and returning to Latvia. The men eagerly speculated that the Russians would not hold out for long, that the war would end after two or three months and, with it, the power of the Soviet Union over Latvia would end. Somewhere at the horizon, in the direction of Smolensk, occasional roar of cannons could be heard. In the camp everything testified to an increase in tension – the loudspeakers had been disconnected, the ration of bread reduced, and the guards had become more abrupt and brutal, more frequently abusing the deported Latvians by calling them Fascists.

By June 25, the transport of prisoners from the camp began, and those that were left tortured themselves trying to guess their fate and that of the men taken away. Again rumours spread about being shot. In some, the insane hope was revived that they would finally be driven to where the wives and children they had been separated from were waiting. On June 29, the last hundreds left the Yukhnovo transfer camp. Thus, between June 25 and 29, also my grandfather again was put in a line-up and, escorted by guards, herded as far as the Babinino station. There he was allowed to collect some of his belongings, which had stood for a week under open skies and now were rain soaked, left in disarray by the other deportees who had handled them again and again. I don't doubt that my grandfather, in his concern for Emilija and Ligita, tried to take as much as he could of the things they needed. Then he was herded into the railway car. I don't know if it was a cattle car, wherein were "transported" about fifty prisoners, or a large "Pullman," in which could be squeezed from ninety to a hundred people. Moscow was only 215 kilometres from Babinino, but the "transport" of prisoners took a roundabout route, with long stopovers in stations, reaching its final destination in two to five days time. The journey was lengthened by an unending string of contingents of soldiers and armaments flowing to the West. It was unbearably hot. They were not given anything to eat. There was lack of air and drinking water. People frequently fainted from thirst and excessive heat. The prisoners were totally isolated from the outside world and did not know on whose side fortune smiled in the war. In the stations even the loudspeakers were silent. Dr. Šneiders recalled that in Moscow, through a crack in the wagon wall, he had seen anti-air-raid balloons – therefore German planes must already have been threatening Moscow. From Moscow the road followed the route Gorky – Kotelnich – Kirov.

In Kirov, the train stood for several days, and all the time the people who were to be transferred were locked in the railway cars. Then the train started to move in a northerly direction to Rudnickaya village, where the Vyatlag camps began. According to Cheka documents, the first trainload of deportees from Latvia reached their place of imprisonment on the 9th of July. The majority arrived on July 10, while the last contingent got there no later than July 13. In total, 3281 Latvian inhabitants were imprisoned in Vyatlag in the autumn of 1941.[74] From what Dr. Šneiders has recounted, I learn more about Vyatlag 7 prison camp, where initially the majority of Latvians were located and where also my grandfather was imprisoned. It is possible that they knew each other, because, being a doctor, Šneiders attempted to relieve the suffering of the weak and the ailing, thus becoming acquainted with many of the deportees. After arrival, the deportees were again searched, lined up in a row and ordered to hand over all their belongings that, on release, they were told, would be returned to them. A receipt was given for the confiscated property, which was taken away already during the first search.

Each time I heard my mother say that the family belongings they had taken along had remained with my grandfather, I consoled myself, that at least they had been of use to him, so he could be more warmly dressed or could exchange them for something to eat. Nary a hope. The belongings were stolen or senselessly left to rot in some warehouse, while my grandfather in Vyatlag and my grandmother and mother in some other corner of Siberia froze and starved.

After their belongings were taken away, the prisoners were herded to some wood barracks. There in the cracks of bare wood plank bunks, numb from starvation, bed bugs hid, waiting for the unfortunates. Sensing the warmth of human beings, they revived and, by the thousands, infested the newly arrived. The barracks were dirty and littered. Refuse was scattered on the floor, and underneath the plank bunks firewood was stored. Although wood was burned in the iron "efficiency" stoves day and night, the walls of the barracks were iced over.[75] The barracks were locked from the outside at night, and the locked in inhabitants had to take care of their bodily needs by using the *parasha* – a large metal bin, which the men carried out each morning. It seemed as if the smell of urine and excrement had impregnated everything – the air, the clothing, the flesh and the food. The stench had permeated everyone so intensely, that it did not leave the prisoners even outside the barracks or while they were working in the woods. Even the privies installed on the prison camp territory were not cleaned and, during the winter, turned into an ever-mounting frozen hill of excrement. The workday started at six in the morning and finished at eight at night. On occasion, the more urgent work needed to be done at night. Before work, the prisoners were lined up and, accompanied by guards, herded off to work in the woods. Those who fulfilled their daily quotas received food ration coupons for a watery soup with a piece of bread or a ladleful of porridge with a piece of bread. On occasion a fish was thrown in with the ration. But what if the quota was not fulfilled? Then incarceration in the cold and the dark, virtually without food, awaited the culprit. In order to "re-educate" the culprit, the guards did not hesitate in applying corporeal punishment.

According to camp rules the prisoners in Vyatlag were divided into three groups. Group "A" consisted of those who could do hard physical work. In the next group "B" were prisoners suited for work around the prison camp. The third group "C" consisted of "off-balance-sheet invalids" and prisoners under investigation, the stronger of whom also performed hard labour. My grandfather Jānis was thus included in the last group. By order of the GULAG administration, food rations were planned in accordance with the specified categories. Workers in the "A" group, after fulfilling their daily quota, had the right to receive 500 grams of bread per day, the "B" and "C" groups – 400 grams.[76] Theoretically workers in both of the first two categories, with good work and if they outperformed their set quotas, could increase their bread ration. However the prisoners very shortly understood that the additional slice of bread did not balance out the expended energy. The prisoners in the third group did not have this opportunity.

When the war began, the food rations for the prisoners were arbitrarily reduced because camp authorities no longer received regular deliveries. The prisoners became even more isolated from the outside world: the number of guards were increased, radio transmitters were disconnected, newspapers no longer were received in the prison camp, correspondence and receipt of packages was prohibited.[77] The prison camps became islands of horror in the middle of a sea of ice and snow. The Latvians had to live in the same barracks as criminals, even murderers. Highly educated and able people were forced not only to submit to the brutality of prison camp personnel, but also to struggle for survival in the environment of a degraded criminal world, regulated by its own laws. In addition, "to maintain order," the administration of the prison camp collaborated with the "criminals" and turned a blind eye to their skulduggery against the "smart-ass intellectuals" and the "contras."

Jānis Dreifelds was 63 years old. Already before he was deported, the first signs of age had appeared, which grandfather, like everyone who enjoys excellent health and great physical strength, looked on with great distress. He grumbled about his wife's warnings to observe moderation in eating or to dress more warmly because he caught colds frequently. In Siberia, Jānis' health no longer allowed him to do heavy work in the woods. Initially perhaps he still had the strength to do something on the prison camp territory, but very soon he became too weak and ill from starvation and cold. From the recollections of others, I learn that the first signs of weakness started to appear already at the beginning of August – boils, festering open wounds, scurvy. In order to somehow combat avitaminosis, the prisoners boiled up a concoction of pine needles and drank it. Most certainly the enforced starvation had changed my stately grandfather until he was unrecognisable: he was either swollen from starvation, or else had become dystrophycally thin. The Latvians who have survived Vyatlag and the nearby Usollag confirm that the 1941–42 winter was the most dreadful. Their weight had decreased more than two times, and some of the deportees had only weighed 35 kilograms.[78] According to the materials gathered by the expedition "Vyatlag–Usollag '95," in the period from 1941 until July 1942, 2337 persons, more than two thirds of all the imprisoned from Latvia had died. Of these, 1603 persons, among them my grandfather Jānis, already died during the investigation period.[79]

The prison camp administration considered people like my grandfather to be an unnecessary drawback that damaged "production statistics," and it was in their interests to have the "off-balance-sheet invalids" die quickly so they could be written off from the live inventory. The administration worries reflected the Soviet style, because in the Soviet Union everything was planned. The production plan of the prison camp was dependent on the number of prisoners at the camp. The higher authorities, in their turn, evaluated the work of each prison camp commander according to his ability to drive the prisoners hard and fulfil the production plan. The camp commander was not interested in excuses or justifications that the "units of labour" could not work without enough food, clothing and minimal rest. When the war began, the already long workday had been lengthened by 3 hours – the war industry had an increased need for lumber and firewood.[80] In conjunction with the war, the flood of deportees decreased, because the regime needed people for the front, and this for a time slowed down the battle with the "internal enemy." The prison camp administration had to fulfil the approved production plan with the existing number of prisoners. How dreadful the conditions of imprisonment were, can be discerned from the speech of the administrator of Vyatlag at that time, Levinson, at a meeting of the local party activists. There are no lights, no heating, no drying rooms, no saunas or mattresses for the wood plank bunks. The prisoners are made to work until total exhaustion for 16 hours per day. Food is pilfered from the kitchen, and the prisoners do not even receive their reduced food rations. Due to lack of clothing and footwear people regularly catch colds.[81] It would be naïve to conclude that Levinson was a generous human being who, without personal interest, had insisted on improvement in living conditions for the prisoners. No, he was concerned for his own fate, because during Stalin's regime no one could be safe from being labelled a "saboteur and enemy of the Soviet regime." The experienced Chekist understood that unfed two-legged cattle would not be able to fulfill the production plan and that the responsibility would have to be assumed by him.

When the list of the 409 Latvians who had died in Vyatlag compiled by Dr. Šneiders was published in February 1989,[82] our family, like the relatives of so many others all over Latvia, avidly read it, searching the columns for the surnames of their own. For many, this list was the first news of the death of their relatives. The name of Dreifelds was not there. At the time of the publication of the list, our family did not know anything at all about the fate of grandfather Jānis, and he could as well have died in some other of the many "prison camps located across the spacious Soviet motherland." It was only in June 1989 that my mother had gathered enough courage to turn to the KGB, to ask for information about her father. In the response received on 21 April, 1990, it was stated that "Dreifelds Jānis, son of Kristaps, born 1878, was held in prison from June 14, 1941, died on 31 December, 1941, in Vyatlag, and had been rehabilitated on April 6, 1990." What Vyatlag was, we learned at a later date. My grandfather, together with Dr. Šneiders, were in prison camp No. 7 until August 14, when the latter, together with 900 other Latvians, was transferred to prison camp No. 11, where they were made to work in the woods. Dr. Šneiders' list of deceased was started on August 26 – that is, after the doctor had left prison camp No. 7.

On Jānis Dreifelds' death certificate it is written that he died from chronic myocarditis and croupous pneumonia. This sort of diagnosis is to be found in almost all the official death certificates. The depositions by doctors imprisoned in the GULAG, but in particular the unique list of Dr. Šneiders, wherein he has compiled information about the deceased prisoners of Vyatlag prison camp No.11, as well as Dr. Silvestrs Čamanis' narrative,[83] there is incontestable evidence that the direct causes for illness and death were the inhuman living conditions, starvation and dystrophy caused by the latter, avitaminosis and hard, superhuman labour. The most prevalent cause of death was enteritis and enterocolitis, meningitis, pneumonia, pleurisy and inflammation of the joints. In addition, the deceased had suffered from tuberculosis, stroke, nephritis, otitis, dystrophy and other illnesses. Similar descriptions of illness and death are also found in the recollections of prisoners from other prison camps. In the infirmaries there were virtually no medicines, and it was not possible to save the dying. As a consequence, the infirmary was called the death chamber. Only the weakest and the most hopeless cases were sent there. Those who ended up there knew that they were going to die. No one returned from there.

Jānis Dreifelds was aware that his hour of redemption was approaching. What were my grandfather's thoughts as he lay on his deathbed? The most tormenting must have been the thoughts he had of his family. He knew nothing of the fate of his wife and daughter. In the first year of the war, any contact with the outside world was prohibited; and grandfather, his heart going numb, would have thought that Emilija and Ligita were suffering similar torture in some other GULAG prison camp and perhaps were already dead. Why should he think otherwise, given that, even among the prisoners in Vyatlag, there were women? It is doubtful that the interrogator Vids was merciful enough to reveal anything about my grandmother's and mother's deportation circumstances to this "exploitative and socially dangerous element" when Jānis Dreifelds finally was called out for interrogation on December 17.[84]

A true Soviet Chekist was hardened by class struggle and did not feel any compassion for the class enemy. Thus, Jānis Dreifelds died not knowing anything about Emilija and Ligita or about his sons Voldemārs, Arnolds and Viktors. He could not know whether they had been taken prisoner on some other day known only to the Cheka, and similarly herded into cattle cars to follow their father to Siberia. Jānis Dreifelds had always felt responsible for his family.

Perhaps with his sense of obligation he blamed himself for what had happened? It is possible that, since that distant night of June 14, right up to his hour of death, my grandfather in his mind blamed himself, asking again and again, why he had not listened to railwayman Šveheimers' warning and saved his family. They could have found shelter in family farm or with Emilija's brothers near Liepāja. But what if his wife's brothers also were somewhere in Siberia? Perhaps all Latvians were deported to Siberia and there was not a nation any more! The same as Latvia was no more …

Jānis Dreifelds died in the freezing cold of December. On the last day of the year, which, according to Soviet traditions, is a day of particular celebration. As was customary on holidays, the prison camp guards got heavily drunk. Vodka melted hardened souls and loosened tongues. They cursed the fate that had brought them to this part of the world, forgetting that the privileges enjoyed by the Chekists protected them from sure death in the battlefield. Now and again, their Slav souls drew refreshment from their plaintive songs. Were they not human like anyone else? Did they not deserve to live the beautiful life their Illustrious Leader Joseph Stalin had mandated for them? Their Illustrious Leader in Moscow, who untiringly cared about them in distant Vyatlag while gazing at a brightly lit fir tree in the Kremlin.

Jānis Dreifelds died alone. In a room that was stuffed with other dying bodies. Some called on God, others cursed fate. Some moaned and screamed for their wives and children. After dying, the deceased were stripped naked; their ragged clothing was steamed and passed on to the still living unfortunates. A metal wire, to which was fastened a wooden tag bearing the file number of every prisoner, was fastened around the neck of each corpse. Then the naked bodies were thrown into a cart and driven to a hole hewed in the frozen soil. The bodies were thrown into the hole and frozen clumps of earth hurled as makeshift cover. Even in death, the martyrs were not given back their name and surname. They had been converted from "units of labour" inventory into the useless commodity list.

My grandfather's body rests near the territory of Prison Camp No. 7. The place of the Latvian burial grounds is now only known to the oldest inhabitants of the nearby Lesnoye village. Wind has sown a birch grove on this lush earth, fertilised as it is with dead flesh. The trees quietly rustle in the wind, in innocent happiness about the short northern summer.

In 1995, the expedition "Vyatlag–Usollag '95" headed for the places where Latvians suffered. The pilgrimage was undertaken by the sons of those who had died in Vyatlag and the people who themselves had suffered there: Ilmārs Knağis and Alfrēds Puškevics, the historian Ainārs Bambals, as well as Zigurds Šlics and the TV cameraman, Ingvars Leitis. In the centre of Vyatlag, on a hill near Lesnoye village, on August 16, they erected a wooden cross they had hewn and tarred. Under the cross they buried a clay pitcher with a handful of earth from the Big Cross at the Forest Cemetery in Rīga where some victims of 1941 lie buried. A handful of Vyatlag's earth was brought back to Latvia and buried at the Big Cross beside many other handfuls of earth from Latvian burial grounds scattered across the GULAG.

At the foot of the Vyatlag commemorative cross is a bronze plaque with an inscription in Latvian, Russian and English: "For citizens of the Republic of Latvia – victims of the Communist terror. Latvia 1995." The cross rises above the woods cleared by the prisoners and above Lesnoye village, where the descendants of Chekists continue to live, themselves now working in the still operative Vyatlag, a closed-type correctional institution – K-231. Prison Camp No. 7, the place where my grandfather Jānis was imprisoned, has burned down. Around Lesnoye village, there are peat bogs, whose area has increased after ruthless clear cutting of forests during the heyday of the GULAG. In the autumn, the roads become wet and muddy, impossible to wade through. Snow starts to fall in September, as it did when the people deported on June 14, 1941, suffered, and very soon the cold reaches the forty, even the fifty degree mark below zero. In the centre of the Lesnoye village, stand the monuments of Lenin and Dzerzhinsky,[85] while on the gravestones in the official cemetery one can read the names of Chekists from Stalin's era. Names of the guards, interrogators and torturers of my grandfather and other Latvians. Their descendants, it seems, still have not understood the inseparable union of the words "communism" and "terror."

War in Latvia

My father Aivars was wounded during the first days of the war, when, as the Red Army was retreating, there was an air raid on the unfinished Russian airfield at Jumpravmuiža near the home of my father's grandmother, Berta Matilde. It happened about a kilometre from the Šķirotava freight station, from which my mother's family was deported to Siberia in a cattle car on June 14. One of the main roads used by the retreating Red Army passed by Šķirotava. In a great hurry, the army fled along the Daugavpils highway heading toward Rīga. Aivars, like most boys, was curious and despite the fact that his grandmother had forbidden it, he prowled among the roadside bushes, so that no exciting events would pass him by. German bombs and Russian anti-aircraft shells were exploding around him. The boy was afraid, but fear of what was happening only increased the fascination. Close by, some Red Army soldiers were trying to find shelter in a ditch. That is the last frame that remained in Aivars' memory before a stunning explosion and a shock wave that propelled him in the air like a rubber ball. As he fell, the boy got a concussion and broke a leg. Grandma Matilde was in despair. Around them bombs were exploding. There was neither a horse with which to get the boy to the doctor nor a doctor to whom she could turn. Also there was no way she could let Milda know about the boy's accident because, due to war, the communication lines with her daughter had been severed. My father's mother only found out several days later that her son had been injured during the air raid. Without the help of a doctor, the leg healed wrong. In normal circumstances this problem could have been corrected, but it would have required the intervention of a qualified surgeon. In the confusion of war and post-war events this was not done, and thus my father became lame for life.

Germany attacked the Soviet Union during the night of June 22 and, a few days later, the German army had already crossed over the border into Latvia. Everything happened so fast that the Red Army was not even able to fulfil Stalin's order to destroy everything that might be of use to the enemy, as well as to evacuate all the inhabitants whose skills might be employed by the enemy forces.[86] The Red Army soldiers and Soviet officials fled in such a panic and in so disorganised a fashion that some of them did not even manage to take along their weapons. From the Jugla bridge near Rīga to the town of Sigulda, the sides of the highway were littered with looted property, uniforms, gas masks, munitions and wrecked cars. On July 1, the Germans entered Rīga. After almost a yearlong interruption, the national anthem "God bless Latvia" again sounded over the radio and the red, white and red flag flew in the streets. Even though the Latvian flag was flown beside the flag of the Third Reich – the red with a black swastika at the centre – in the eyes of the Latvians, it did not overshadow the beauty of the national flag at that moment. People came to lay flowers at the Freedom Monument for Mother Latvia to show their joy about the liberation and, in churches, sermons of thanksgiving were said.

Probably nowhere else in Europe were the German armed forces awaited with such enthusiasm. Or perhaps only in the two other Baltic States. To this day it shocks Europeans, who know so little about the sudden reversals of Latvian history and the criminal offences committed by the Communist regime. Western Europe has experienced the horror of Fascism, but Communism, in the opinion of many, had seemed more like an innocent intellectual infatuation, idle living room chatter about equality and social justice. In reality, they both were criminal totalitarian regimes, which practised racism and national intolerance and were responsible for mass genocide. Because of a historic twist of fate, Latvians became acquainted with Communism and its governing methods first. Therefore, after the just experienced year of Soviet occupation and the mass deportations of June 14, the German soldiers were awaited as liberators. After the war, Soviet propaganda took advantage of this fact, in order to convince their Western allies about the Fascist and anti-Semitic sentiments of the Latvian people. Film clips of the German invasion can still be seen in European television programmes, and the producers of these transmissions usually forget or simply don't know why Latvians felt this way. They do not explain to their viewers or listeners what happened in Latvia during the first year of Soviet occupation.

On July 4, Rīga was shocked by the news that 98 bodies had been unearthed beside the Central Prison, and crowds of Rīgans descended on the prison looking for their missing relatives. The retreating Chekists had hurriedly shot people en masse all over Latvia. At last it was possible to talk aloud about the horrors of the year under the Soviets, about deported and missing relatives. Long columns of death notices as well as a column "In Search of the Missing" were published in the press. Every day new facts were uncovered about the crimes committed by the Chekists – officials, officers, old people, students, women, even children had not been spared from the torture chambers of the Cheka.[87] Under Soviet censorship, people had lived with their own pain and fear, thus no one had had full knowledge of the extent of the horrific crimes. For their own selfish motives, the Nazi propaganda machine took advantage of the events of the Year of Terror, as it became to be known, in order to further inflame and feed the fear of Bolshevism and reinforce the belief that only under the wing of Third Reich the Latvian people could hope for a future. At that moment this propaganda seemed irrelevant to Latvians, because the corpses were real and the pain was real.

This tragedy touched almost everyone, and also children grieved alongside the grownups. Among my father's closest relatives no one had been shot and killed or deported, but Aivars remembers with what sadness and anger never experienced before by his child's heart he had watched the victims of Communism that were being driven past grandmother Matilde's house during that first summer of the war. The tortured victims were being dug up somewhere beyond the village of Rumbula. Carts of corpses wrapped in white sheets passed by accompanied by German soldiers and local Home Guards. Among the many people shot at the Central Prison there was also a doctor, with whom my father's mother Milda had worked for many years in the Red Cross hospital. I remember well that once, when I was a child, my grandma forgot caution in my presence and, on reading an article in the Soviet magazine "Health" (*Veselība*) about a previous colleague, she let slip a story about how brutally the Chekists had tortured the doctor before shooting him. They had driven nails under his nails. I listened, my eyes wide with disbelief, and could not believe what my grandma was recounting. That is how the Fascists could have acted but not the Chekists, who, as I was being taught in Soviet school, were an example of everything that was sublime and human. I was still a child and believed everything that I was taught in school. On the other hand, my parents, in order not to get into trouble, were careful not to dispute the Soviet inventions, which I enthusiastically recounted to them after school.

How great my shock would have been, if my father had told me what he had seen in the Cheka cellars, where he had gone driven by teenage curiosity in order to ascertain for himself whether the horror stories he had heard corresponded to reality. They did! His inspection of the Cheka started in the exercise yard for the prisoners, followed by the cellars, which, for propaganda reasons, the Germans had opened to the public. The prisoner cells had depressingly low ceilings, and in each cell there was a list of surnames of all the victims tacked to the wall. Even though no signs of bullet holes could be discerned in the walls of the death cell, the drain to collect the blood spoke its own language. The interrogation cell with a portrait of Dzerzhinsky on the wall left the most harrowing impression on my father. The eminent Super Chekist gazed down with arrogant indifference at the various means of torture placed right there, the assorted instruments for hitting and the box with the torn off human fingernails on the table.

This and much more my father unwillingly recounted when I started to work on the book. In my childhood, the past was only mentioned in connection with household incidents and family events, but almost never in its political or historic significance. I grew up under the influence of Soviet propaganda, knowing almost nothing about the real history of Latvia. The latter was totally buried in silence. This self-imposed censorship mirrors the desire of my parents not to complicate the life of their child with unanswerable questions and dangerous doubts. Above all, they wanted to protect me from a repetition of their own tragic fate. Only now, am I able to evaluate how beneficial their silence had been – my childhood was not ruined by fear, because I was not aware of the danger that could threaten free thinkers and of what horrific acts the Soviet regime was capable of performing. They kept silent. I, therefore, did not have to lie or pretend in school, on the street or among people. This helped me evade a tortuous dualism in my character. Later, when I started to think in more depth about the cause and effect of things, the negative truth I discovered about the essence of the Soviet regime no longer threatened the integrity of my personality. This awareness led me to those who were turning against the Soviet regime.

Latvians very shortly recovered form their gullible enthusiasm about recurring "liberations." The German authorities firmly resisted all the recommendations by local politicians to form a self-governing administration and pleas for equal participation in the governance of Latvia. On July 17, Hitler made Latvians happy with the announcement that, in the future, they together with Estonians,

Lithuanians and Byelorussians would live in Ostland province and would be called Ostlanders.[88] Rīga was granted the great honour of being the capital of Ostland, with all security and administrative structures centred in the city. What Latvians themselves thought of this decision was never asked. Newspapers and cultural life were subjected to stringent controls, the same as they had been during the Soviet period.[89] All things Latvian were not persecuted as brutally, but the practise of Latvian traditions was limited, strictly restricted to the domestic level. Parallel to the Soviet period, the celebration of the Independence Day of Latvia, on the 18th of November, was prohibited. The national flag vanished, and the national anthem no longer was heard. Brīvības iela – Freedom Street – was renamed Adolf-Hitler-Strasse. In the newspapers Father Stalin's photo was replaced by a portrait of Führer Hitler; in place of songs of praise for the Red Army, now praise was sung to the heroic liberators, the *Wehrmacht* soldiers, and admonishments to learn Russian were replaced by advertisements of German language courses.

Approximately 25,000 officials arrived in Latvia from the Third Reich to administer the new territory.[90] Among these state-employed Germans were many repatriated Baltic Germans who returned with their families and thus enjoyed the sweet taste of revenge. Their representatives had made certain to that the Führer was reminded of their historical rights to the Baltic States. They had whispered into the Führer's ear that this, after all, was the rightful political inheritance of the Third Reich, which it had been deprived of in 1918. This coincided marvellously with the plans of the leaders of the Reich to colonise Latvia after the war. Thus buildings, property and land were needed for the colonists to relocate in Latvia; hence the German authorities not only were reluctant to return the properties nationalised during the Soviet period but also covertly continued nationalisation.[91] Germany did not recognise the legality of the agrarian reform implemented in Latvia during 1920's and planned to renew "the proprietary status quo that had existed for 700 years." Until these plans were put in force, the Latvian farmer legally became the tenant of the state property he had owned; now it was the property of the Reich, which was only made available for temporary use by the farmer!

Whatever had not been exported to Moscow in the first year of occupation, now was exported to Berlin. The Germans bought out the stores within a few months, because the Reich administration froze the prices of goods and set a fixed exchange rate for the Reichsmark that did not correspond to its real value. Effective September 1, a system of ration cards was introduced, which, in German style, was precise and minutely detailed. The section read most carefully in the official newspaper *Tēvija* (Fatherland), was the one outlining the regulations on supply booklets, ration cards, and food rations, wherein the specifications and norms were published on a regular basis. As the war continued, the supply of food products and other necessary goods ration per person continued to diminish. An extensive black market flourished, and the Germans responsible for order cashed in generous duties from the speculators. This was a statewide form of racket. The Latvian countryside was being buried under tax burdens, but the farmers at least were fed and could still managed to exchange some things with the city folk, who, in violation of the ban on such activity by the German administration, still went to the country in search of food. Germans without trepidation accepted the regulations and orders that reinforced the differences between the "Reich Germans" and the "natives." The food rations for local residents were lower by up to 33% and salaries by up to 50% than those of the Germans.[92]

Seeing these and many other instances of inequality, within a few months the initial enthusiasm about the "liberation" had changed to bitterness as the "liberated" understood that another occupation had started and that there was not even a hope of self-rule in the territory of Latvia. Latvians had again become the "*Bauer*" (peasants) ruled by German overlords. After twenty years of living in an independent state it was hard to become reconciled to being subjugated again!

Sometime in autumn, Aivars' broken leg had healed, though improperly, and he returned to his mother's house. They lived in a one-room flat on Mēness iela in a blue-collar district that had not suffered the ravages of the battles over Rīga. Not a window was broken in the house, while the windows of the buildings in the centre of the city and the Old Town looked at the heavens through black and shattered eyes. Old Rīga was in total ruins. St. Peter's Church had burned down. So had the pride of Rīga, the Blackheads Society building. Bridges over Daugava River had been blown up. That is how Rīga looked when Aivars arrived in autumn to return to his studies in primary school. My father's class no longer was located on the bright second floor. Now a pension had been installed on the top floors for the German officials and families who had arrived from the Reich. Also, beside the school, the previous inhabitants, the Baltic Germans, had returned to the block bounded by Hospitāļu iela and Miera iela, the area popularly called the German Garden. In the school, the first floor and the cellars had been left for the Latvian children. The teachers were Latvian, and even though they tried to hide their true feelings, the boys sensed how they felt. In the same way that the boys waited for the "*Krauts*" in their Hitlerjugend uniforms to descend from the upper stories to beat them up, the teachers never forgot to emphasise discreetly what was Latvian and patriotic. Aivars remembers the solemn silence that fell over the class when the literature teacher Mežgailis read to the boys Aleksandrs Grīns' novel *Soul Storm* (*Dvēseļu putenis*) about the freedom battles of the Latvian army.

It was only after the war, when my father started to study at the Polytechnic College, that he began to understand what large gaps the education of the German period had left in his knowledge. The "Ostlanders" were only taught the most elementary things in preparation for becoming a suitable workforce for future German colonists. My father had to be satisfied with arithmetic and the history of the Third Reich, because an expanded curriculum including algebra, geometry, physics and chemistry was perceived to be an unnecessary luxury. The creation of an Ostlander intellectual elite was not part of Hitler's plans. The Baltic had to become a Germanic country. Some of the more "humane" Reich theoreticians did allow for the idea, that the racially more worth-while Latvians could be Germanised, but for the "incorrigibles" – the intellectuals – plans had been drawn up for evacuation to Russia, so that these "second-class persons" could help the Germans subjugate the "third-class persons" there.[93] Whether it was Soviet or German occupation – the fate for Latvians continued to be the road to the East.

Latvians gradually became accustomed to the many *Verordnung* (decree), *Bekanntmachung* (announcement) and *Anordnung* (regulation), and life assumed a certain order. When the war began, my grandmother Milda worked at Rīga First Hospital as a nurse. After the German invasion, a German infirmary was installed in the hospital, and Milda was initially assigned to the section that treated Soviet war prisoners. She did so conscientiously. At that time, my grandmother could not even imagine that she was nursing patients literally destined for death, who were sent directly from the hospital to prisoner-of-war camps. Later, war prisoners who had escaped from the Salaspils prison camp knocked many times at the door of the house of my father's grandmother Matilde in Šķirotava. Once my father also came face to face with one of these men. It was in winter 1942, when my father had trudged on foot from school in Rīga to visit his grandmother. A war prisoner dressed in a Soviet army uniform knocked at the door and entered. He begged permission to warm himself. In empathy, Matilde ladled soup into a bowl for him. The gaunt man started to eat the warm soup. He patted my father's head and said that he also had a son. Unfortunately, precisely at that moment, someone from the township arrived at Matilde's house and saw the stranger. After having eaten and gotten warm, the prisoner asked permission to stay overnight, and my father's grandmother, with a heavy heart, responded that she could not risk violating the orders of the German commandant's office by giving shelter to prisoners. The next morning Aivars saw footsteps leading to the hay barn in the distance, where the man had spent the night. The subsequent fate of the war prisoner is not known.

Injured German soldiers and officers were also treated in the German infirmary. After nursing the Soviet war prisoners, Milda was promoted and given the honour of taking care of Aryan-born patients. My grandmother also cared for the Germans conscientiously. The well-kept, expressly polite and elegant German gentlemen gladly showered the vivacious and compassionate nurse with gallant compliments and gave her a chocolate bar on occasion, which Milda immediately saved to give to the children. However, the superficially civilised behaviour no longer deceived Milda. My grandmother's sympathetic heart could not comprehend how people could behave so inhumanly to war prisoners and Jews. When she had gone by herself or together with Aivars to her mother's home in Šķirotava, she had often seen the Soviet war prisoners who were employed in construction work. In the freezing February weather they looked blue with cold, because their emaciated bodies were only covered with flimsy clothing made of sacking. To protect themselves from the cold, they had dug burrow-like holes in the ground that provided some sort of shelter from the harsh winds. Occasionally, trainloads of war prisoners stopped at the Šķirotava station. Aivars remembers how the people in the train had let down tin cans tied to a string through the small window of the cattle car and, while the train was moving, had attempted to scoop up small amounts of snow. On occasion they succeeded, but it also happened that the tin would snap off from its string and, with a jangling sound, disappear beside the railway track, taking along with it last hopes for quenching thirst.

The Germans were so convinced about the superiority of their race that they did not even attempt to hide their inhumane treatment of the war prisoners and openly herded them in columns through the centre of the city. One morning, contented with his "wheeler-dealer" skills, Aivars returned from the market where he had successfully completed a barter deal for a small amount of food. Along Brīvības iela (Latvians never called it the Adolf-Hitler-Strasse) the German guards were herding the prisoners of war. There were about a hundred prisoners. All of them were ragged, wearing whatever they had found to put on their back. Some of them had wrapped themselves in cement bags. So emaciated they were that they barely dragged along. One of them fell, and the guard – an eighteen-year-old – began to hit the unconscious man with his rifle butt. Having got rid of his rage, the soldier stopped. The others lifted up their fellow prisoner and limped on. It was very painful to watch, but the passers by, including my father, could do nothing else but lower their eyes and continue on their way. All felt as if they were equally guilty in what was taking place, and their own powerlessness was humiliating.

Since 1940 a sort of a curse hung over Šķirotava. It had become the place of misfortune, the crossroads for the many who were fated to die. At first there was the mass deportation of the 14th of June. Then, after the German invasion, came the huge trainloads of prisoners of war and West European Jews, who were either "unloaded" at Šķirotava station or transferred to further destinations. All of this happened in front of the eyes of the people who lived in the area, but the most horrifying days were the 30th of November and 8th of December, 1941, when in nearby Rumbula 24,000 Latvian Jews from the Rīga Ghetto and about 1000 from Germany were exterminated. Even though General Jeckeln had planned everything perfectly, with great attention to detail so characteristic of him, it was not possible to conceal the extent of the mass exterminations. My great grandmother Berta Matilde was also a witness to what happened.[94]

During the Soviet occupation, the army personnel had started to build a military airfield a few kilometres from my father's grandmother's house. Because of war, they had not managed to finish the airfield or the road leading to it. Only the embankment of the road, which now has been levelled, had remained. It was located some four hundred metres from my grandmother's front door. One Sunday morning Matilde was startled by loud moans and screams. She ran outside and saw that along the road embankment, an interminable column of people was being herded under heavy guard. They were Jews – women and children, old people and men. It was a terrible sight. Guards' curses could be heard in both German and Latvian. Now and then one of the persons being herded stumbled and fell either from exhaustion or despair. Matilde also heard shots. As if frozen, my father's grandmother stared at the unfortunates being herded in the direction of Rumbula. All day long, without cease, the echo of shots resounded in the neighbourhood. And even when it was dark the shots reverberated again in Matilde's head. In shock and despair, she did not know what to do. Matilde did not dare discuss what had happened with the neighbours. The neighbours, too, pretended that they had not seen or heard anything. Only when Milda and Aivars arrived the following weekend was it possible to discuss the dreadful events. Although Matilde and Milda had made the boy promise to keep his mouth shut and not to go near Rumbula, as spring approached, he disobeyed and skied over the strips of remaining snow to the place of execution. Grandmother's story would probably have faded long ago for Aivars, but what he saw became forever imprinted in his mind.

There were two clearings among the pines. One larger, the other – a bit to the side – smaller. The snow had already partly melted. The smallest clearing was literally covered with Latvian and foreign passports, as well as other documents written in strange languages and foreign paper money. Also among the litter were Red Army and Latvian Army identification papers. Aivars was also surprised to find a Lāčplēsis Order Certificate.[95] In the larger clearing clearly visible were six cone-shaped pits, which, as the snow had melted, had sunken in. Right nearby were abandoned shovels and other digging implements. Various small items were scattered all over the place – a broken leather strap, a soaked stocking or a dirtied torn strip of clothing – that the innocent victims had discarded before lying down in the grave and being shot. There was a discernible smell of decay in the air. Aivars could feel his knees shake and a wave of nausea climb to his throat. Turning swiftly, he skied off as quickly as his legs could carry him.

How much greater would my father's revulsion have been had he known then how the extermination had taken place. The victims had to undress in the smaller clearing and separate their belongings into precisely marked little piles, so nothing of value would be lost for Third Reich. Then, stark naked, the people had to move toward the dug out pit and wait their turn to climb into the grave to lie down on top of the still warm, just executed bodies. The last thing that the unfortunates perceived was the cold barrel of a weapon at their heads, and then a shot extinguished their lives forever. Later, in 1943, when the Germans felt that they would not be able to hold out against the Soviets much longer, in order to hide any traces of their crimes and in response to an order by Himmler, the digging up and burning of the corpses began. A swath of thick, malodorous smoke and the stench of burning bones and decaying flesh hung across the houses in the neighbourhood. When the wind was easterly, this smell even reached Rīga.[96]

Fleeing from the place of execution, my father could not imagine that five years later, during his exile in Siberia, the first task assigned to him would be to transport the corpses of people who had died in the transfer camp to the anatomical theatre of the Tomsk Medical Institute. The majority of these consisted of ten to twelve year old children who had died some days ago so that rats had managed to feed substantially on their faces. It is a blessing that their relatives never found out about this.

Already during the first days of the German occupation, the Nazis began an intense anti-Semitic campaign, blaming the Jews for what took place during the Year of Terror. The word "Jew" became synonymous with the words "Chekist" and "Bolshevik." Even President Ulmanis[97] and other members of the Latvian government were accused of having acted "according to the directives of the Jews and Freemasons."[98] This propaganda was fully consistent with Nazi attempts to compromise Latvian statehood. It was a true eruption of hatred that descended over Latvians, who had not yet recovered from vivid recollections of the horrendous scenes of mass graves of victims tortured by Chekists and the deportations of the 14th of June. The despairing relatives easily believed these unsubstantiated claims,[99] and thus a new mythology that all Jews were Communists was created. The need to find the guilty was satisfied. Precisely the same happened after the war, during the 1970s, when the Soviet propaganda machine turned Latvians into evil "Jew killers." In reality it was a Soviet objective to compromise Latvian community in exile, and for this purpose new "facts" were needed, hence a series of KGB publications were created, which surprisingly became a "source" for many researchers of the Holocaust.[100]

Both these myths continued to be propagated in European political science and historical essays, despite the efforts of many scholars to prove factually that these myths are unsubstantiated. Each time that I read again as axiomatic about the particular Latvian sympathy for Fascism or about our inborn anti-Semitism, it hurts me. It insults and humiliates me. My great grandmother

Matilde was a simple countrywoman, who without hesitation shared her bread with prisoners of war who strayed to her door, or with the imprisoned Jewesses at Jumpravmuiža[101] who had been fortunate enough to crawl out of the camp and to slink to the nearest house. My grandmother Milda took care of injured Soviet soldiers and knew that her friend, a dentist, was hiding her husband, a Jew, in her apartment. I have no doubt that many Latvians behaved in the same way, because elementary humanity demanded it.[102] I do not accept this label of "inborn guilt" on me and other decent Latvians only because a group of ambitious adventurers under the leadership of Viktors Arājs formed a brigade, whose main task became the shooting of Jews, Communists and Gypsies after the Nazi invasion of Latvia.[103] This fact alone is not proof of the aggressive anti-Semitism of Latvians. Every society has its dregs. A totalitarian regime and occupation create a particularly favourable medium for all ilk of adventurers and amoral people to surface and become obedient instruments performing the dirty work of a particular regime. But Latvia and its people under foreign domination must not bear the burden of the responsibility for the decision made by Nazi Germany without our consent to use our occupied country as a place to exterminate the Jews of Latvia and Western Europe. That responsibility rests exclusively on the rulers of the Third Reich.

Occupation is an abnormal situation. For decades, its consequences continue to torment the people of a country freed from occupation and those that are "in the right" blame those who were "in the wrong" for the misfortunes experienced and the crimes committed. The Nazi occupation lasted five years in France. It was very much the same in other occupied European states. In these countries, there are still questions that have not been answered satisfactorily today, as well as individuals whose degree of collaboration is the subject of hot debate. Latvia experienced three occupations, one after the other, whose combined length – fifty years – exceeds anything that Europe has experienced in the twentieth century. The question about the compliance and collaboration of each individual with the various regimes, therefore, is particularly painful. Only after the renewal of independence have we regained the freedom to judge our history and to cleanse it of the lies and propaganda introduced by foreign regimes. Both the Fascist and the Bolshevik regimes committed crimes in Latvia. The guilty, irrespective of whether they worked on behalf of Nazi or Communist doctrines, the same as their collaborators, who committed crimes against the civilian population, have to be found liable for their acts. Crimes against humanity have no statute of limitation.

The Blitzkrieg planned by Hitler against the Soviet Union failed, and after the capture of the army of General Paulus in Stalingrad on the River Volga in January, 1943, it appeared to the Nazis that the enemies of the Reich and the "lovers of Jews," Roosevelt, Churchill and Stalin, would find a common language. In October 1943, a conference of the Ministers of Foreign Affairs of the US, Great Britain and the Soviet Union took place.[104] It was the cause for major consternation in Berlin, and instructions were sent to Ostland to organise mass protest demonstrations of Ostlanders in Rīga, Tallinn and Vilnius. The *Reichskommissar* in Latvia issued instructions to suspend work and education, and, ostensibly at the invitation of the Board of Trade, people were sent to the Dom Square with pre-prepared placards on the morning of 13 November. How very reminiscent these "spontaneous demonstrations" were of the Soviet style of manipulation with people during the "socialistic revolution of working people" in 1940! My father Aivars, too, was among those "100,000 who protested against the Anglo-American supported Bolshevik initiative to once again enslave the Latvian people."[105] His class stood on the side of the square where the Unibanka is now located. The facades of the Radio House and other buildings were brightly decorated with flags of Third Reich and the red-white-red of Latvia. The boys had been in the square since early morning and had become bored. The announced meeting time was approaching, but no activity could be seen on the rostrum. Talk was spreading that Lohse, the Reich Commissioner for Ostland, was going to speak. While the boys pushed and shoved, a loud bang was heard. In the garbage tin attached to the wall of the Radio House a bomb exploded at nine thirty. The crowd of people became animated, shouts and squeals could be heard, but there was no panic, and no one was allowed to leave. From mouth to mouth, the news travelled like lightning that three, among them a ten-year-old boy, had been killed instantly, while two had been critically injured. One of the injured later died.[106]

Traces of the explosion can be seen even today on the granite trim of the Radio House. Once, during the 1980s, my father showed these to a woman guiding an excursion, who was telling a group of tourists in the Dom Square about the courageous Soviet underground army whose "explosion echoed throughout Latvia and all of Europe and was proof of the unyielding resolve of the Latvian people to remain in the brotherhood of the Soviet peoples."[107] My father could not keep silent and said that innocent people had been hurt by the explosion – which was in contradiction of the official Soviet version. The woman listened in silence. What could she say? To ask something in front of the tourist group would mean that she questioned Soviet honesty. Who would dare do that? I, too, had to learn in school that this explosion was the most distinguished anti-Fascist act of resistance performed during wartime. Each year this day was especially commemorated, and students had to write essays about the heroic young men of the Young Communist League – Imants Sudmalis, Maldis Skreija and Džems Bankovičs. My father had not ever even mentioned that he had been in the Dom Square during the explosion. God knows what my father thought reading my "correctly" written essays. How did he manage not to comment on them with irony?

Up to now I have not mentioned my grandfather Aleksandrs. Starting in 1941, he worked as an auto mechanic in a German armed forces division and was well thought of there. Aleksandrs, who had no training in mechanics, had golden hands and a natural talent. He managed to bring the most hopeless motors back to life, motors on which others had worked without success. With the beginning of war, Aleksandrs' and Milda's relationship had become even more complicated, because Aleksandrs had become, if possible, more jealous. The most innocent things served as a pretext for a scene. Milda would clink glasses with someone at a party and, as etiquette prescribed, look into the man's eyes, and Aleksandrs would immediately accuse her of having pointedly flirted with him and then grill her on what exactly was between her and the man?

Aleksandrs Kalnietis' employee ID.

The patients in the hospital would leave her a small gift or bouquet of flowers – and for Aleksandrs these gifts could not be given just because of beautiful eyes, there had to be more. Aleksandrs would destroy the flowers in blind rage. Milda would be late because of a meeting with her dear friend Lidija in some café, and again Milda's husband would make a fuss about assignations with a lover and try to get her to reveal his name. At the beginning of their marriage, like many wives tormented by a jealous husband, Milda tried not to do anything that would provoke Aleksandrs. But he still could blow up a stormy scene from nothing. Milda finally decided not to alter her behaviour and continued to live as if her husband's jealousy had nothing to do with her.

This was hard and demanded great spiritual strength from my grandmother. When I was a young girl and discussed my first romantic feelings with her, she warned me not to ever fall in love with a jealous man. "There is nothing worse," she added after a long, silent pause. Their relationship on occasion reached true crisis, when Aleksandrs, slamming the door, would "leave forever." But he always returned, because he loved Milda, though inadequately and in a tormented way. He just could not content himself with his wife's independent nature. Thus, during the hardest period of the war, my grandmother could not count on Aleksandrs' support and she alone had to take care of feeding her two growing sons Aivars and Arnis. She herself ate at the hospital and sometimes brought a bowl of soup for the boys. Also their country relatives and mother Matilde helped as much as they could, but their food rations were meagre. My father remembers the constant hunger that tormented him as a growing boy. In order to have the boy recover, regain weight and health, Milda could do nothing else but send Aivars to the country to work as a shepherd. Thus he at least was fed and earned his suit of clothes for the winter, as well as five kilograms of country bacon. So during the summers of 1943 and 1944 my father worked as a shepherd boy in two different farms. The farmers he worked for were kind and decent people who treated the boy well. He could drink as much milk as he wanted. To this day, however, my father does not fancy fried or smoked carp, which were served almost every day at the farmstead.

Sensing the Eastern front approach closer and closer, the leaders of the Reich began to be more yielding about increasing Ostlander rights. They had to regain the sympathies of the inhabitants lost due to their discriminatory policies. Beginning in 1943, now and then, the word "Latvia" was to be heard in official speeches and again the red, white and red flag appeared in the streets. In February, with the agreement of Hitler, it was decided to partially return private property that had been nationalised by the Soviets.[108] At the beginning of the war the Germans did not even want to hear about the formation of Latvian military units, but, with the changes in fortunes of war and because of lack of soldiers at the front, the so-called Latvian "Self-Administration" leaders were given oblique hints about the renewal of statehood after the war,[109] on condition that Latvians would selflessly fight against the Bolsheviks. In February of 1943, Hitler ordered that a Latvian volunteer legion be established, structured as a part of the "*Waffen SS*."[110] The word "volunteer" helped the Germans hide that the Hague Convention of 1907 on the conduct of war had been violated, specifically the stipulation that prohibited the mobilisation of the local inhabitants of occupied territories into the armed forces of the occupier.[111] The mobilisation was planned with German precision, dividing the men to be mobilised into age groups with implementation occurring in several stages – convincing evidence that the Germans themselves did not count on any volunteers. On the 9th of March, the youngest group of men was mobilised, and so it continued until July 15, 1944, when total mobilisation was announced. Initially, my grandfather was not touched by the mobilisation because of his age. But a mobilisation notice arrived on the 26th of March 1944. With only short breaks,

Aleksandrs served as an auto mechanic in the 19th Division right up to capitulation. After that, like thousands of other Latvians, he became a "Forest Brother" – a partisan.

Even though during the fall of 1943 and the winter of 1944 newspapers and radio continued to talk about "tactical retreat" of the *Wehrmacht*, which was supposedly done in order to concentrate their forces for the next victorious strike, nonetheless the Eastern front was approaching irreversibly. The residents had not had their radios confiscated, and Aivars, the same as many others, regularly listened to English broadcasts. He had obtained a map, on which, he marked with paper flags the changes in the frontier line in accordance with the news broadcast by the English. In February of 1944, the Soviet army troops had reached the border of Latvia. The air was heavy with fear. People by now had come to know the Germans. Even though they were not likeable, at least they were a known quantity. Memories about the Year of Terror and the horror stories of atrocities committed by Soviet soldiers in their reconquered territories magnified the fear of Bolshevism. Rumours were rife that the Russian revenge would be horrendous after their return. Aivars was scared. So, too, were Milda and grandmother Matilde. People tried to hold on to the illusion that a miracle would happen and that, with German support, the Latvian Legion would be able to defend Latvia. Talk was spreading about a miracle weapon that almost, almost was ready to be used by the Germans, and then the fortunes of war would turn. For the Latvian Legion this was a holy war for their homeland. They sang, "We'll beat up the lice-ridden ones, and afterward, the blue-grey ones" – and they died with Latvia on their lips. For the moment they had to tolerate the German "blue-greys," in order to protect Latvia from the return of "lice-ridden" Bolsheviks.[112] When this would be accomplished, then the leaders of the Reich would have to fulfil the promise given to the legionnaires about the renewal of the state of Latvia.[113] The men truly believed this.

By mid-summer of 1944 there was no doubt any more about the impending catastrophe. In August the Germans started to evacuate.[114] People were being hunted down in the streets in order to be sent to work in Germany or dig trenches in Kurzeme.[115] Milda did not have to be afraid because she was working in a German military hospital and was needed by the Third Reich right here. Also Aivars was safe doing his shepherd work in Carnikava. The youngest son Arnis had been taken to Matilde's in the suburbs of Rīga. From time to time, a letter arrived from Aleksandrs. Milda was offered the opportunity to evacuate along with the German infirmary. For a moment my grandmother was tempted to leave, but the risk of losing her children was too great. A promise had been made to evacuate them separately and unite them at a later date with their parents, but Milda was doubtful – what if something would happen en route and they would not manage to meet up? What would her life be like without Aivars and Arnis? So my grandmother decided to stay. In this confused time the most important thing was to gather the family together in one place. Despite the objections of the farmer who employed him Aivars interrupted his shepherd duties and returned to Rīga to his mother's house. After a few days also Arnis and Matilde managed to find their way to the Mēness iela flat, and they, all together now, started to wait for the end. Where Aleksandrs was, or if he was even alive, the family did not know.

Air raids had already started over Rīga. Sirens wailed in the city. People hurried down into cellars. Milda, being a fatalist, decided that the cellar would not save them in any case, so all of them sat in the room and waited. It was dreadful to hear the roar of the bombers become louder and louder. Then the first explosions started: Boom! Boom! Boom! With only one thought after each blast – this time it's sure to hit! A new "Boom!" and again abysmal fear! Until finally the roar of the bomber engines started to retreat and ease off. Not this time. Not yet! To save them from this chilling fear, Matilde's brother Eglīte, the owner of the "Ārgaļi" farmstead, together with his son Arvīds, came in two horse drawn carts to collect his relatives and take them to shelter in the country. Matilde, Aivars and Arnis headed for the village of Straupe. It was a night of horror. The Sigulda highway continued to be sporadically bombed. As they drove north-eastward, German army vehicles and horse carriages headed toward them in the oncoming lane. The horses neighed frantically. Cars honked. Aivars, as the oldest of the boys, had been entrusted with driving the second cart. Despite the surrounding confusion, he had dozed off for a moment and the horse cart had almost run into an approaching car. An angry German soldier had slapped the boy – what business did he have to be on the road! Then he let him go to jolt along further. Thus, with difficulty and in fear, the Rīgans arrived at their destination the next day. After the insanity of Rīga the silence and peace of the countryside seemed totally unnatural. Immediately black rye bread, bacon and cottage cheese were put on the table for the overtired travellers. After the meagre fare of the city this was a true feast. For a moment it seemed as if the war did not exist and that is how it would be forever. Like paradise.

My grandmother Milda alone remained in the city. In August, the German infirmary was evacuated and the German personnel left, taking along with them all the medication, the hospital equipment and the instruments – everything that the Third Reich could use. The occupation authorities ordered the Latvian doctors to take over the ruined hospitals, and thus the German infirmary once again became the First Hospital of Rīga. On October 13, Rīga was occupied again. Once more it belonged to the Soviet armed forces. In the opinion of the occupiers, the Latvians were Fascists who had no rights. They could be looted, beaten up, shot or raped. One afternoon a gang of Russian soldiers had wandered into the Mēness iela courtyard. Milda watched the ragged and badly dressed soldiers through a slit at the side of her curtains. They had stopped on the steps and were passing around a flask, loudly jeering. One of them was pointing at his boot sole tied with a rope and asking "*A sh'*, *do Berlina doydu*"[116] Milda shook her head in disbelief – such raga-muffins! Who would let them get into Berlin! At that moment she believed that the English and the Americans would come to their senses, re-evaluate their friendship with the Russians, and not let them expand into Europe.

The only part of Latvia that the Soviet army did not succeed in occupying was the region of Kurzeme. Up to May 9, fierce battles continued there, in which also the men of the 19th Division of the Latvian Legion fought.[117]

"I beg you – shoot me or exonerate me"

On May 8, 1945, at 23:01, Admiral Dönitz signed the unconditional surrender of the Third Reich to the victorious Allies. The German armed forces fighting in Kurzeme and the Czechoslovakian capital of Prague surrendered only on the next day. The Soviet Union, therefore, always celebrated its victory on May 9. My grandfather Aleksandrs Kalnietis was stationed in Kurzeme at the moment of capitulation, not far from the village of Vāne. At the end of the war he served in the 19th Latvian Legion Division as the staff auto mechanic for the 6th Corps. When on the evening of May 7 it was announced to the soldiers that they could disperse wherever they wished, Aleksandrs together with several of his fellow soldiers attempted to get to Ventspils in a truck so they could board a boat leaving Latvia. Nearing Ventspils, he found out from people driving toward them that there were no more boats. Even wrecks had put out to sea.

Aleksandrs could not decide what to do next. To head for Rīga seemed risky, because Soviet agencies there were avidly hunting down "traitors of the Soviet Motherland" like him. Confusion still reigned in Kurzeme; thus it seemed better to remain there. First he had to change clothes because to wander around in a legionnaire's uniform was madness. In an abandoned house Aleksandrs found some clothes that fitted him. Now he felt safer. Near the house he also noticed an abandoned car. It was not working, but there was gas in the tank. It seemed like a fateful omen signifying that everything was not yet lost. Aleksandrs quickly got the motor in working order and decided once more to look for his fortune in Ventspils. If only he could manage to get to Sweden somehow! But he did not succeed. For several days he roamed the city. The Germans had not been able to clear out the army warehouses and goods that were stored in them. All sorts of delicacies and liquor were now accessible to everyone. What was happening was reminiscent of a feast in the midst of the plague when people tried to drown their despair and sorrow in alcohol. This was Latvia's funeral, in which Aleksandrs, too, took part. He drank in rage about the damned wars that twice had wrecked his life. The first time depriving him of his parents, and now depriving him of everything – his homeland, health and family. Seeking oblivion, wishing no longer to feel anything, he drank until he passed out … Coming to his senses the next morning, Aleksandrs decided to leave this place of disaster where the first Red Army vehicles were patrolling already. The only safe place was the forest. This is how my grandfather became a "forest brother" – a partisan.

The woods were not a free and considered choice for Aleksandrs. He, like many other legionnaires, did not have any choice.[118] He had served in the German army. In the opinion of the Soviets he, therefore, was a traitor. Knowing how the Chekists had treated totally innocent people during the Year of Terror, Aleksandrs, like other legionnaires, could envisage the torture that was planned for the "traitors of the Soviet Motherland." None of the officials of the new regime would have been interested in the fact that Aleksandrs had been assigned as a mechanic to a German army unit in 1941 by the Labour Administration.[119] A living had to be earned in order to survive. Later, in March 1944, he was mobilised into the Latvian Legion despite the fact that he had active tuberculosis in his right lung. He could not, like some other civilians, hide out with relatives in the country or desert from the Legion. He already was working in a mechanic workshop of the German army, and if he had refused induction, he would have been court-martialled.[120] In January 1945, due to his state of health, Aleksandrs was released from active service, but he was sent to perform labour service in Germany. As the final hours approached for Latvia, my grandfather again was mobilised and ordered to serve in the 19th Latvian Legion division, which was fighting desperately in the Kurzeme pocket of resistance. Like for millions of other people, the war robbed Aleksandrs of the opportunity to decide his own fate.

After this, there is no reliable information about where and with whom Aleksandrs spent time. After his arrest and imprisonment, when the Cheka interrogation experts were torturing him, trying to force Aleksandrs to reveal the surnames and locations of the forest brethren, my grandfather several times changed what he said. However, beginning with the third interrogation, his statements started to acquire some stability. A few days after leaving Ventspils, Aleksandrs had wandered alone to the village of Zūras, where he had met some fellows in adversity. After some discussion, the men had asked Aleksandrs to join their group, which in the Cheka documents has been named Sils, meaning pine forest. He had remained with the Sils men until mid-July, afterward joining Olģerts Stūris, called Labietis, whose group of partisans was active in the Kuldīga district. By mid-August, Aleksandrs already was in Birzgale and from there, according to his statements, he headed to join his family in Rīga at the end of October. My grandfather did not reveal to the Chekists that he had, together with some other men, crossed the Daugava River at Jumprava and from the beginning of September had been active in the region of Vidzeme. Obviously, Aleksandrs did not want to put at risk the many relatives of his wife Milda, who lived in the Straupe area and would have immediately become suspects to be interrogated if not arrested. Aleksandrs very sketchily recounted where he had been after returning to Rīga. In Vidzeme, the support base for the forest brethren was the Ceplīši farmstead. There he could for a short while feel like a human being – eat, bathe and warm up in a sauna, put on a clean shirt and have a peaceful sleep.

One night at the end of October, when the men were readying to go to sleep in the hayloft, shots were heard outside. Chekists had surrounded the barn. Not hesitating even a moment, Aleksandrs jumped out of the loft hatch door. He fell, somersaulted once, and, zigzagging to evade bullets, headed toward the nearest woods. With bullets whining all around him, my grandfather ran like crazy. In his white underwear he made an excellent target. He was hunted among the undergrowth and bushes like a rabbit. Miraculously Aleksandrs escaped.

Having finally reached safety in the woods, Aleksandrs, exhausted, collapsed and lay for a long while in the cold, damp moss. He was alive, but for how long? It was late fall and a cold winter lay ahead. He no longer had either his warm clothing or boots – just his undershirt and underpants. Aleksandrs shook in tubercular fever, his lungs not suited to the harsh life of the forest brethren. Grandfather was tired of hiding out in the woods, spending nights in haylofts and ditches. Peace could not be found anywhere. After the fall of Kurzeme, the Russians had herded all the men aged 16 to 60 years of age into "filtration camps."[121] Shortly thereafter they started to comb the woods, attempting to drive out the "bandits." For a while it seemed that it would be safer in Vidzeme, but even here the Cheka raids became more frequent against the forest brethren. Aleksandrs did not believe the hopeful rumours about English and American assistance. These seemed to him to be only empty promises. Because the Allies had allowed Russian incursions into Europe and begged for Soviet assistance in the war against Japan, why would they, for the sake of some Balts, destroy their relations with the mighty USSR? No, there was no future in a continued life in the woods. He had to get to Rīga. There would at least be hope of finding shelter and surviving winter if he could lose himself in the big, crowded city. Aleksandrs did not put much hope on Milda's help, because their last parting had been cool. He had done too much harm to his wife for her to forgive him. But he desperately wanted to see his son Arnis. At least for one more time.

Early in the morning, Aleksandrs gathered courage to knock at the window of a house. Everyone in the parish already knew of the shooting at Ceplīši, and people were afraid that, for the grace of God, the same could happen to them. Aleksandrs was given something to wear made of coarse sackcloth and had a hunk of bread shoved in his hand for the journey. Just so he would leave the sooner. My grandfather, too, was in a hurry – he wanted to return to the safety of the woods. So going from woods to woods Aleksandrs started to march toward Rīga. He couldn't walk fast because he had no boots. In order to protect his feet from the cold and the rough and sharp forest floor, he wrapped his feet in rags he had found in ditches along the way. The hunk of bread given to him dwindled away, and soon my grandfather was tormented by hunger. But he was afraid to approach a house. Once, meeting a lone man walking toward him, Aleksandrs dared talk to him and beg for something to eat. Waiting for the stranger to return, Aleksandrs hid and fearfully watched to see if the man was being followed. But everything was fine, and he finally got something to eat. Beside the stone fence of the Līgatne cemetery, grandfather buried his handgun. Later he told my father where to find it and gave him instructions to hide it carefully. The next summer Aivars went to find the pistol and brought it back to Rīga to hide in the attic of the house. It could be that the weapon is still hidden there today. Aleksandrs finally reached Rīga on the 30th of October.

It was late evening. The doorbell rang. In post-war Rīga, a ring like this did not augur well, and my father was thoroughly startled. He was alone at home because Milda was working the night shift at the hospital, while Arnis was in the country at his grandmother Matilde's house. Cautiously, Aivars asked: "Who is it?" After a moment of silence, came the response: "Your father." Aivars quickly opened the door. The light flooding from the kitchen lit up Aleksandrs' figure against the dark of the stairwell. His appearance was appalling – he was dressed in dirty, ragged sackcloth with a wood saw slung over his shoulder. An odd, padded cap covered part of his bearded, unshaved face. His feet were the most wretched sight – wrapped in rags and tied with string. This is how my grandfather Aleksandrs returned home.

Milda took Aleksandrs in. Their previous disagreements now seemed distant, part of some inconsequential past, totally overshadowed by the catastrophe at the end of the war – the hundreds of thousands of refugees and the Bolshevik terror.[122] After the long period of uncertainty, Milda was happy to see her husband alive. She hugged gaunt Aleksandrs and for a brief while felt like a woman again. At that moment, she did not know that only thirteen more days remained until Aleksandrs' arrest and imprisonment. That it would be the last time in her life as a wife. Milda was thirty-seven years old. Her joy at the return of her husband was overshadowed by the realisation of how threatening his presence was for Aivars and Arnis. After a struggle with herself, Milda decided that Aleksandrs had to report to the militia and thus "legalise" himself. From what I was told as a child, I know that my grandmother had felt deep down in her heart that nothing more than prison threatened her husband. Now I understand that in that critical moment she had self-censored her reason. Wanting to protect her sons, she had blocked out the experiences of the Year of Terror and allowed herself to be deluded that "this can't happen to us," "we always have been people of modest means," "my husband has done nothing wrong…" – as if the degree of guilt would be of any interest to the Soviet executioners! Aleksandrs agreed, though he did not believe that the Bolsheviks would keep their promise and absolve the "sins" of former "Nazi collaborators" only because they had "legalised" themselves. The same as on the day of capitulation, my grandfather again had no choice. Certain death awaited him in the woods.

There was not the slightest hope of surviving winter with his damaged lungs. By handing himself over to the Soviets, he was doomed to be deported to Siberia and to his death. He was beyond exhaustion and fatally resigned himself to the inevitable.

Warm clothes and boots had to be provided for Aleksandrs. At least this much needed to be done to protect him from the unforeseeable, before he went to register. He had a coat that had been saved from the pre-war period. Other pieces of clothing were collected from friends, but the boots had to be bought. The family kitty was, as always, empty and they had to wait until Milda's payday so they could buy what was needed on the black market. In the meantime, a primitive hiding place was constructed under the kitchen table where grandfather could hide during the day from uninvited guests. Aivars was told firmly not to breathe a word about his father's return. Aivars himself understood how important it was to keep this secret. So much had been experienced during the war years that his childhood had ended before it had been lived.

At the end of October 1944, when Aivars had again returned from the country to "liberated" Rīga, total licentiousness and violence reigned. During German occupation at least there was a certain order in the city. After the Russians marched in, chaos began and people did not feel safe even in their homes, much less on the street. Not only armed bandits robbed and raped, but so did also the soldiers to whom it seemed that these were the legal rights of the victor. In their opinion, Latvians were Fascists and did not deserve anything better. Even though people talked only in half-whispers about the robberies and the rapes, Aivars knew very well that in his house, too, several women had experienced this. Right here on the corner of Mēness iela armed thieves had robbed a small shop three times. Rīga was changing. There were many empty flats in the city whose proprietors had left for the West as refugees.[123] The Red victors installed themselves in these flats. In my father's house one of the previous neighbours, who had left together with the retreating Soviet army in 1941, had returned. This neighbour firmly believed that all who had remained in Latvia and had not died were Fascists or their sympathisers. He would be the first to inform about a "bandit" being hidden, therefore precautionary measures had to be so stringent that Milda decided to leave Arnis, who was in the country, uninformed about his father's presence in Rīga. Arnis, with seven-year old naivete, could unintentionally let it slip to someone that his father had returned. Thus Aleksandrs' heart-felt desire to see his son was not fulfilled.

My grandfather Aleksandrs Kalnietis was arrested on the night of the 13th to the 14th of November, two days before Milda's payday. Someone knocked loudly at the door. The parents were sleeping in the kitchen. Aivars, who was sleeping on a small couch in the living room looked on petrified at what was happening through a crack of a door left slightly ajar. He saw how his father quickly crawled under the table. Milda swiftly smoothed out the bed so the impression of another head would not be seen on the pillow. Throwing her dressing gown on her shoulders, she went to open the door. Two armed men broke into the kitchen and aiming light and their weapons directly at the hiding place, shouted: "*Vykhodi bandit! Strelyat budu!*"[124] They obviously knew where Aleksandrs was hiding. Someone had informed the Cheka about the return of Aivars. Who? It could be no one else except the wife of Milda's brother Voldemārs, who had been in the flat. Only she knew that Aleksandrs had returned.

After the shouted order and threat to shoot, Aleksandrs crawled out from under the table, raising his arms above his head. The Chekists screamed at him to give up his weapon. Having made certain that there was no weapon, they ordered him to follow them. Aleksandrs slowly got dressed. He put a yellow billfold that held his personal documents and family photographs in his pocket. Taking the small bundle of clothing Milda had prepared, he embraced his wife in farewell and patted the head of Aivars, who stood frozen with fear. Thus, in flimsy summer shoes, Aleksandrs began the last stage of the journey he had not chosen. The last memory Aivars has of his father is his dark form silhouetted in the kitchen doorway. Neither Milda nor Aivars were to see Aleksandrs again, either alive of dead.

Aleksandrs was taken to the Cheka building at the corner of Stabu and Brīvības iela. As requested, he filled out the prisoner's personal questionnaire. Then they ordered him to undress and took away his billfold. The contents of it today are still in Aleksandrs' personal case file in the National Archive of Latvia.[125] The Chekists did not even allow the "bandit" to keep his son's photograph. On that same day, at 14:10, the Chekists started to interrogate my grandfather. The first session lasted eleven hours, during which the man recording the session covered ten pages written in a liberal hand. The average writing speed, therefore, was little less than one page per hour. The record, the same as the rest of the interrogation documents, was written in Russian. Having read over the testimonies of the forest brethren who had been through the Cheka cellars and who had survived Siberia, I can envisage the torture and agony that my grandfather had to endure. The interrogator did not inflict the physical blows. Neither did the man recording the proceedings. For this there was a man specially designated to do the beating. He hit unexpectedly and in the most painful places. When the interrogated person fell, he continued to be kicked. A foot in a heavy army boot was an excellent means of torture.

Did Aleksandrs come to experience other Cheka interrogation "refinements" – being hung from the ceiling, arms wrenched behind the back, forcing of knees up to the chin, pressing bones in iron shackles – can only be guessed. That it was horrendous can be gleaned from the six letters that reached my grandmother Milda when she was already in Siberia. Aleksandrs wrote: "After all that I have endured, death seems to me like a friend, a saviour, and for a long time now death hasn't seemed dreadful to me. I could also no longer be among the living, but stubbornly I persist – I live!"[126] When he collapsed semi-conscious and was brought down from the fifth floor torture chambers of the Security Committee Building, he was thrown into a damp, cold cellar where night and day a bright light burned on the ceiling. The light was so disturbing and piercing that it interfered with sleep. "Light therapy" and sleep deficit were additional methods for wearing down the prisoners, because interrogation, for the most part, took place during the night. After interrogation, the tortured persons were allowed to sleep only on their back and forbidden to cover their eyes with hands. The guards carefully watched that this rule was observed.

The next interrogation took place two days later. Obviously my grandfather had been reduced to so poor a condition after the first "conversation" that it was not possible to deal with him sooner. Altogether Aleksandrs had to endure seven such interrogations, which, in comparison to what other forest brethren had to suffer, was not much, but it was enough to meet with the Chekists, masters in their "profession," even once for a person to become crippled for life. After each "session" he again was returned to the cellars, so intensifying grandfather's tuberculosis. Every time my grandfather had to submit to another interrogator, who again and again repeated what had been asked many times before, until my grandfather started to get confused from pain, exhaustion and thirst about what he had said. The Chekists were interested where and with whom he had been; what weapons the group had; what other groups were operative in Kurzeme, as well as elsewhere in Latvia; how communication among the groups was organised; whether the roads to their encampments were mined; who were supporters of the bandits, etc.

During the first interrogation sessions Aleksandrs muddled up everything that came to his mind. It did not occur to him that all the interrogation records would be carefully read and every place name, surname and date underlined in red and checked afterwards. The Chekists quickly caught onto the contradictions in my grandfather's stories, and he was given an increased dose of beating. In the third interrogation session Aleksandrs promised to reveal all that he knew. But the Chekists were in for a letdown, because my grandfather knew very little. This was the longest of the interrogations, which continued for almost two days. The record of the proceedings was interrupted many times and continued after a few hours. Did Aleksandrs lose consciousness? What my grandfather said harmed no one, because the men whom he named were deep in the woods and still continued to operate there for many years. Proof of my grandfather's self-control lies in the fact that he did not say a word about his activities in Vidzeme, thus protecting Milda's relatives from certain arrest and deportation. After the last interrogation, my grandfather's signature was almost unrecognisable – so distorted it is and tortured. Finally, after the seventh interrogation the Chekists understood that they wouldn't be able to beat anything more out of him and decided to begin closing down the case. Aleksandrs was transferred to the Central Prison and placed in a gigantic, overcrowded cell where there were about forty people. Besides political prisoners there were also criminals in the cell.[127] Now a new, trying period began for my grandfather: he had to learn to live by the ruthless rules of the criminal world. Finally on May 6, 1946, his day in court arrived.

In order to improve statistics, individual "bandits" detained by the Chekists were arbitrarily grouped into "armed gangs." By this method, impressive court proceedings could be fabricated and awards earned for the struggle against Fascist bandits. On March 30, Aleksandrs was acquainted with the materials in the interrogation case. He found out that he would be prosecuted for being part of the so-called Ragnija Jansone's gang, whose case materials were collected into nine volumes. During the interrogation my grandfather had not named any of the people who were now being prosecuted together with him. Similarly, the rest of the twenty-four "gang members" had not mentioned Kalnietis' name. Thus, for the sake of credibility, the Chekists had assigned my grandfather the role of liaison of the National Partisan Association of Latvia. This would explain why no one would know him. Attached to the case file is the liaison scheme for the resistance movement group,[128] where my grandfather's name is written into a distant square. From my correspondence with some of the prosecuted persons who have survived and are still living, I understand that in this group of twenty-five people only five had acted together prior to the court case. The rest were included to make the case more impressive – they saw each other for the first time in the courtroom.

The war tribunal was closed and not open to the public. As was common in Soviet court proceedings, judges, prosecutors and, what surprises me the most, also a lawyer participated in the session. In total, 31 witnesses were heard. The court proceedings were conducted in Russian, thus most of the people prosecuted did not understand what transpired. The servants of the Goddess of Justice – Major Ragulov, Lieutenant Oleinikov and Lieutenant Levan surely were bored, because this was not the first time they had to pretend that justice was served here. The roles were well known, and no surprises were expected. The investigators had worked with precision, and the set procedures had been observed faultlessly. Each of the accused was questioned once more. Aleksandrs denied that he had tried to escape to Sweden; that he had disseminated anti-Soviet leaflets or gone to Rīga in order to establish links with other "armed gangs" – but it was useless. This was followed by the prosecutor's scene: frothing at the mouth, with fervour worthy of Vyshinsky, Stalin's star prosecutor during the purges, he proved the offences of the bandits against the Soviet regime. In the charges against my grandfather it was stated:

> Kalnietis Aleksandrs Janovičs [...] until the day of his arrest on 11.11.45 fulfilled his function as a liaison among Northern Kurzeme bandit groups, actively participating in the underground diversionary, counter-revolutionary organisation, the 'Latvian National Partisan Association'. As a participant of the bandit group, he terrorised the residents of Northern Kurzeme, among them the Soviet and Party activists, worked to sabotage the delivery of state grain quotas and other levies by the farmers. He disseminated anti-Soviet leaflets, in which he called for active resistance to the Soviet regime.
>
> The conclusion: to indict Kalnietis Aleksandrs Janovičs in compliance with the RSFSR [Russian Soviet Federated Socialist Republic] Criminal Code, Paragraphs 58–1 "a," 19–58–8, 19–58–9, 59–10 Part 2 and 58–11."[129]

Similar charges were brought against the rest of the prosecuted persons. After a feeble defence by the lawyer Kusin, the judges adjourned to deliberate. Strange as it seems, the judgment had not been pre-prepared. It appears that a five-hour recess was called in order to increase the appearance of legality. Perhaps the explanation is even more banal – it was lunchtime. While lunch was enjoyed in a leisurely fashion and various small, collected tasks disposed of, five hours had passed. On May 10 at 17:45, the sentence was read in Russian. It was of no interest to the "most humane court in the world" that the prosecuted did not understand what was said. In Jansone's group no one was given a death sentence. Five persons were given a sentence of twenty years in maximum security prison camp, followed by five years of forced settlement. Aleksandrs was among those whose guilt was viewed with more leniency – ten years in a maximum security prison camp plus five in settlement.

My grandfather's final words before the sentence was read were: "I beg you – shoot me or exonerate me..."[130]

His plea was a rhetorical cry of despair, because Aleksandrs knew that he would not be exonerated. He had hoped for a death sentence as redemption. The thought alone that what had been endured in the torture chambers of the Cheka and the Central Prison would continue over and over was unbearable. However, it did continue. Like my mother's father, Jānis Dreifelds, Aleksandrs, too, had to survive the long voyage in an overcrowded cattle car. In contrast to Jānis, however, who during his transport to the prison camp was together with decent people and protected from contact with criminals, in Aleksandrs' convoy, political prisoners were transported together with criminals. This made each of the kilometres in the rattling train, as well as the tormenting thirst and summer heat, even more unbearable. Thus going through stage by stage, from prison to prison, Aleksandrs reached his first prison camp, about the location of which his family has no knowledge.

The first contact Aleksandrs had with his family occurred in 1950, when he had already been transferred to the prison camp in Archangelsk Region, Velsk Departament, P.O. Box No. 219. It is not known if my grandfather had been forbidden to write,[131] or if he himself had not wished to do so earlier. The letter sent from the prison camp infirmary through friends of friends reached Milda's mother Matilde and her son Arnis in Latvia. In the letter, written in response by his son, Aleksandrs found out that on March 25, 1949, Milda and Aivars, as the family of a "bandit," had been deported to Siberia. What Milda had most feared had come to pass. Aleksandrs found it very painful to read the uncaring accusations by Matilde written in the childish handwriting of Arnis. He was called the cause for all the misfortunes experienced by the family. This accusation Aleksandrs received instead of the empathy that he had hoped for. What an injustice! When his great sense of insult and injury had somewhat diminished, my grandfather understood that anger was useless, because Matilde had a right to her feelings as a mother. In the first letter Aleksandrs wrote to Aivars, which, in reality, was meant for Milda, he asked: "... do other mothers think that their sons, brothers and husbands are guilty, or do they mean the others, the really guilty ones!"[132]

The first letter sent by my grandfather was on May 5, 1950. The last one – the sixth – was sent on April 27, 1951. He died on February 18, 1953. All the letters were written from various GULAG infirmaries. Tuberculosis and ruthless interrogation in the Cheka torture cells had done their work. From October 26, 1946, Aleksandrs had been declared unfit for work and had received the food ration of an "off-balance sheet" invalid of 400 grams of bread per day. However, it had not stopped the prison camp administration from sending him farther and farther north. Grandfather's last letter, dated April 1951, was sent from Ustyvimlag,[133] but the death notice was issued in Pechorlag AA–274 prison camp.[134] Relative to the previous place of imprisonment in Velsk, Ustyvimlag was located about 400 kilometres further to the northwest, but Pechorlag was right at the polar circle. This camp was created in order to provide gratis labour for the construction of a railway in the permafrost zone. What an absurd act – the decision to sentence an invalid to such extreme conditions! It seems like reason for the relocation is not rational. It is to be found in the bureaucratic execution of Stalin's vision of a prison system, when each of the administrators of the prison camps tried to literally and precisely fulfill the most absurd of orders of the central authorities only to protect himself from being charged with sabotage. The orders to deport arrived, and people were transferred.

In his third letter Aleksandrs wrote to Milda: "Nothing lasts forever! I am in a new 'workplace,' farther north! They don't let you die in one place, but lead you on like the devil the Saviour, and no matter what, it's just not possible to kick the bucket. I'm very ill right now – the result of the exemplary cattle-car transport, and it seems I won't get well soon. I am writing lying down, and, because of this, probably, not clearly. I'm somewhere far North beyond the polar circle beside some large river, which, it's said, flows from the Urals and on which also riverboats course – it's relatively large and supposedly flows into the Northern Dvina. But I miss the old place where I was for two years and seven months and had already settled in. I had my own patch of land with potatoes, red beets, carrots, a few onions and garlic, salad and radishes. The radishes and the salad were given to me for my effort. The rest I had to leave behind. I have to establish my roots again on my own, if only I don't kick the bucket first. My health is not the best, and if after a while my letters stop, then you'll know that I'm no longer among the living. That's how it is; I won't live forever and won't forever be able to endure this hell. I regret nothing!"[135]

Puriņš, the past director of the Tērvete Tuberculosis Sanatorium, who had treated Aleksandrs, was at Ustyvimlag at the same time as my grandfather. After examining his ex-patient, the doctor confirmed that grandfather's condition was hopeless. Under normal circumstances, with fresh air, good food and rest, there might have been some hope of saving him, but in the prison camp, except for fresh air, dry and icy as it was, everything else was not available. They were surrounded by such hopelessness: the tundra, snow and virtually a polar night. How could one, in the shadow of death, not sink into depression in such circumstances? In Velsk, the music making of the small prisoner ensemble, in which grandfather had played the violin and mandolin, helped people hang onto life. Aleksandrs had some artistic talent and perhaps at times, when a scrap paper or the butt of a pencil could be scrounged, he also drew something – some northern landscape or an innocent cartoon. Perhaps he managed to feel like a human being during these moments. The rest of the prisoners in Velsk were not as depressed as those in Ustyvimlag, because the living conditions in Velsk were somewhat better. In the new place the camp authorities did not concern themselves with such superficialities as providing a social life for the prisoners, however minimal, and there was nothing here that could pull my grandfather out of dreary hopelessness. He wrote to Milda that he tried to walk a lot, but the minus forty freezing air was so cold that each breath stung the lungs with a thousand small pins. Thus he had to brood in the semi-dugout infirmary and stare at the whitewashed walls until he sank into apathy.

Aleksandrs felt very lonely. Lonelier than many of the others, because correspondence with his family was so sporadic. The waited-for letters were few and sometimes lost en route. It seemed to Aleksandrs that everyone had forgotten him. He was most hurt by the indifference of his son Arnis, who, in his childish self-preoccupation, did not yet realise how much his father waited for his few, unwillingly written lines. Arnis almost did not remember his father, because the war and parental disagreements had allowed them to be together for so short a time. His father remembered him as a six-year-old boy, whom Aleksandrs had seen for the last time in 1944 before his mobilisation, not the teenager, who, with stubborn perseverance, struggled to survive, because both he and his grandmother Matilde had a very hard time after the deportation of Milda and Aivars. They lived off the generosity of others and often were half starved. Aleksandrs, in his despair, self-righteously, could only see himself and his own suffering. All of his orphaned life he had waited for love from others, not ever learning to really give it.

Aleksandrs' last letter to Milda was a confession and an accusation at the same time, a closing of accounts with life and a last testament.

"I thought for a long time, if it would be worth while to respond to you, because you will have to come to terms and get used to the idea that I am no more. This possibility is not so distant, because over time even iron corrodes, much less even the best of health in the living and climactic conditions that I have had to survive. [...]

I have reconciled myself to the thought and am prepared. If we have to come to this, I can tell you that I shall leave this life not as someone who regrets, but as someone who has lost. [...] I have acted in accordance with my conscience and have been guided by a healthy, logical human mind. I could do nothing else. If I have harmed you, I have been punished by my conscience, and this is a heavy punishment. The harm you have done to me has been punished by your conscience. [...]. We often did not agree. I admit my guilt in regards to you, and I consider my guilt absolved by your parallel guilt. There is still Aivars. For his sake, I would need from fate a few years of life together with him, for I am more than convinced that we would understand each other and be good friends. [...] from the bottom of my heart, I wish him the best and my wishes go with him and he will be fine.

"If you are of the opinion that I'm the cause of your current misfortunes in life, you simply are mistaken and do not know the truth of the situation. You don't have to feel particularly sad, because it is not much better for our countrymen than it is for you. [...] The last letters that I wrote to you were on August 20th and November 2nd, and to Arnis – on November 13th. Since I have received no response from anyone, I decided not to write to you any more. [...] Arnis also hasn't written all this time and I, too, don't intend to do so in the future. He is big enough to understand the essence of the situation. If he does not, it's his business. Fate has meant to have him face the realities of life early, and he has to live his life his own way. The only thing that I recommend and wish for Arnis is that he should start to learn a trade a year from now. Do write this to him.

"Greetings to everyone back home. Greetings and a happy birthday to both of you. All the best. A. Kalnietis."[136]

Milda wrote several more letters to her husband but did not receive an answer.

Aleksandrs was dying in the dark polar night. Slowly and in agony. First, the dry, habitual cough changed to bloody phlegm. Aleksandrs was bathed in sweat, shaken by fever. There were better days sometimes when the desire to live returned with overpowering force. Then he tried to get up and feverishly bustled about in the poorly equipped camp infirmary. When Aleksandrs for the first time felt his mouth fill with something repulsively slimy and warm and a stream of red blood spewed from his mouth, he understood that this was the end. From that moment onward, with distanced indifference, he watched as from his mouth, bit by bit, his lungs were spit out – in porous, pale and bloody lumps. He fought for air as something heavy and immobile lay on his chest. Even the smallest move created a sharp, piercing response and raging pain in his body. In his mind, Aleksandrs travelled separate paths from his emaciated flesh. During his comatose state of pneumonia and high fever, time had lost its cruel reality and irreversibility. Aleksandrs again was a small boy playing with his best friend, who turned out to be his own son Arnis. His mother and father, who had died long ago, were again together with little Sasha. Finally he was with his own people – loved and cherished. Thus, drowning in blood, my grandfather Aleksandrs Kalnietis' life ended.

My grandfather died not knowing that his granddaughter Sandra had been born. Milda's letter with news of this reached the prison camp after Aleksandrs' death. One of his fellow prisoners notified my grandmother of her husband's sad demise. When, after Stalin's death, a review of the case files of the people prosecuted during the "cult period" began in 1954, the court decisions against many legionnaires were reversed or altered. Against my grandfather's name the commission of the "just" had written: "The judgment is considered to be correct."[137] The next review of the "Jansone Group Case" was in January 1990, and the LSSR Assistant Prosecutor V. Batarags decided that "there is no basis for reversing the judgment of the war tribunal of May 10, 1946. The guilt of all of the twenty four persons in the case has been proved and none are eligible for rehabilitation."[138] At that time it was only three months prior to May 4, when the newly elected Supreme Council of Latvia would approve the Declaration on the Renewal of the Independence of Latvia, which would reinstate Aleksandrs Kalnietis' rights to rehabilitation. After his death.

Forced Settlement and Starvation

Three weeks after parting with Jānis Dreifelds at the Babinino station on the 20th or 21st of June, Emilija and Ligita were nearing the end of their journey. The Ural Mountains had already been crossed and the cities of Chelabinsk, Kurgan, Petropavlovsk and Omsk had been passed through and left behind when an order was shouted to get ready to get off at the next station. Throughout the journey my grandmother and mother had not left their wagon. They had not washed nor put on clean clothing. Many of the other women were in precisely the same state, since their belongings had remained with their menfolk. The ones who had been separated from the men in their family already at the "loading" station in Latvia could at least change into the clean clothes they had brought along even though they also had not been able to wash. Of course, this luxury was only possible if at the moment of arrest, overcome with confusion, they had managed to regain their senses enough to take something along for the journey. That is if the Chekists had not arbitrarily forbidden them to do so. Fortunately in my mother's wagon there were not many small children and, therefore, it was not necessary to stand by and watch helplessly the little ones suffer. The only child in the wagon was Mrs. Balodis' three-year-old daughter Inta. The young woman was expecting another child, and her only wish was that the hour of birth would not arrive on the train. Her prayer was answered, and the baby was born in the first place of forced settlement. Because of poor nourishment and her terrible experiences the mother did not have any milk to keep the baby alive. Thus the baby soon died. Inta survived and together with her mother returned to Latvia.

News of the German attack on the Soviet Union reached the train on Midsummer night, June 23. This seemed like miraculous news promising change and an early return to Latvia. For the first time after the dramatic night of June 14, people became more spirited because hope again had been rekindled. In the light of this hope even Midsummer night seemed beautiful, because after crossing the Ural Mountains, they were permitted to keep the wagon doors open except when the train passed through cities. Emilija and Ligita gazed at the dark star-filled heavens, sang Midsummer songs along with the others and for the moment forgot the stinking wagon. The songs also sounded from other wagons, and it was very pleasant to entertain the illusion that right here, beyond the dark trees, was their own seashore where people were celebrating Midsummer night and singing joyfully. They also talked about dear papa Jānis, whose name day was the following day. About those lovely things that they would do when they returned to Latvia. There, older brother Voldemārs would take Ligita and Emilija to the Opera, and they both would be wearing the prettiest dresses in the world. Holding their breath they would watch as the lights of the magnificent crystal chandelier slowly faded. And then the music would sound … During all the interminable years in Siberia this image – the slowly fading lights of the Opera chandelier – had been my mother's dream symbolising a civilised life that was so unattainable. Now, every time that the both of us are at the Opera and I gaze at the chandelier lights fading, I know that this is a sacred moment for my mamma. As it is for me.

The train stopped in Novosibirsk. Everyone was ordered to get off and go to the shore of the Ob River, where a gigantic barge lay waiting for them – so large, that it was able to accommodate all the people who had been on the train. They had become unaccustomed to walking. Some of the smaller children were not able to walk anymore. There, at the shore of the Ob, Emilija and Ligita were able to wash themselves. Without being embarrassed by the all-knowing glances of the guards, the large crowd of deportees washed themselves. It was an almost forgotten feeling of well being to sense the cold, fresh water on their skin. Dirty flesh, wilted and stale, was revived, and together with this revival, interest in their further fate was revived as well.

The women started to question the guards about their husbands – where and how were the families to be reunited? The standard answer: just get on the barge to clear space for the arrival of the men's train. It had not arrived yet, the guards said. Hadn't they seen that they had been the first to leave? Just go on to the place indicated and get ready to wait for the men. The women could not comprehend that the guards were accustomed to lying because to tell the truth to such a large crowd was dangerous. Even totally worn out women can become uncontrollable in their anger. What the guards said seemed credible. It was true – their train had pulled away while the train the men were on had remained standing in the station. Therefore, their reunion was still to come. When I asked my mother when had she finally understood that these had been false promises and that no reunion and living together had ever been intended, my mother sadly kept silent. She no longer remembered this – she had experienced so much callousness and lies that in her memory everything had become tangled and could no longer be unwound.

After the long train trip my grandmother Emilija had become very thin and weak. She had contacted dysentery from the dirty drinking water that the guards most often drew from the ditches beside the railroad. Supported by Ligita she somehow staggered to the large barge and there, half-sitting, collapsed. She was not the only one who was ill. Almost all deportees on the train were suffering from the same malady. Ligita soon fell prey to the illness, too, but not in as heavy a form as Emilija. She at least was able to walk. Over the edge of the barge were positioned two wood cabins, where the ill stood in an unending line. Soon after you had been in the hut, you had to stand in line once more to wait your turn again. After a few days of the journey, the first instances of typhus appeared, and the healthy panicked. There was no possibility of avoiding the disease. The deportees were so crowded, with so little space granted for each, that all of them did not even have the opportunity to stretch out to sleep, and thus, half-sitting, half-prone, the sick ones pined away side by side with those who still had managed to stay healthy. At the landing stops smaller boats pulled up beside the barge and groups of deportees were ordered to transfer to these boats. These were sad moments, when the ones who remained listened as their travelling companions departed until the farewell song sung by the people leaving no longer could be heard. Finally Ligita's and Emilija's turn came to transfer to another boat.

On July 10, 1941, after a voyage that had lasted more than a week along the Ob and its tributary Parabel, they reached the kolkhoz "Bolshoy Chigas," which became the first forced settlement location for my grandmother and mother. At the time they did not know that Latvia was an impossible 6000 kilometres away, which Emilija was never destined to conquer, while Ligita had to cover this distance twice. For the first time it would happen, with high hopes, in the spring of 1948, when the deported children and some young people were allowed to return to Latvia. But after a year and four months the security agencies would recover from such soft-heartedness toward the children of the class enemy, and many, among them my mother, were sent back to Siberia like criminals from prison to prison. Only in 1957, after a long sixteen years, the Soviet regime would recognise Ligita Kalniete, née Dreifelde, as a worthy Soviet citizen and renew her right to live in Latvia.

The distance from the river shore to the village was about eight kilometres, and even though Emilija had recovered from her illness to the degree that she could manage to step ashore by herself, she could not walk such a distance. The person leading them was a kind-hearted farmer, who allowed her to clamber up to a ramshackle cart, and thus, through a marsh, along an almost non-existent road, they trudged along to the kolkhoz. Ligita walked beside the cart. In order to save her only pair of shoes – the dance shoes given to her as a gift by her brother the night prior to their deportation – my mamma took the shoes off. Her feet were tender and pampered, not accustomed to walking barefoot along a bumpy road riddled with stones and sharp branches. Ligita's feet hurt, and now and again she cried from despair. That did not help because they had to move forward nonetheless. She had also become accustomed to crying.

The arrival of strangers was a major event, because never before had the locals seen such well-dressed people. Or – only in Soviet propaganda films, in which neatly dressed kolkhoz inhabitants and workers happily sang about their beautiful life under Stalin's sun. Now such film stars had arrived in their own village. The villagers, too, were class enemies, but ones of longer standing. During the 1930s Stalin had deported them to Siberia, because they were either wealthy landowners – *kulaks* or *kulak* yes-men, in either case – saboteurs, as it was assumed *a priori* by the Soviet regime, hostile to the collectivisation process and a worker-farmer state.[139] The sad story of these people was devastating because, after everything had been taken away from them, they were left, without seed or farm animals, in the taiga to die. They dug themselves into the earth and when, after a few years, those that had not died from starvation and the cold, had somewhat settled and acquired a cow, pig or sheep, they again had become *kulaks* in the eyes of the Soviet regime and were to be transferred somewhere else. The incomprehensible senselessness had stultified the locals to such a degree, that they now did not try in any way to improve their lot but passively worked in the impoverished kolkhoz, waiting until once again the accusation of sabotage would descend on someone. They knew what suffering was and were sincere and helpful. My mother recalls the people here with gratitude. In their poverty they shared what they had with the Latvian deportees to a greater degree than the true locals, the natives who had already lived in Siberia for several generations.

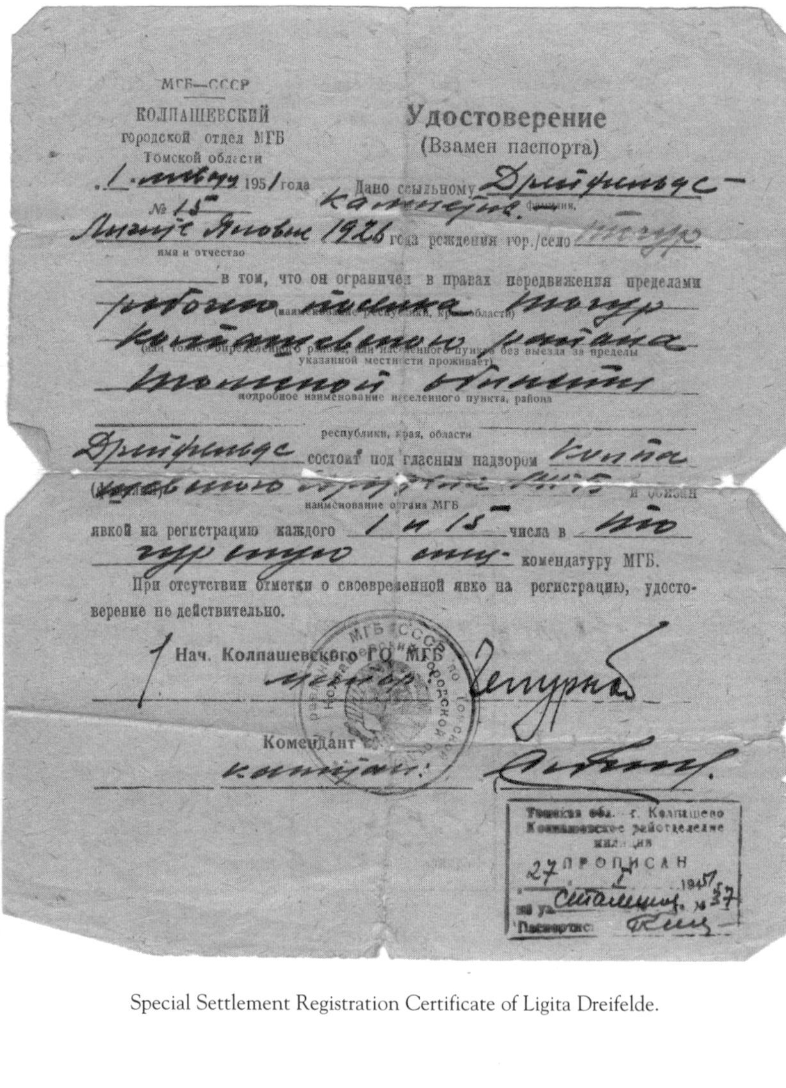

МГБ—СССР
КОЛПАШЕВСКИЙ
городской отдел МГБ
Томской области

1 ... 1951 года
№ 15

Удостоверение
(Взамен паспорта)

Дано ссыльному ... фамилия
... 1926 года рождения гор./село ...
имя и отчество

в том, что он ограничен в правах передвижения пределами
(наименование республики, края, области)
(или только определенного района, или населенного пункта без выезда за пределы указанной местности проживает)
подробное наименование населенного пункта, района
республики, края, области

... состоит под гласным надзором ... и обязан
наименование органа МГБ
явкой на регистрацию каждого 1 и 15 числа в ... комендатуру МГБ.

При отсутствии отметки о своевременной явке на регистрацию, удостоверение не действительно.

Нач. Колпашевского ГО МГБ

Комендант

Томская обл. г. Колпашево
Колпашевское райотделение милиции
ПРОПИСАН
27 I 1951
№ 37
Паспортист

Special Settlement Registration Certificate of Ligita Dreifelde.

The crowd watched in silence as the new arrivals settled down into the local school. This was a recently erected building with two quite large rooms, in which some twenty-five people settled to live. A few days later the Commandant arrived in the village and ordered all the adults to confirm with their signature a document stating that they were deported for twenty years without the right to arbitrarily leave their place of settlement.[140]

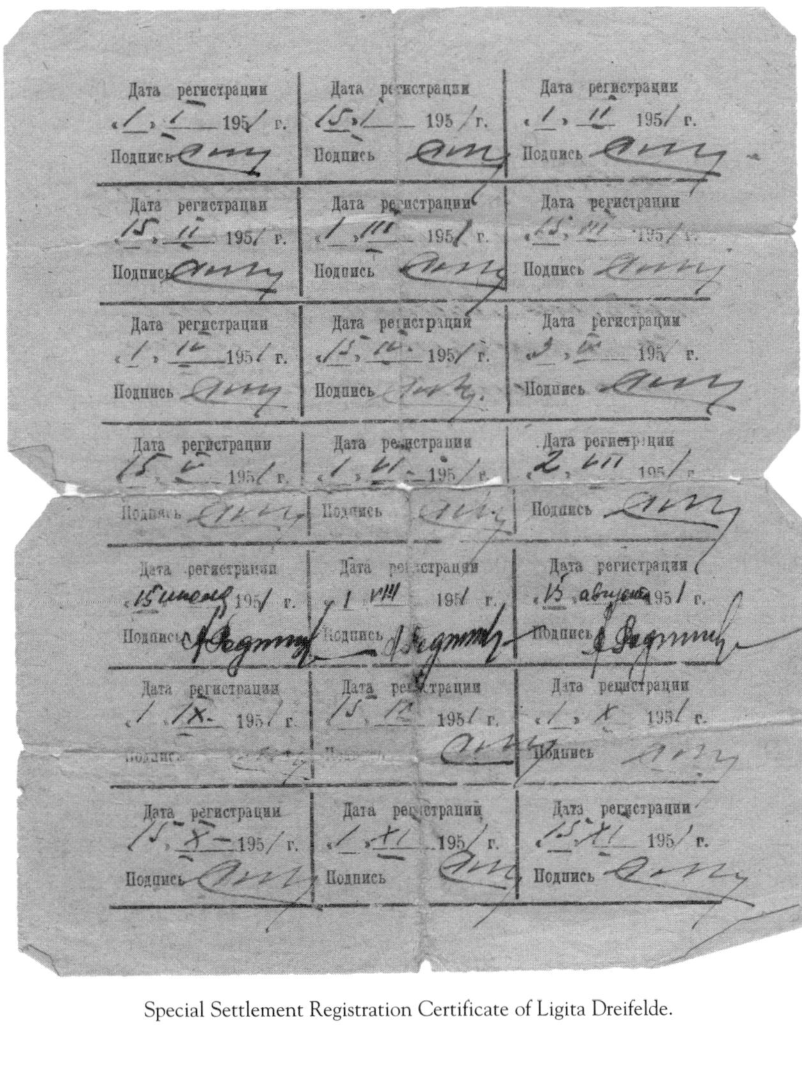

Дата регистрации «1» I 1951 г. Подпись	Дата регистрации «15» I 1951 г. Подпись	Дата регистрации «1» II 1951 г. Подпись
Дата регистрации «15» II 1951 г. Подпись	Дата регистрации «1» III 1951 г. Подпись	Дата регистрации «15» III 1951 г. Подпись
Дата регистрации «1» IV 1951 г. Подпись	Дата регистрации «15» IV 1951 г. Подпись	Дата регистрации «3» IV 195 г. Подпись
Дата регистрации «15» V 1951 г. Подпись	Дата регистрации «1» VI 1951 г. Подпись	Дата регистрации «2» VII 1951 г. Подпись
Дата регистрации «15» июля 1951 г. Подпись	Дата регистрации «1» VIII 1951 г. Подпись	Дата регистрации «15» августа 1951 г. Подпись
Дата регистрации «1» IX 1951 г. Подпись	Дата регистрации «15» IX 1951 г. Подпись	Дата регистрации «1» X 1951 г. Подпись
Дата регистрации «15» X 1951 г. Подпись	Дата регистрации «1» XI 1951 г. Подпись	Дата регистрации «15» XI 1951 г. Подпись

Special Settlement Registration Certificate of Ligita Dreifelde.

Subsequently a representative from the Commandant's office arrived each month and checked if anyone had escaped. As if they had somewhere to escape to! In later years the registration papers were handed out to the deportees and everyone had to go to sign themselves in at the Commandant's office on the first and the fifteenth of each month. The form was divided into twenty-one boxed sections. When all the spaces had been filled, ten and a half months had passed and a new form had to be filled.[141] This was the only proof-of-identity document that the deportees had. In it the district was specifically defined, within whose boundaries the deportee "under open supervision"[142] was allowed to move with a special permit from the Commandant's office. Without such a permit no one had the right to leave the forced settlement place beyond a distance of more than three kilometres. Right there below the warning was a printed note:

"Without a notation of punctual registration this identity card is not valid." The signature of two officials of the respective regional or city KGB and two official seals validated the identity card.

During the first six months of deportation Emilija and Ligita were forced to change their settlement place nine times. There was no logic in their moves. The order to move usually arrived without prior notice and had to be immediately executed. No one was interested in what the deportees had to suffer, having to leave their small vegetable gardens that they had created in order to guard somehow against starvation. "They," the powers that be, decided, and again Emilija and Ligita had to move to a new place, often totally unsuited for human habitation. When I asked my mother, why the deportees were so often relocated, she replied dryly: "So that a human being would not able to settle anywhere and would die sooner." It is now known that the USSR People's Commissariat of the Interior had in its official memoranda expressed the opinion that specifically in the Novosibirsk region "the living conditions for the deportees in settlement are extraordinarily unsatisfactory"[143] and "the deportees in settlement find themselves experiencing very difficult living conditions. Starvation, poverty and 'unemployment' are prevalent. [...] no one from the PCI apparatus is assigned to deal with the deportees in settlement, and no one has responsibility for their conditions."[144] However nothing whatsoever was ever done to even minimally improve the living condition of these poor unfortunates.

As September approached, the school had to be left and new shelter had to be found with the villagers. For a few roubles Emilija and Ligita settled in with a woman, whose husband had been killed in the war and who was happy about the unexpected extra income. They were given a place to sleep on the kitchen floor near the stove. Emilija's and Ligita's neighbour was a gaunt cow belonging to the woman owning the hut, who did not dare to keep the cow in the barn because of the cold. All the cracks between the logs were teeming with bedbugs, while clothing and heads were slowly becoming riddled with lice. Since that time right up to the autumn of 1946 these vermin became an unavoidable part of life for Emilija, Ligita and the other deportees. The locals lived with these bugs as a matter of course without feeling any discomfort. The vermin travelled together with the deportees from one settlement place to the next, and there they mated with the bugs already there waiting for them. After renewal of the genetic pool, more and more new generations continued to feed off the emaciated flesh of the deportees. They had neither the strength nor means of hygiene to combat the parasites. The only aid was a lice comb carved out of a cow's shank bone that travelled from hand to hand, if only to relieve the unbearable itching of heads for a brief moment.

The first winter the deportees managed to survive because they had enough belongings and clothing they could trade in for potatoes or some other food. The only luxury that Emilija and Ligita had was the small pot of butter they had managed to hastily take along. For some time it enriched the potatoes they ate, but very soon it was used up. The money that grandmother had managed to hide under her vest at the moment of arrest had no normal value in the disastrous conditions of the village, but from time to time someone appeared who was willing to sell some tit-bit of food. The locals were much more interested in the belongings of the deportees, however, Emilija had almost nothing to barter, because everything had remained with Jānis. There were no blankets, sheets or pillows. Only what they had on their backs and some odd pieces of clothing that had been shoved into the small suitcase they had brought along from Babinino: Jānis' long underwear, some women's underwear and one woollen dress. Everything they could do without was sold. Emilija even unstitched the lining of her coat and sewed a bright silk dress, which they exchanged for a pail of potatoes. Her diamond earrings also went for the same price. For sure, the woman who bought them did not understand what she had acquired and was rapt in wonder at the brightly glittering pieces of glass. Old boots were bought for Ligita so she would have something to wear when she could not avoid going outside. In order to guard her legs from freezing, my mother wore her father's long underwear, in addition wrapping her legs with rags for warmth. Certainly everywhere in Siberia where the Balts had been deported even today odd things unfamiliar to the local inhabitants and whose origin they no longer know can be found in the small villages and homes. Clothing has been worn out. Watches have been broken. Jewellery has been lost.

After having spent the first winter with a place to sleep in the Sidorenkov hut, Ligita and Emilija together with the three girls from the Upītis family[145] moved to a small barn that a local woman had agreed to rent. The barn was half in ruins and filled to the rafters with dried out manure. But after they had cleaned out the barn, had covered the roof with birch bark and the floor with wood boards filched from the kolkhoz stables, it was turned into an acceptable home. It only remained to make bunks from birch poles and to create a hearth from homemade bricks. No matter how despicable this shelter was, it was, nonetheless, more pleasant to be together with one's own. With winter approaching, they surrounded the small barn on all sides with heaps of straw, so it would, as much as possible, retain heat. In the semi-dark, snowed-in hut they spent the second winter in Siberia. For Emilija and Ligita it was much harder than the first one.

In this second winter all of the reserves they had brought along from Latvia had been used up and they had to live from whatever they were able to gather during the summer and autumn. Emilija had to go to work in the kolkhoz, but their earnings were so meagre that it was not worthwhile to work. The most that she could earn was 300 grams of bread per day. Together with the Upītis' girls, Ligita went mushroom and nut hunting, as well as tied brooms, which she traded in for potatoes and salted fish. Berries were preserved without sugar for the winter. The gathered nuts were very tasty, energising and rich. Towards autumn everyone joined in to pluck flax and gather grain. If the day's quota was met, a ration of bread – approximately a half a kilogram – was received in return. It was most advantageous to dig potatoes, because the locals gladly employed the deportees knowing that they would be ready to work almost for a song. The potatoes were saved in the little barn in a dug out pit under the floor, without consideration that the earth would freeze in winter and the potatoes would be ruined. Nonetheless, irrespective of what had been stored, there was not enough food, and constant hunger reigned in the small barn. Emilija had found under a roof some quilted jackets that were so old and ragged they were no longer of any use to the locals. Carefully, stitch-by-stitch, my grandmother sewed the scraps of disintegrating cotton unto the remnants of padding with fish net thread. They turned out so beautifully, that they came to be called astrakhan fur jackets, because the black and grey stitches from a distance gave the impression of frizzy Persian lamb fur. When these new overcoats had been completed, they decided to sell both coats from Latvia, however the couple of potato pails that were obtained for them satisfied bottomless hunger for only a short while. Everyone had become thin to the point of being unrecognisable. On March 31 the Upītis grandmother died. After her death the two youngest Upītis girls together with their mother headed out to look for work in the nearest town. The third – Rūta – remained with Emilija and Ligita in the little barn.

Despite this devastation, an inner light warmed Ligita, because she had been visited by the miracle of love. She had noticed the young, handsome man already on the barge en route from Novosibirsk to the Bolshoy Chigas. Their next meaningful meeting took place at a party for young deportees. The local teacher, deported from the city as enemy of the people, had a record player with a few records of waltzes, foxtrots and tangos. The kolkhozniks did not know how to dance such city dances. Their merriment was associated with drinking, followed by fighting and then staggering home. After these rowdies had cleared the club hall, the teacher brought in her record player, and the "foreigners" started their dancing. Some of the local young men and women looked on with wonder and curiosity, perhaps also with longing at what, in their opinion, was an odd style of courting. But the deportees did not care. Their youth demanded joy and a life without care, even if joy and being carefree was denied to them.

That evening Ligita again had a sparkle in her eyes and an impish smile. She once more felt like the queen of the ball. From the heights of her beauty she enchanted those Latvian boys who due to some inexplicable coincidence of circumstances had had the fortune to remain with their family and who now were enjoying themselves with three times as many girls. Her elation at that moment felt as radiant as at it had been at the Dubulti high school dance, when the boys from the senior classes and her own brother's friends had competed to see who would be allowed to dance with the sparkling Miss Dreifelde. Other girls had looked on at what was happening with a sour smile, and that only had served to increase Ligita's joy at her victory. She tilted up her chin, threw back her blonde hair and fearlessly whirled round and round, dance after dance. This evening Ligita did the same, only each smile and dance turn was intended for Him. He did not dance, but looked on silently and reservedly. My mother knew that a few days prior to deportation he had married, but on June 14 he had given it all up as lost. Finally Ligita heard the eagerly awaited words: "May I have this dance, Miss Dreifelde?" Overcome with confusion, Ligita fitted into his arms. My mamma wanted to enjoy a shared silence and just experience the miracle of first touch. The foolish fear that He would sense how she felt, made her twitter and flirt. They danced a few more dances, and then the evening was over. He walked her home to the wretched small barn and did not even kiss her. This is how my mother's first love began. It was never meant to be fulfilled, because the reality was too harsh. After a while he was sent to the coal mines in Prokopyevsk. My mother was transferred to Bilina, the Death Island.

In 1945 they started to exchange letters. Being aware of the two young people corresponding and fearing that her son might marry some local girl, his mother suggested in every way possible that Ligita should go and visit her son. With the support of her mother, Ligita secretly escaped from the settlement. She had to get to Prokopyevsk by hitchhiking because, without a permit from the Commandant's office, train tickets could not be bought and besides that she had no money. Traversing six hundred kilometres during winter was a hard and dangerous journey. When Ligita finally met her beloved, it turned out that the harsh experiences had tested them sorely – they both had changed and had grown apart. After a few months, with a heavy heart, the defeated Ligita returned to Emily. When I try to imagine the feelings of these two people who were destined to live in captivity, I marvel that they even had the strength to love during such disastrous times. He, not knowing anything about the fate of his wife, and my dear mamma, dressed in a skirt patched together from pieces that could be salvaged from a worn-out wool shawl. She was wearing a blouse she had knitted herself from unravelled cotton stockings and her bare feet were clad in heavy, laced boots. Both of them were half-starved. How was it possible in such circumstances to look at each other with rapture and eyes full of love?

The long awaited spring arrived cold and rainy. Bread no longer was given to the deportees, and there was nothing else to be done but to comply with the orders of the Commandant's office and work in the kolkhoz. Almost all the kolkhoz horses had died. None remained to pull a plough; therefore, the "witty" idea occurred to the kolkhoz chiefs to use the deportees instead of horses and ploughs. Thus the emaciated women were made to spade the field to plant potatoes. The first frogs started to croak, and Ligita learned how to catch them. Boiled in water, they tasted like chicken. All winter long small pieces of potatoes and potato peels were saved so they could be planted in the just unfrozen, loosened earth. All of these efforts were proof of small, courageous acts of will when irreplaceable morsels of food were torn away from hungry stomachs. It turned out that the sacrifice was futile, because on May 27 an order arrived to transfer the Latvians living in Bolshoy Chigas to the adjacent small town of Parabel, where deportees were being gathered together from the surrounding area. Emilija was ill with malaria. Prone and half-conscious, she was driven from Bolshoy Chigas and laid to sleep on the floor in the erstwhile church of Parabel, which now sported the name of a club. People were lying on the floor one beside the other in such close proximity that there was nowhere to step. The meagre meals were prepared on the riverbank on bonfires, and people washed up in the same place. When after a month they were transferred again, my grandmother had conquered her malaria.

There on the shore of Parabel River, Ligita for the first time was harnessed to a barge and made to pull the barge upstream in the river. This was convicts' work well known since ancient times in Russia. However, during the Czarist period women were spared the hard work of barge pulling. My mother remembers that the hardest part was crossing the small tributaries, because the cold water often reached right up to her neck. In this fashion, soaked to the skin and hungry, for hours on end she had to slowly work her way along the soft, rain-saturated clay of the shore. The boats had to be loaded and unloaded as well. Salt and bricks had to be carried for several kilometres from the warehouse to the riverbank and vice versa. Bricks were tied up unto a rope, four up front and four at the back, and two hundred people in single file dragged to the riverbank and back again. Feet sank into the trampled clay up to the knees. From the side it must have looked comical, because the walkers slowly raised their legs high as if executing some sort of ritual dance. It was torture because feet clad in bad shoes got soaked through, swelled and became inflamed. The ropes rubbed and cut into shoulders, but, rain or shine, in two weeks of work the load of bricks had been transferred to the barge.

The majority of the people gathered in Parabel were transferred by the riverboat "Tarass Shevchenko" to Bilina, a small island located at the confluence of the River Ob and its tributary Ket. The island was flat, and with the exception of a few willows nothing else grew there. On the island squatted four fishermen's huts and a somewhat larger building – a fish processing plant that had never operated. The boat left, leaving three hundred people – Latvians and Bessarabians – in an open field without a roof over their heads to serve as food for mosquitoes and small, biting flies.

The sailors, on leaving, snickered – these have been brought here to croak! Already the next day what they had predicted became fact. The first one to die was a small boy. Bilina became the last resting place for many. Of the 200 Latvians brought there, 50 died.[146] Emilija and Ligita had the fortune to return from this Island of Death.

It often rained in Bilina, with the only shelter being a woodshed. There was not enough space for everyone in it, and the people who were left without a roof over their heads somehow managed to set up temporary tents with blankets and sheets. The next day after arriving, by an order from the Commandant, they were told to dig sod to build a dugout for shelter. A rectangle of 80 x 5 metres was drawn on the field. Posts were dug in at each corner of the rectangle and a timber foundation was put in around the perimeter. The sod was cut in equal-size quadrangles, which were placed tightly one above the other creating a metre-thick wall, leaving holes for windows and doors. With time, these pieces of sod grew together.

The building of the dugout did not employ everyone, thus some of the deportees were mobilised to pick berries, nuts and mushrooms in the taiga. Emilija and Ligita were fortunate to be included among the pickers, who were taken by boat some ten kilometres from their camp and were left there until late autumn. The splendid nature in the taiga, the sound of birds, wind and the river for a while allowed them to forget wretched reality and be carried away by the illusion of freedom. Nature in Siberia is beautiful and magnificent. In the face of it, a human being feels small and reverent. The encampment in the taiga has remained in my mother's memory as a bright intermission from the hopelessness of Bilina. All around grew large and sweet lingonberries. Black currant bushes stretched above the picker's heads. They were able not only to gather the assigned quotas but also eat their fill, as well as cook up jam in birch-bark pails for the winter. In the evening bonfires were lit, on which berries were cooked in pots or nuts roasted for supper. When hunger had been sated, they shared recollections of life in Latvia. When such reminiscences grew too sad, they told funny stories and sang songs. A singer from the Moscow Bolshoy Theatre worked side by side with Emilija and Ligita. After a concert in Moscow, she had unwisely made the statement that the old songs were her favourites. That was enough to have her deported to be with the "white bears." She occasionally sang opera arias and romantic Russian songs to her fellows in calamity, melodies that sounded strange and savage within the circle of splendid nature and the glow of the fire. At the end of September it grew cold, and in October together with the first snow boats arrived to take the berry pickers back to Bilina. The most heartless thing happened on their return. The guards searched the belongings of the returning workers and confiscated their jam in the birch-bark containers...

Life in Bilina in no way differed from imprisonment in a prison camp.[147] Everyone had to live in an overcrowded dugout, and there was virtually no contact with the outside world. The only difference was that the forced settlers did not have to be so heavily guarded, because in the summer you could not escape from the island, while in the winter no one wanted to. In Bilina it occurred to the Soviet regime for the first time to deal with the deportees' clothing, and they were handed out high felt boots with wooden soles and rough half coats patched together from variegated colour pieces of goat hide. The food rations too were the same as in the GULAG, and there was nothing else to be obtained to eat. At least on dry land you could earn a potato or two or a drop of milk by doing some work for the locals. Some of the most enterprising crossed the ice to the nearest village in order to exchange their few remaining belongings for bits of food, but the locals no longer were so eager to trade for the property of the foreigners. The bartered trivia did not balance out the energy expended in the trek across the ice. True starvation set in: they ate straw, tree bark and fish that had smothered under ice. People turned into ghastly shadows of themselves and became covered with boils. In April, after a harsh, and for many the last winter, just before the start of the floods, the deportees who had survived were transferred to the "big land" and were settled in the village of Petropavlovka. Emilija and Ligita, together with some "comrades-in-arms" from Bilina[148] settled in one of the unfinished huts, which had originally been intended for housing deported Russian Germans. The roaring, swelled spring waters of Rivers Ob and Ket washed away the dugout, which had been built with such difficulty, as if it were just a trifle. It is probable that the mortal remains of Latvians buried in shallow graves under ice were carried away with the floods, scattering the bones of the unfortunates as far as the Arctic Ocean.

The winters in Bilina and Petropavlovka had apparently been the harshest, but starvation was an integral part of Emilija's and Ligita's life until 1947. Starvation and hard, minimally productive slaves' labour. The chairman of the kolkhoz used the deportees to perform various ancillary tasks, for which only with difficulty one could earn a daily ration of bread. This work involved making nets, salting fish, transporting logs, erecting barracks, hewing wood, spading, loading barges, reaping grain, digging up potatoes … It was particularly hard to work in winter, because there was neither suitable clothing nor proper footwear. People had become gaunt from starvation, only to be further tortured by senseless work.

When I talked to my mother about the Bilina and Petropavlovka period during the preparatory phase for this book, I did not allow myself to feel. My objective was not to interrupt the thread of recollections and to question dispassionately in order to learn as much as possible how starvation emaciates a human body and alters the spirit. When I later listened to the taped conversations, their calm flow seemed unbearable to me, so abnormal was their content. The sad story told in my mother's everyday voice singed me with sudden waves of pain. My body shook and I had to hang onto my desk to contain my uncontrollable sobs. I could not listen to my practical voice, repeating a question about how a rat tastes or wondering how mother had not died from eating a horse cadaver. Just as matter-of-factly, without the slightest hint of emotion, my mother answered that a rat tasted of dust and mould and chuckled: "They weren't so easy to get either. Grandmother had connections in the kolkhoz chicken coop!" Even I laughed together with my mother because there wasn't anything in the Soviet Union that did not require "connections" or the so-called *blat* – even to get rats to add to a nettle stew! When we had wiped away the tears of laughter, mother added: "It truly is a miracle that we survived after eating the flesh of horses, calves and rats that had died from God only knows what disease. The rats were no less dangerous, for they had been killed by poison. When we ate them, it didn't taste at all unpalatable. We needed the food then ..."

Only once did my mother get food poisoning from eating a fish she found. She lay for several hours unconscious, and after coming to her senses for a time lost her memory. She didn't even recognise her own mother.

Starvation changed everything. Hunger became so unbearable that it overtook every thought and every conversation. The established norms of politeness and morality fell apart. Everything that previously had been prohibited was allowed: for the sake of food it was permitted to steal and to lie. My grandmother like the others headed out at night on potato stealing expeditions to the kolkhoz potato fields. The penalty for such sabotage was prison, but what was prison in comparison to starvation, and how did prison differ from the existing calamity! Once a distant neighbour's ducks happened to wander as far as the deportees' hut. Ligita with her friend Aina, not exchanging a word, just threw each other a meaningful glance, and the fowl were caught before even a minute had passed, plucked right away, fried and eaten. When the neighbour later asked if they had seen some ducks, Emilija, without the slightest qualms of conscience, lied that she had seen them that morning because they usually wandered here every day, and waved in the direction of the woods. Everything was edible. Grass, tree bark, nettles, rotted potatoes, linseed, frogs and carrion. Stomachs went on strike from the enormous amounts of stewed nettles and other surrogates; hence what was ingested came out almost undigested. The roasted linseed stupefied, and after eating them a state of semi-consciousness set in, but starvation was so horrific that seeing in one's excrement undigested seeds, the deportees were ready to rinse them off and eat them a second time. Starvation changed the human body. Some became emaciated, others swelled up until excretory systems no longer functioned due to internal organ oedema. Ligita's menstruation ceased. This also happened to the other women. Their menstruation only restarted in 1947 after they received the first food parcels from Latvia, together with the improvement of general conditions after the war.

Emilija looked on powerlessly as her child slowly wasted away. In Bilina, Ligita's splendid blonde hair was cut off, leaving only a symbolic strand of hair on her forehead. Her bald head had broken out in boils oozing pus. Head lice, showing off their shiny well-fed behinds, fed in the boils as if they were bowls of meat. In Petropavlovka, Ligita fell ill with malaria, which was a terminal illness for her body wasted away by long-term starvation. Emilija only had a damp cloth at her disposal to use as a cooling compress to put on her daughter's forehead while she lay half-conscious with starvation and malaria. Emilija herself was only skin and bones, but she took every morsel of food from herself and gave it away to her daughter. What was most dreadful was that Ligita wanted to die and Emilija was neither able to rekindle her will to live nor pull her out of the apathy resulting from starvation. In the moments when Ligita regained consciousness, the mother talked to her daughter about her father, who loves his "Ligucis" so much, and fervently begged: "You must not do this to papa. He won't survive this." She drew vivid scenes from memory about life in Dubulti and the pranks that Ligita had worked together with her brothers, who now were waiting for their little sister to return. She conjured up tables breaking from being overloaded with steaming cups of cocoa, rosy Daugava salmon and aromatic smoked Rīga ham that both of them would eat in Latvia. She only had to hang on and survive. Ligita gazed at her mother with large, shining eyes that slowly became more and more transparent. Each time that her daughter again slid into unconsciousness, Emilija shouted at God in her despair. Everything had been taken away from her – her husband and her sons. Only don't take away the only thing remaining from me! A miracle happened. Someone was fortunate enough to obtain several packets of quinine, and they succeeded in tearing Ligita away from the jaws of death.

In her mother's despair Emilija regretted that because of age and lack of strength she could not work more to be able to get food so that after the heavy illness Ligita would regain strength sooner. Even her body was too old to sell to some covetous man for a few potatoes. But Emilija was able to arouse the pity of the local storehouse supervisor, who agreed to employ grandmother occasionally in some house or field work in exchange for some potatoes or leftover fish bones. This was very magnanimous, because the villagers themselves lived in semi-starvation in spring. Emilija still had about twenty matches saved from Latvia. For these, she had obtained from a farmer a calf that had died several days previously and now was already bloated. She cut out the best meat pieces and cooked them for a long time before giving them to Ligita. With these trifles and the symbolic daily ration of bread given to them, Emilija succeeded in pulling her daughter through till true spring. Then they were able to begin eating more wholesome things – nettles and frogs. Later incredible good fortune befell Emilija. A local supervisor showed up, who, being somewhat of a dandy, desired to buy a gold watch that up to now no one had wanted to buy. He had previously lived in the city and knew the value of the watch; thus Emilija traded the watch for an unbelievably high price: a pood of rye flour,[149] a pail of salted carp and ten kilograms of fresh fish. Now the worst was behind them.

The spring brought long-awaited happy news. "The war is over! The war is over!" Emilija heard. She looked out the window and saw the deported German, Kaufmann, arms raised, waving and jumping comically, loping across the field still covered with snow in patches and full of puddles, shouting again and again. Emilija felt her legs go weak, and she collapsed on the bed. So great was the news. Slowly from the depths of her being rose an irrational hope: "Liguci! Home! We'll finally be able to go home!" Joyfully, Emilija and Ligita hugged each other and started to cry.

The days came and went, and slowly the hope that had stirred with the news of the end of war dissipated. My mother remembers with what agitation and conviction they had debated that now the West would help. They would not allow such horrors to continue! As soon as Latvia would be free, everyone would be able to return home. The voices saying that no one in the world had the slightest interest about them here, in distant Siberia, were drowned in protest. A human being had to believe in the good. The fantasy created by hopelessness turned the English, French and Americans into knights meting out justice, whose mission it was to defend the poor unfortunates and to punish evildoers. Most of them had forgotten or seemed not to remember the dirty pre-war games – the Munich deal or Finland's solitary battle with the USSR. It was naïve wishful thinking, totally removed from reality. However, it helped to keep hope alive and to survive.

In the summer, Emilija and Ligita were moved once more. They were ordered to move to the neighbouring village Borovoy. This did not make any sense whatsoever, because for work they still had to go back to Petropavlovka. Because of this senseless walking and confused from feebleness, Emilija got lost in the winter of 1946 and nearly died. The brigadier had sent her with some news back to Borovoy. It was not far, only about five or six kilometres along a well-travelled and familiar path. In the evening it was discovered that no one had seen Emilija. People were called together, and all of them set out to search for the lost woman.

When Emilija got lost, Ligita panicked. The mothers of friends of her own age, Māra and Aina, had already died, not having survived the inhuman conditions. For Ligita it almost seemed like a logical outcome that now it was Emilija's turn. As if half-insane, she cried and cried. Emilija's love was so great, so self-denying, creating such security and feeling of shelter that Ligita, with an egoism characteristic of a child, had perceived it as something self-explanatory and inalienable. Now my mother understood with harsh clarity that without Emilija life would not be possible. Each evening the searchers returned and with each day hope of finding the lost woman alive grew less, because outside the temperature stood at minus 30 degrees Celsius. They searched for her for three days and three nights. On the fourth morning, children going to school from the neighbouring village found her. For all this time my grandmother had been wandering nearby. She had been led in circles by an evil spirit.

Wandering in the freezing weather through the woods, Emilija realized that the only hope of survival was to keep moving, and she forced her totally exhausted body, emaciated from starvation, not to stop. She could not allow herself to give in to the temptation to sleep – to lie down in the snow and fall asleep. Emilija knew it would be certain death. She had to live because her child could not be without a mother. On the third night Emilija no longer had the strength to walk. In order not to fall asleep she gathered the branches blown down by the wind and broke them into little pieces, to make a deathbed. Emilija knew that this was her last night. That she would not be able to survive more. When in the morning she heard the children's voices, she cried out gathering the last vestiges of her strength. Fortunately, the children heard her weak cries. When Emilija was brought by sled to the village, her frostbitten nose had already started to fester. Later the tip of her nose fell off. Her heels and fingers had also frozen, however, gangrene fortunately did not set in and they healed. Only one of her thumbs remained blue and stiff to the end of her life.

The nearest hospital was located forty kilometres away in the town of Kolpashevo. Emilija was wrapped up in some rags donated by neighbours, placed in a sleigh, and the hours-long journey could begin. Only once did they stop at a house where they warmed up and drank tea. Ligita did not have warm clothing, only a ragged quilted jacket. Under her cotton skirt she only had brief panties. Her thighs were naked, while on her feet she wore felt boots with wood soles. When they finally reached Kolpashevo, Ligita's bare thigh skin crackled dryly on touch. Later it turned black and peeled. Ligita was not allowed to remain in Kolpashevo. Having made certain that her mother's life was no longer threatened, she left to return the next day. The driver had already left, and Ligita had no other recourse but to walk. It took the whole day to walk the forty kilometres. Walking she did not feel the cold so much.

Emilija spent several months in the hospital getting well. The poor food seemed absolutely royal in comparison to the starvation suffered in the village. Kolpashevo's Latvians took care of my grandmother as much as they were able to. Each brought some small trifle from the little food they had: a boiled potato or carrot or a piece of fish. Ligita only visited her mother once, because half-starving and in the freezing cold she did not have enough strength to walk the forty kilometres there and as many back. She wrote letters and sent them to her mother with people who were going to Kolpashevo. Emilija recovered around springtime. The sun was already high in the skies, but the snow still held. Ligita asked the kolkhoz for a horse to bring her mother back from the hospital, but her request was denied. There was nothing else to be done but to borrow a sled and to pull her mother back herself. Emilija tried a few times to walk on her own, but she did not have the strength and had to sit down again on the sled. My grandmother cried from despair, because she could not bear to watch Ligita like an old women making one weak step after another, moving the sled ahead bit by bit. It was good that daylight was already longer in April. As the dark set in, the forty kilometre tortuous journey was finally over. During the walk they had had a few potatoes along for sustenance. They both knew that in their hut there was also nothing to eat.

Changes

The first letter arrived in spring 1946 from Emilija's sister Anna. Grandmother and mother had written many times on birch bark[150] to their relatives in the Kurzeme region, but they had not received an answer.[151] They had not realised that the letters could not reach the addressees because Latvia was on the other side of the front line. After the war, Anna received the accumulated letters and now was able to communicate with her sister. From Anna's letters Emilija finally learned that her sons were alive and that she was a grandmother. Voldemārs had married Zenta. They had two sons – Juris and Jānis. Arnolds had a daughter Mārīte and a son Andris. Anna intimated that Voldemārs and his family, Viktors and Arnolds were safe, while Arnold's wife Nellija with their children were living in Ventspils. Anna's letter was read and reread not only by Emilija and Ligita, but also by all the Latvians living in Borovoy, until the letter disintegrated. News from home did not only belong to the person it was sent to but to everyone, because the fate of the deportees had bound them so closely together that they all felt like one family, whose sadness and joy was mutually felt and shared.

Anna wrote in a roundabout way, not stating anything directly, but Emilija sensed that her sons were living abroad, outside Latvia, because only there they could be safe. As the end of the war had approached, Voldemārs, Arnolds and Viktors had left Latvia. There was no definite news of where they had settled. The refugees were reluctant to write to their relatives afraid to cause difficulties for them or to reveal their own location. In Germany rumours spread in refugee camps that one could not rely on the Allies, because, on Soviet request, they were said to hand over Balts to the Russians.[152]

In the opinion of the refugees coming into Soviet hands was equal to a death sentence. Everyone knew some horror story about the cruelty that had taken place in the part of Latvia that the Soviet army had occupied in October 1944. It was horrendous to think of the fate of the unfortunate compatriots who had found themselves in areas occupied by the Red Army in Germany. They all had been shoved into cattle cars and deported to Siberia.[153]

The second greatest event was the arrival of a package from Latvia in spring 1946. It arrived sooner than for other people, because Anna had had the foresight to send it by train to Moscow to her husband's sister, who then had sent it on to Emilija and Ligita. At the time Latvia's communication channels with the "great Soviet motherland" had not been fully restored yet. They had to walk sixteen kilometres to the nearest post office in Ustychaya to get the package. The first half of the journey wound through a marsh along a small path fashioned of branches, sticks and other remnants of wood. In places small runoffs of melting snow ran across the path and had to be waded through. Weak after her illness, Emilija did not have the strength to go on; hence at the halfway mark she was forced to remain in Petropavlovka while Ligita continued on alone. The package was a heavy plywood box that weighed more than ten kilos. Having escaped the curious glances of the postmistress, my mother hurried outside to open the box – there surely had to be something to eat in it! It was very thoroughly nailed shut. Having unsuccessfully struggled to open the box using chips of stone and wood splinters, Ligita finally remembered to try her hair clip. Wonder of wonders, the nails gave way, and the lid of the box moved. On top was clothing. Ligita quickly pulled it out and right at the bottom saw what she had hoped for – tins of food, sugar and a large piece of smoked country bacon. With relish my mother bit into the fatty pork. How good it tasted! How good it smelled! In savage hunger she bit and tore with her teeth, until in shame she recalled her mother. Somehow managing to shove all the sent items back into the box, Ligita tied the box with rope and, hoisting it on her back, started to walk. The burden was very heavy! She had to stop more and more often to rest. From the sun it could be seen that afternoon was dangerously closing in. Ligita was overtaken by a local woman, whom she begged to tell Emilija, that her daughter did not have more strength to continue further. Thus, having exhausted her strength, Ligita sunk down in a heap and waited. "My dear mamma hurried up on her thin, thin legs, took the box and carried it ... She, so wasted away ..." my mother sobbed out, remembering.

All the Latvians in the Borovoy settlement came together for this major event. In the package were three warm jackets and a couple of flannel nightgowns, several dresses, shoes and underwear, a blanket, sheets, towels and soap. These were amazing riches that everyone touched and patted. For a long, long time no one present had held something so beautiful in their hands: since the day they were deported, their clothing had shrunk and become threadbare, turning into pitiful, mended rags. For a long time now no one had had any shoes, all of them wearing the padded felt long-boots with wood soles. As if it were the greatest of delicacies, Emilija cut a small, small bit of the country bacon for all of her guests. The women magnanimously tried to refuse, but such politeness was beyond human endurance, and the tasty titbits disappeared in eager mouths. After so many years they finally had fragrant soap with which to wash and a clean bed in which to sleep. Emilija commented shyly that it would be enough to have one sheet, that the other could be saved, but Ligita would have none of it, so both of them happily fell asleep with a blanket and two sheets. Each time my mother mentions this episode, the long ago experienced feeling of well being once more shines on her face.

In May 1947, Anna forwarded Viktor's letter to Emilija and Ligita, which through an indirect path had reached her from abroad. In reading it, Emilija and Ligita never managed to get past the words " Dearest mamma and sister" without crying. Again and again they would cry, as a surge of emotion and happiness overcame them. Viktors had said these words so very, very long ago. He wrote about wonderful things: "When we'll be together again, then, dear mamma, you'll have to live a while with one son and then the other." Viktors, too, had gotten married, and he had a daughter Dace, lovingly called by the diminutive Dacīte. "I have five grandchildren!" through tears, Emilija exclaimed joyfully. That evening she believed what Viktors had written: soon, very soon they would return to Latvia. A reunion was in the near future! Each day that had passed in starvation and calamity Emilija and Ligita had dreamt about this, thinking of their dear husband and sons, father and brothers. Each of their birthdays and name days were remembered with solemnly shared reminiscences that helped forget the hunger and hopelessness, allowing them to return to the distant, happier days when the family was still together. Emilija never let Ligita sense how much she worried about the unknown fate of Jānis and her sons. My grandmother talked with such conviction about them that my mother firmly believed that her brothers were fine and her father was still alive. Despite everything they had survived after all. Viktors' letter to Emilija and Ligita was like a message of hope, like destiny's promise. Soon! Very, very soon!

That same evening Ligita wrote a letter to her brother, which she begged to be forwarded from Latvia to Viktors. The first words of joy were followed by a description of the bitter reality: "We both live in a bleak village. Mamma has grown old, old. I have grown up, and my main task is to saw timber. Mamma has already not worked for approximately a year, because in the winter of 1946 she got lost for three days in the woods, in the marshes and froze terribly. She has regained her health, only her nose now is shorter and she has no feeling in one of her fingers. You probably know that I am now 20 years old. [...] In our talks with mama, we still call you the boys.

But you're surely not boys any more! …"[154] How hard it was for Viktors to read this letter! What had those damned people done with his gentle mother and pampered little sister! However, Viktors did not dare to write any more. He understood from aunt Anna's response, written in the handwriting of her husband Jānis but with an unknown signature "Ruta" at the bottom, that letters to relatives were too dangerous. There was a hidden warning in the letter for the brothers not to return to Latvia.[155] Uncle Jānis wrote: "Ligita is living with her mother, […] in the same apartment where they used to live in 1943. If you were to return, you would have to settle with them for the rest of your life, because they have very spacious premises and there would be enough room there for all of you."[156] Their communication was only renewed in 1955 after the unmasking of the cult of Stalin, when a letter from relatives abroad was no longer as dangerous to the people who had remained in Latvia or who were deported to Siberia.

Emilija was never destined to see her sons again, nor was she to meet her grandchildren. She died, not ever learning that she had fourteen grandchildren. My mother only met her brothers after many years had passed. Her older brother Voldemārs returned for a visit to Latvia in 1982. He knew that it would be unbelievably hard to see what the Soviet occupation years had done to his homeland, but he gathered courage and came, because whatever hope he had left that his sister would visit them had vanished. My mother had handed in an application to the visa section of the Ministry of the Interior, asking that she be allowed to visit her brothers in Canada, and she was refused sixteen times.[157] In each instance in the printed form a typewritten comment was inserted "Your trip is not considered expedient." What a Soviet style formulation – as if the relationship between family members could be viewed as being a question of State "expediency." Only in 1987, under the influence of the new policies of Mikhail Gorbachev, procedures for visits with relatives were simplified, and my mother received the long awaited visiting permit. When Viktors and Ligita met in the Montreal airport in Canada, forty-seven years had passed since June 14, 1940, the night when Viktors had watched in despair how the Chekists had taken his parents and sister away in a lorry. Arnolds, the middle brother, flew to Toronto, Canada, from England to meet his sister. That was their last meeting, because Arnolds died a year later.

Already in the summer of 1946 the news had spread with lightning speed in Krasnoyarsk territory and Tomsk region that a Commission had arrived from Latvia to collect the children who had been deported in 1941. This was a work group formed by the Ministry of Education, which had been assigned the task of returning orphans or partially orphaned children, four to sixteen years of age, back home to Latvia.[158] Seeing the sickly thin children dressed in rags who started to stream to Krasnoyarsk from the neighbouring villages, Anna Lūse, leader of the work group, violated the stringent directives of the Ministry of Education regarding who was to be transported and who was not. She could not refuse the despairing mothers who begged for their children to be saved, and thus, many were entered into the orphan lists. The local governing institutions had received a directive from Moscow to create lists of Latvian children and to offer all possible assistance in their re-evacuation; however each local chief interpreted the order arbitrarily. Some helped, others – in every way possible – put obstacles in the path of the re-evacuation, for various petty reasons not confirming the lists compiled by Lūse. Without a permit from the Regional Department of Internal Affairs, no one could leave. Nonetheless, overcoming various bureaucratic obstacles and material difficulties, until the end of the 1946 navigation season 1425 children were successfully re-evacuated to Latvia.[159] The mothers of the children who stayed behind were promised that re-evacuation would continue starting next spring. The promise was not kept, because the Soviet Regime decided to the contrary. The prepared lists were placed in archives and the "socially dangerous children" continued to pine away in Siberia.[160]

Seeing the children depart, it had seemed self-evident that after a while their mothers would follow, and then it would be the turn of the others. Everyone in the neighbourhood hurried to write petitions. Also Ligita decided that she must do this. In the petition, she elaborated on her own and Emilija's innocence, the incomprehensible circumstances of the deportation, begging that the case be reviewed. She also swore that she was now ideologically rehabilitated and fit to build socialism in Latvia. A futile period of waiting began, because no one received an answer. When I became acquainted with my mother's case in the archives, I did not find any of the many petitions that she had written to the Presidium of the Supreme Council of the USSR and to the Central Committee of the Communist Party of the Soviet Union during the early years of deportation. It was obvious that these petitions had never left the Tomsk Region and were either destroyed or to this day are lying in some dusty archive of the local Cheka.

By the winter of 1947 only a few Latvians remained in the Borovoy kolkhoz. The rest had managed to get away and find some other work. From her fellow sufferers of the Bilina period the first to get married was Aina. Together with her husband Juris Baginskis she moved to the distant town of Kolpashevo. A small group of Latvians lived in Togur, a village where a sawmill, a wool processing plant and a log floating station were located. From the Togur Latvians Ligita learned that there was a need for workers. She and her friend Māra decided to try their luck and, without a permit from the Commandant's office, one night headed out to the village.

The story of this trip is one of the rare light-hearted moments during the long years of deportation that has stayed in my mother's memory. They hitched an ox filched from the kolkhoz to a sleigh, wrapped their heads in wool shawls and their legs with rags, and took off. The girls were in a joyful mood, because the trip ahead seemed like a grand adventure. Having left their village, the girls squealing and laughing urged the ox down a steep slope. Both sang at the top of their voice a German song they had learned from some deported Germans: "*Mahle ist von Afrika. Mahle ist nicht schön!*"[161] Ligita sang the female "part," Māra – the male voice. The terrified ox, his head twisted sideways and squinting with one blood-shot eye at the strange creatures behind him, in fear galloped faster and faster. Slowly coming to the realisation that he would not be able to escape his mischievous drivers, the beast tired and started to move at his customary apathetic pace. The original high spirits of the singers, too, became more subdued, and they both fell silent. Thus, around lunchtime, frozen and shaken by the ride, they arrived in Togur. The plant was short-staffed, hence the director gladly agreed to organise with the Commandant's office transfer of the Borovoy Latvians. Having visited with their Latvian friends in Togur and happy about the impending changes, Ligita and Māra left to go to their village.

During the return journey, the ox grew more and more restless. Nearing his native fields, he became uncontrollable, no longer heeding the snapping whip and the angry voices. Suddenly, to the great consternation of the drivers, the beast veered off the road and headed into the field. Fiercely lowing and foaming at the mouth, he scrambled in the snow so deep it reached as high as his stomach. Only after seeing the vague outline of a haystack in the middle of the field in the moonlight, Ligita and Māra understood that the beast had not gone mad but was hungry. They had forgotten to feed him, and the poor animal had made the journey without eating. The girls again were overcome by a bout of laughter. Laughing once more, my mother recounted the story of this crazy trip and the fearful misunderstanding, finishing with a proud observation: " Crazy, we were absolutely crazy!"

Togur was the first place to which Emilija and Ligita moved by choice. It was the last settlement place for my mother, where she, with only a brief interruption, lived for almost ten years. My grandmother Emilija died in Togur. My parents got married there, and I was born there.

Again the air grew tense with the excitement of hope. Some of the deportees had received permission to return to Latvia, and all, as if electrified, waited to see who would be the next on whom fortune would smile. Emilija and Ligita discussed returning from exile almost every day. It was unclear by what principles the Cheka was choosing the candidates to be freed. The majority were of the same young age group as Ligita, but there were rumours that also older people were among those released. There were also no signs that would allow them to know if both of them would be allowed to return or only one. If only one of them, then Ligita was almost certain that it would be her mother, who, as a useless invalid, would be sent home, while she, Ligita, would be kept to work in the forest. Each time when their talks turned in this direction, Emilija exclaimed indignantly: "What nonsense, Liguci! I won't leave without you," immediately adding: "You must go, though!"

In April 1948, my mother received a notice to present herself at the Togur Commandant's office. Both Emilija and Ligita were very agitated. They had waited so long for this! But they would not allow themselves to hope, because disappointment would be too hard to bear. All the way to the Commandant's office Ligita repeated to herself – it can't be! But nonetheless again and again the thought – what if? – washed over her being like a hot wave. Ligita sat down in the waiting room. It seemed to her that the Commandant's secretary was looking at her in a special way. Finally she was called in. Commandant Kukushkin, called *Dzeguze*,[162] sat at his desk. To underline the importance of the moment, there was a pregnant pause followed by some irrelevant comments, and then, finally, without taking his eyes off my mother's face, he announced: "Ligita Janovna, the Soviet authorities have evaluated your behaviour and

First photo of Ligita and Emilija
taken in Siberian exile 1948.

grants you permission to return to Latvia. You are given the opportunity to prove that you are worthy of this trust." Ligita grew pale and gasped: "And my mother?" she asked. That would happen at a later date, first permissions to return being given to the people born after 1925. She should feel happy about herself. As if intoxicated, my mother went out into the street. She was free! On April 15, 1948, the last registration entry is noted on Ligita Dreifelde's identity card issued by the Commandant's office.

Less than a month remained until the start of the navigation season. In joyful expectation Emilija started to prepare for Ligita's long journey. As well as she could, she refashioned some of the clothing they had received by mail. Relatives from Latvia sent money to cover the cost of the trip. My grandmother had a special talent in maintaining friendly relations with useful people, which she put to use for the umpteenth time, managing to obtain flour from the local warehouse supervisor to bake bread for the journey. Ligita was not the only one who would be leaving Togur. Olita Siliņa also had received a return permit. Māra and Aina had to stay, because they were a few years older. Finally, at the beginning of May, Ob was free of ice and the spring floods had ended. Everyone was waiting with great anticipation for the arrival of the first boat in Kolpashevo. Ligita tried not to think about parting from her mother. Emilija had hidden her pain deep down, because she was most afraid that Ligita would change her mind and decide to wait until the two of them could return together. That could not be allowed to happen, and Emilija externally showed a brave smiling face. Murmuring in her soft Kurzeme dialect, she convinced Ligita to go, saying: "Soon, my sweetie, I'll join you."

All the Latvians living in Kolpashevo and Togur had gathered at Aina's, to say good-by to Ligita and Olita. The mood was joyful rather than sad, because the people staying behind saw in the girls' departure a firm confirmation of their own future release, which would come sooner or later. The young people accompanied the girls to the boat. Ligita asked that her mother not come to the port, because she was afraid that she would not be able to leave. They had to say their good-byes at Aina's. Emilija was crying. She had resolved not to sadden her child, but the parting tested her resolve. Ligita, too, was crying. Thus, at the beginning of May, dressed in her "Sunday best" sewn from old pieces of clothing, her grandmother Lība's shoes and carrying a bag of her belongings, Ligita began her 6000 kilometre long return journey.

When the boat began to sail, Ligita saw Emilija on shore. As if gone mad, she started to scream and wave, but her mother stood frozen, not turning her wide-open eyes away from Ligita. To the very last, Ligita stared at Emilija, until the grey, tiny figure disappeared behind a curve of the river. Ligita has etched this moment forever in her memory – the last time that she saw her mother alive.

My Grandmother Emilija

After Ligita left, Emilija's life seemed to split into two distinct parts. Although she worked in order to somehow obtain food and keep herself alive, this part of her life seemed of little consequence to her. She lived only for the day when she would again be reunited with her daughter. Since this was not possible, Emilija created a special mind space for herself, in which she could always be together with Ligita. It was like a never-ending handiwork, a gigantic embroidery, at which Emilija's soul could labour drawing inexhaustible inspiration from Ligita's letters. Her eyesight being too poor, my grandmother was not able to read these letters herself, hence she always had to find someone to help her. When a letter had been read and reread several times out loud, it became etched in her memory and continued to live there, increasing in significance and becoming more real. With great persistence my grandmother worked each person or episode mentioned in the letters into the existing fabric of her thoughts, until through a thousand interconnections and imagined details the new became inseparably linked with previously mentioned persons and episodes. The further she delved into the past, the more densely and intricately woven were the threads of her imagination. The closer she stayed to the last letter, the lighter and more transparent her mental creation became. Unanswered questions stretched like long, loose threads from the fabric – questions, which with disturbing force attempted to conquer the vacuum of not knowing. But each answer she found gave rise to new questions. And thus she continued to live Ligita's life, convinced that this mental space, where the two of them met, was more real than her miserable daily existence. This space belonged only to her, and no one could by any kind of order or interdiction deport or force her to move from there to another place.

Fifteen of my grandmother Emilija's letters have been saved in the family archive. The first few are written with a pencil on pages and scraps of paper obtained from God knows where, because paper was a rarity in Siberia after the war. Later, after receipt of the first parcel from Ligita, Emilija wrote on notebook pages in ink. The handwriting is uneven, laboured and occasionally difficult to read. She wrote spontaneously, as if talking to her daughter, but it can be sensed that her thoughts hurried faster than her unexercised hand could follow; hence a sentence is not always finished or a thought clearly stated. As a true native of the Kurzeme region, she preferred to use masculine endings for feminine gender words and often dropped the flexional endings, all of which personalised the letters. In reading them, I can imagine how the words, many of them no longer in use today, could have sounded from my grandmother's mouth because, after the return of our family from Siberia, I heard similar expressions from my grandmother's sister Anna, who also talked in the drawn-out intonation and the special linguistic rhythm of Kurzeme. In Emilija's letters her gentle and sincere nature is revealed in full. Affectionate words are scattered throughout, and each letter closes with a 1000 kisses, never forgetting to mention Ligita's friends, who were still in forced settlement. In each letter they sent greetings to Ligita. Of particular significance to me seem the dreams recounted by Emilija, because they allow me to look into the subconscious of my grandmother. In dreams she again is reunited with her family, however in these happy scenes there is always some note of alarm that incorporates unfulfilled hopes and concern about the well-being of her beloved ones.

Ligita, too, wrote much and often, because she and her mother were united by special bonds stronger than bloodlines. Such bonds form between people who together survive existentially extreme situations. They both, at different times, had almost stepped over that dangerous boundary that leads into extinction, hence they knew how irreplaceable they were for each other. Everything had been experienced – the sublime as well as the base, and there was nothing that Ligita could not tell her mother, because deep down she knew that Emilija loved her and accepted her as she was.

According to Emilija's calculations, around the tenth of June the first letter from Ligita was supposed to arrive, because Ligita should have arrived in Latvia by the end of May. There was no letter. With each passing day Emilija's concern and worry grew. What if something had happened en route? Horrendous stories circulated about disorders along the railway. Perhaps her child had fallen ill? Emilija began to go to the post office every second day. The postmistress empathetically chatted with the concerned "Janovna,"[163] but these post office visits only offered a brief respite. Emilija had to return and continue her occasional work as a housemaid. For a couple of days a week she washed laundry in one house, and then did the same in another. Finally, on June 26 three letters arrived all at once.

Emilija hurried to Ligita's friend Aina, and the reading began. Ligita had encountered the first difficulties in Tomsk, from where she had to travel further by train to Novosibirsk. In order to buy train tickets, a delousing certificate was required. It could be obtained in the public bathhouse. She and Olita had headed there, but in error they had entered the men's section. Then the "fun" had begun! The certificate had not helped much, because the line-ups were so long one would have needed to stand for several days. Finally the two of them had gotten on the train. In Novosibirsk everything had started all over again. Except that they had had a harder time there, because there had been no Latvians who could advise them. They had met a Russian soldier who was on his way home. He had been so taken by Ligita's blonde hair and blue eyes that he had arranged tickets for them taking advantage of the privileges he was entitled to because he had served at the front. Emilija smiled. Yes, that was her Ligucis, reckless and able to arrange anything. In Moscow the two girls had stayed at the home of Anna's sister-in-law, who very hospitably and kindly had welcomed the young women in her humble flat. On hearing this, Emilija, immediately liked Alīda, though she had never met her. And Alīda had even given silk stockings to Ligita and Olita! Yes, the first silk stockings that her dear daughter had ever worn. After the dark hole that they had lived in for years, Moscow had seemed such a large and magnificent city to the two girls. Tears sprang into Emilija's eyes, when Aina read that on the train to Rīga Ligita had heard Latvian spoken for the first time. The next sentence in Ligita's letter was bitter – that the majority of the travellers had, however, talked Russian only. Emilija and Aina exchanged glances and sighed. Ligita had disembarked in Zilupe, the first station after the Latvian border, so she could feel her homeland under her feet and breathe the fresh spring air. Emilija understood her daughter so well. Oh, just to touch Latvian soil! Aina's voice woke Emilija from the sweet daydream. A Russian soldier had screamed at Ligita – why had she left the wagon without permission! He even threatened to take her to the militia. Her child, crying, had jumped back into the wagon. So that's what Latvia was like now!

The train pulled into the Rīga railway station. Now both Emilija and Aina had to cry again. Each had their own memories of Rīga, of their previous life there. Ligita wrote about her happiness and confusion standing after so many years in the Rīga terminal, where she had been so often on her way from Dubulti. There were so many people there; her head was spinning. Where to go? She had no more relatives in Rīga or in Jūrmala. She could not go to her aunt Anna's in Liepāja, because the city was now off limits and one could stay there only with special permits. Olita had invited her to come along to Mazsalaca, but fate had intervened – Mrs. Emersone had, by chance, walked toward them in the station square. The same Mrs.

Emersone who had been deported together with them and who had received permission to return to Latvia earlier. She had immediately invited Ligita to come with her. Now Emilija knew that Ligita was near someone whom she could trust and who would be able to advise her.

Ligita had left the hardest part to the last. It was the news about the death of her father. She had learned the sad news in Tomsk from a Latvian who had been in the same prison camp as her father. Jānis Dreifelds had already died at the end of 1941. Emilija found it hard to believe. Every time she asked at the Commandant's office about the fate of her husband, the answer was always the same: Jānis Kristapovičs Dreifelds has been sentenced to ten years in high security prison camp without the right of communication.[164] Therefore he must be alive! Emilija could not imagine that in accordance with GULAG instructions an old man's death could be classified a state secret, not to be revealed even to close relatives. But her thoughts returned again and again to what Ligita had written, and slowly doubt crept in. If Emilija herself had aged so much, had become so wizened, and was so feeble, then how was Jānis? Her husband was, after all, fourteen years older than she. Perhaps he had not survived … One night she saw a prescient dream. She was in Dubulti again, at their home. She was sitting in the bedroom combing her hair. Her husband rushed into the room. He had a sly expression in his eyes that signalled a secret. It surely must be a gift. "Which hand do you want," Jānis asked. Emilija flirtatiously answered, but she chose the wrong hand each time. Jānis, in despair, asked again and again. Emilija began to become upset: why was her husband stretching out the teasing to such a degree. Suddenly she noticed that after each wrong answer Jānis was shrinking and becoming smaller. Horror washed over Emilija, and she hurried to save him, to hold him, but to no avail. Jānis vanished. The only thing that remained was the gift box. Looking in the box, she recognised the wondrous light blue dress, which her husband had at one time begged his friend to bring her from Paris. Emilija woke up. So it must be true. Jānis was no longer.

Usually letters took three weeks to arrive in one direction and three weeks in return; therefore both Ligita and Emilija received news from each other with almost a six-week delay. In the meantime Emilija fretted about the unbreakable vicious circle in which her daughter had come to be: she couldn't get work without registration of residence, and no one would register her if she didn't have work. In the interim Ligita had started to work as accountant in the Tukums bakery and had registered to live with some woman who was willing to risk and rent a bedstead to a person marked by Siberia. During her long return journey Ligita had dreamed that she would again live in Dubulti, but she was not permitted to do so. Also the larger cities were off limits to these deportees. Thus she had to content herself with Tukums, where several other ex-Siberian exiles had found shelter. Emilija consoled her daughter that it probably was for the best because it would be too sad to live in Dubulti. Everything there would only serve as a reminder of their past life.

For the first time in her life Ligita received pay for her work. In the beginning the 270 roubles her daughter earned seemed to Emilija like an enormous sum.[165] But she lived in a different world where money had virtually no value. All of them had become accustomed to subsistence farming and were scrambling to survive as well as they knew how. In Togur people did not receive pay for months and even years. Instead of pay each worker on the list was given 800 grams of bread, and each dependent family member was allotted 300 grams.[166] Emilija was not a dependent, and she had to manage as best she could herself. Somehow she had to work enough to earn 20 roubles so she could pay for her bedstead. To pick two or three glasses of berries she had to walk for half a day. A glassful of berries only earned her one rouble, but there were scarcely any buyers. In addition, one had to be careful that a militiaman would not see the transaction and threaten to put such a "speculator" in prison. For delivering three kilos of wild mushrooms at the collection point Emilija received a half-kilo of bread plus 57 kopecks. For a pair of mittens Emilija knitted from raw wool made into yarn by twisting manually she received 10 roubles.[167] After her rent was paid, almost nothing remained for bread. My grandmother survived almost exclusively on potatoes and salted fish.

However, very soon Emilija came to understand that Ligita's pay in the circumstances in Latvia was very meagre, and she started to worry how her child would pay her rent, buy firewood and still have something left for clothing. About her food at least she did not have to worry, because Ligita could eat her fill in the bakery, and knowledge of this fact warmed Emilija with constant joy. "My dearest child," she wrote, "if only you knew, how happy it makes me, to hear that you have enough bread to eat. Often, I don't have bread. Just a potato, though that's good too."[168] Ligita was bitterly aware of her helplessness. There was nothing, absolutely nothing she could do to help her mother.

Emilija had to pine away alone in Siberia, living from the pity of others and having to work very hard. Ligita was only able to save and lay aside a miserable few tens of roubles now and then to send to her mother. Each time that she received the money transfer, Emilija felt great pride about her daughter. These roubles meant much more to her than just the possibility to buy a couple of loaves of bread or a handful of sugar. It was a visible demonstration of love, which proved what a good daughter Ligita was. Emilija didn't need this gesture to know this, but it was important for her self-respect, so that no one would dare even think that she had been abandoned and forgotten. Nonetheless, my grandmother painfully realised how hard it was for Ligita to set aside the thirty or fifty roubles and wrote in each subsequent letter that she didn't need any more money, that she had enough of everything. But Ligita didn't listen. A few times she even managed to scrape together a package of food. She also put in these packages some small thing for the friends she had left behind. She had not forgotten her life there and knew too well what it meant to survive in Togur.

Frequent perusal of Ligita's photographs, showing them to her friends and talking about them helped Emilija keep in constant touch with her daughter as well. Whenever there was a spare moment Emilija carried the photos to the window, in whose faint light she gave herself over to examining them. Her eyesight was so poor that on occasion she did not even notice that she was looking at the photograph upside down, but that did not interfere with her seeing what her heart wished to see at that moment. On each of these occasions, she discovered new nuances in the so familiar facial expressions of her daughter. These were more a reflection of the state of Emilija's own soul or the impression left by the last letter that Ligita had sent, rather than the frozen moment fixed by the camera. Morning and night, when nothing could be seen in the dark of the hut, all my grandmother had to do was to look in the direction of the shelf where the photos were arranged and, without the slightest exertion, in concentrated contemplation she could envisage every small detail of her daughter's face or clothing. When Emilija felt particularly sad, she thought of their parting photo. Just before Ligita left, they both had gone to Kolpashevo to have their photograph taken together for the first time after the long years in Siberia. The bitter mood of parting permeated the photo, cruelly reflecting the reality – the evil that deportation had wrought on both of them was clearly visible. On occasion Emilija asked herself whether that old, totally run down woman with the disfigured nose, who stared hopelessly into a vacuum, was really she? Ligita, too, looked stiff and bloated from eating the unhealthy diet that consisted primarily of potatoes. However, Emilija more frequently liked to contemplate the photos that Ligita had sent from Latvia. She

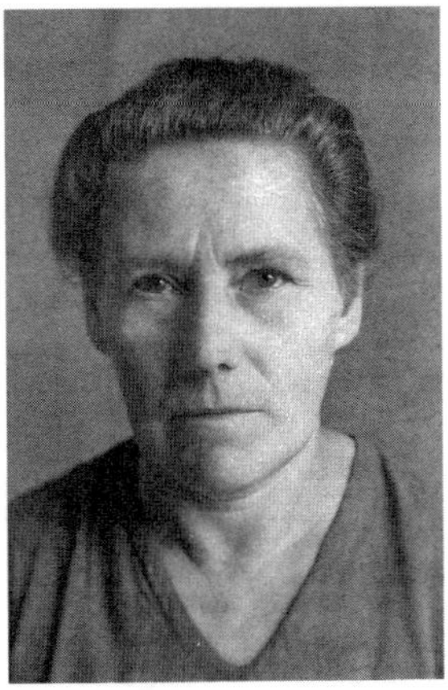

Last photo of Emilija Dreifelde 1949.

couldn't contain her joy how lovely her sweet child looked. As a young girl from a good family should. With pride, the photos were first of all discussed within the circle of friends, with each trying to say something nice about Ligita to cheer up the lonely Mrs. Dreifelde. Emilija could not resist showing the pictures to the local villagers as well. Let them see how the poor Cinderella had changed. The villagers shook their heads in unfeigned admiration and offered unstinting praise: a real city girl, which, in their value system, symbolised an unattainable, happy life of ease.

With love and gratitude, Emilija thought about her brothers and sisters, who had welcomed Ligita with such kindness and showered her with gifts despite their post-war poverty. There was wool for knitting, which Ligita could do magnificently. Emilija remembered how, during the Petropavlovka period, with tacit approval by the local executive, they had formed a sort of knitting co-operative. Having closely examined the complicated patterns of some old sweaters, Ligita had taught these to her friends Aina, Māra and Olita. Together with Emilija, the five of them could knit a sweater in a day and get three pails of potatoes for it. Emilija's fingers were too stiff, so Ligita also knitted her part. Now finally her child could knit for herself from real wool, not from cotton unravelled from old socks or net string, with which they had to content themselves in Siberia. The Liepāja relatives had also given Ligita a gift of a couple of lengths of material for dresses and even some black broadcloth for a coat, as well as money, which Ligita immediately shared with her mother.

Before being deported, Emilija had taken several bolts of dress material to the seamstress that had remained uncut. Given the poverty of the war years, the bolts had been sold; hence the seamstress considered it a matter of honour to repay the debt and thus sewed a couple of dresses for Miss Dreifelde for free. As a result, Ligita, without any further expenditure, obtained new and elegant clothes. In looking at her daughter's photo, Emilija sighed in satisfaction: "Now you can count yourself a rich lass. Now you have everything."[169] Yes, in that world where Emilija was now living, a couple of dresses and a coat constituted incredible wealth. The eight years of starvation and poverty that had been lived through had cut into Emilija's consciousness, so that her own well-to-do previous life seemed something distant and almost non-existent. How could the mending of felt boots and old cotton dresses be compared to the once so self explanatory feminine rituals – the annual sewing of the most fashionable season's dresses, the fine gloves, high-heeled shoes and weekly visits to a salon to have hair done and nails manicured? Only after eight years of exile did my grandmother for the first time have an opportunity to ride on a bus!

Ligita did not write anything about their ancestral home. Emilija remembered the family home as it had been when they left it on the night of June 14 – a light-coloured masonry building with beautiful glassed-in verandas and white curtains. She often saw the house in her dreams. In these dreams, all the family was again together in one of the many happily spent summer afternoons. Emilija and Jānis calmly looked on the boys fooling around, whooping and shrieking,

The Dreifelds family home in Dubulti.

while little Ligucis was playing with the dog. That was one of Emilija's happiest dreams without a trace of Siberian shadow. Surely, now strangers were living in the house, but Emilija could not envisage that. Sometimes she visualised Ligita standing by the fence at the small gate not being able to gather enough courage to open it. She would have felt the same, because it would be incredibly painful to enter her own property as a stranger without any rights. Finally Emilija asked her daughter in a letter: "Please write to me about our home. How does it look? Is the sidewalk still intact? Who is living in our flat? Have you been inside your room?"[170]

Ligita had taken a train to Dubulti the day after her return to Latvia. In the train she had stared fixedly in the direction of the turn-off for Lielupe, waiting when the familiar corner of the house would appear. There it was! Her heart leapt with joy, the same as in her childhood when she had pressed her nose to the window calling out joyfully to her mother and father: "Home! Home!" Ligita got off the train and stood for a long time in front of her high school building. It was located directly in front of the station. She thought about her classmates, who now were dispersed across the world. About a third had escaped and now were abroad. As was her best friend Marianna. In her class only Uldis had experienced Ligita's fate. She did not know if he was still alive. She also did not know what had happened to the rest.

Ligita started to walk up Slokas iela. A strong pulse throbbed at her temples and in her throat there was a lump. Soon, very soon she would arrive at her ancestral home. As if on a carousel, all sorts of remembered scenes raced disconnectedly through her head, reminiscences that her subconscious had fixed with amazing precision, the criteria for their selection known only to itself. Ligita saw herself as a tiny girl standing with a checkers board at the door of her father's office, unable to gather courage to enter, knowing that the game would be lost again. A tiny chick. Its limp and still warm little body lying in the child's palm – she, with ardent love, has smothered it and, totally distraught, is crying. Sunday morning. In the dining room the maidservant is good-naturedly scolding, because the imp of a child again has scooped off and eaten the skins from the steaming cups of cocoa. Mother and father are off on a visit, and the girl is in her parents' bedroom delightedly looking into the mirror. The chit of a girl is wearing her mother's high-heeled shoes and her lips are smeared with red lipstick. She feels like a lady and is totally unaware of how ludicrous she looks. In the nearest corner store mother has "opened" a running tab for her daughter. Each day she is allowed to eat some sweets. Ligita worries about the accumulating debt, but she can't contain her craving for sweets. But mamma only laughs about the spent *santims*. As she does about all the rest of Ligita's pranks. Pampered by her parents, she was a wilful girl.

Ligita stood by the garden gate. Her eyes quickly traversed the yard. It was littered with refuse, the sheds half in ruins, the fence in need of paint, the sidewalk crumbling. Through the kitchen window could be heard a shrill woman's voice screeching something in Russian. Ligita choked up. So unprepared she was at such a blow. So their house has been handed over to Russians! Occupiers! The ones who had taken everything away from them! It was a blessing that mother and father were not here to see it. Ligita turned on her heel and hurried off. Then she stopped and turned around. It was the Dreifelds' house that father had built for his family after all, and she had a right to enter. With determination, Ligita knocked at the door. No one came to open. Hesitantly she tried the door handle. The door opened. A pungent smell billowed out at her, a combination of the smells of a toilet, rotting food and gasoline fumes. Sickening. Earlier everything had smelled of dried orange peel and mint. Ligita opened the kitchen door. The white sideboard with the green glass still stood in its old place. The strange woman who was working at the stove, looked up questioningly at the visitor. Ligita wisely asked for directions to a neighbouring house, pretending that she was a stranger in the neighbourhood and had got lost. She would not, for sure, say that she was the daughter of the previous owner, who wanted to see what strangers had done to their home. Having managed to make her exit, Ligita hurried to the sea and for a long time wandered on the seashore. She wanted to save her mother from what she had experienced and now responded to her mother's questions with just a few matter-of-fact lines what the house looked like after an eight-year absence. Emilija sensed that her daughter was trying to shelter her, and never again mentioned this painful subject in her letters. Ligita also hid from her mother that their country house "Upītes" had burned down during the war.

It just so happened that the sister of Arnold's wife Nellija, Irene, was assigned a living area in the Dreifelds house by the executive committee. Now Ligita had a reason to visit the house as frequently as her heart could bear the experience. Irene lived on the upper floor in the erstwhile rooms of the "boys", as my mother always had called and continues to call her brothers. Each time Ligita visited there, she conjured up the noises and sounds of the past in her imagination, until it seemed to her that she really was hearing her brothers' voices. It was a kind of self-torture, but my mother's feet again and again carried her there, because she had to reach out to her childhood. For a moment then she felt closer to her own people.

When our family was allowed to return to Latvia in 1957, I too frequently visited my grandfather's house because Irene still lived there. At that time I did not understand what it meant to my mother to see how carelessly and negligently the newcomers carried on there, knowing nothing about the cruel fate of the previous inhabitants. The old sideboard, worse for wear, still squatted in the same place. It had lost its coloured glass and had been painted a repulsive green. My father could not bear to stand by and watch how it took mother several days to recoup from the negative experience of our visits to the house and begged us not to go there any more. But the experienced pain subsided after a while, and mother again went to see Irene, taking me by the hand. I was bored, because I wanted to go out in the courtyard to play with the children, but mother strictly forbade me to do so. I became crabby and sulked. I had no idea how impossible it was for my mother to see me in the miserably looking yard, where nothing remained from her childhood world. In despair, my mother often repeated to my father: I have my ancestral home, but I have no right to even have a room in it![171] It was particularly unjust, because the four of us had to live in a walk-through room, where only a wardrobe and decorative drapes helped us escape the "landlady's" curious glances. Our family had no hope of getting on the waiting list for a flat, because in accordance with Soviet regulations we had enough living area "per person," and thus my parents were not accepted on the waiting list.[172] They did not give up and decided to save money for a co-operative flat, for which the down payment must have seemed astronomical – 1760 roubles! The remaining sum of 4600 roubles had to be paid over a term of sixteen years![173] Father started to work in several workplaces, and nine years after returning from Siberia, in January 1966, finally my mother's most fervent desire was fulfilled – she held in her hands the keys to her own flat. Grandfather's house was demolished in

1971. In its place was built one of the grey and uniform-looking multiple flat tenement houses that got planted all over Latvia during the Soviet era.

In all of Emilija's letters her longing for her daughter could be sensed again and again like a constant, repeating refrain – a yearning for her honey, her chick, her baby, her little girl, her sweet little sugar lump. Ligita found it very hard to read how much her mother had to work, but even harder to know how unhappy she was: "In my thoughts I am with you each day. Especially in the mornings, when I sit in the kitchen and clean the potatoes. You're still sleeping then. I am with you. Without you noticing it I pat your curly-haired head. A long year has passed when I haven't seen you or heard your voice. And there is no one who calls me mommy. Now they call me Emilija Ivanovna, and my landlady is Olga Vasilyevna."[174] There was so much bitterness and hopelessness in the words "Emilija Ivanovna." Ligita remembered how much she despised the patronymic Ivanovna, Petrovna and Viktorovna that the local Siberians immediately attached to Latvian names. It was good that Emilija did not know that in Latvia now her daughter also was customarily addressed as Ligita Janovna. Why did'nt they allow her mother to come back to Latvia? Immediately after her return, Ligita had handed in all the necessary documents to the Ministry of the Interior to issue an official invitation to her mother to come and live with Ligita in Latvia. But a response did not arrive, and the irrational distressful separation continued. Each succeeding letter brought a different reminiscence and expression of longing, intensely echoing the emotions Ligita herself was experiencing: "Good morning, my dearest. Everyone is still sleeping, and you too must be asleep. It is only seven, but I got up already at five. I want to go to you. By the time I walk there, it will be time for you to get up. How I would like to wake you up and say: 'Wake up, wake up Liguci, breakfast is ready.' But Ligucis doesn't care to get up yet. To be sure, it doesn't seem believable that it would someday happen like this."[175] Oh, just to experience once more mama's quiet steps and the gentle touch of her hand!

Emilija was constantly concerned about Ligita. She worried about her daughter's immaturity, which could not be otherwise, given the eight abnormal years experienced in Siberia. It was a brutal cleavage where the experiences and values of a previous life lost their meaning and all the energy of an individual was devoted to physical survival, leaving almost no resources for maturing and spiritual development. It was a traumatic shock for everyone, but particularly affected by the cleavage were the children and teenagers, for whom the gentle and careless world of childhood was replaced in one day by constant suffering, hunger, and death. This trauma is the greatest harm that deportation caused the deported children and teenagers, leaving non-erasable and crippling traces in their immature personalities. Deeply buried in the subconscious, people carry this trauma until the end of their life. One can try to forget, but it is not possible. Emilija realised that the struggle for survival in Siberia had not prepared Ligita for adult life. Her daughter totally lacked that emotional experience, which under normal circumstances every girl would receive, gradually learning unwritten social laws and maturing emotionally as a woman. Siberia had robbed Ligita of all this, and she returned to Latvia externally a twenty-three year old woman, but with a young teenager's understanding of the world and human relationships. Her daughter did have her first love behind her, but even that had blossomed in abnormal conditions, and the inability to overcome these conditions resulted in love not being fulfilled and experienced.

Emilija understood very well her daughter's profound need to experience joy because joy had been denied to the child for such a long time, but she was frightened of the reckless way Ligita threw herself into compensating for her stolen youth. She had no intention of listening to her mother's pleading reminders to take care of herself, to dress warmly and to get adequate sleep. Ligita was brimming over with the joy for life. She had been released from prison and once more was living in the land of her dreams, Latvia, where nothing evil could happen. To Ligita it seemed that she was surrounded only by good and honest people who treated her with the same openness and directness as she treated them. She did an honest but boring day's work in the office, because it was necessary, but real life began after work on Sunday. On Saturday night somewhere in the near neighbourhood there was a dance to which Ligita went together with her girlfriends. She danced till morning without ever feeling tired.

With the same enthusiasm as in her high school years she teased with the boys; at times she flirtatiously arranged to meet someone but sent a girlfriend in her place. There was nothing wrong in this, but it was childish, and precisely because of this Emilija thought it dangerous. From Ligita's candid letters she gathered that Ligita's interrupted life had almost restarted, as if the Siberian cleavage had never happened. With the enthusiasm of a fifteen-year-old school girl, Ligita continued playing, not realising that with her actions she was misleading, confusing and provocative, if not hardhearted and not nice. They were no longer the shy and naive boys from Dubulti High School, but grown men who saw Ligita as a young, attractive woman, not being aware that behind the exterior hid an inexperienced girl. It would not be hard to imagine that life in Siberia had made her unusual, different from others and branded for life, but looking at the laughing, sparkling Ligita, the dreadful shadow that hung over her was not apparent. She herself never talked about Siberia. She remembered it with horror when she was alone or when she read her mother's letters, but after the moment of sadness there was again a new morning, the world once more shone back at her, and the quest for joy continued.

Emilija could do nothing to help her child fight worldly temptations. She was denied the possibility of being beside her daughter and watching over her. Her sister Anna lived in Liepāja, and the only worldly-wise person near Ligita was Mrs. Emersone, to whom Emilija's daughter often unburdened herself. But no one, absolutely no one, could replace her mother, whom Ligita missed so dreadfully. Emilija tried to write about her concerns and worries, but it was not possible to talk about these in a couple of sentences. How much she was concerned about her daughter's behaviour can be seen in the courage Emilija gathered to say a few harsher words, which my grandmother found very hard to do, because she had a gentle nature. Toughness, scolding and sternness were not part of her educational arsenal. However, because she was concerned, she "read a sermon" in her letter to her daughter: "When will you come to your senses? You can't control yourself and like to drag others by the nose. Would you like it if someone did it to you? Each one of us has been young and had fun. Me, too. [...] Dearest daughter, you'll probably be angry with me. As you wish, but I don't mean any harm. It's only because I love you so very much. You are the only one in this world for whom my heart beats."[176]

Like a thunderclap news arrived that Ligita had become engaged. What Emilija most feared had happened. Her daughter, not mature enough for married life, had decided to get married. Despite the fun-filled social life of the young people – girlfriends, dances and men's attention – Ligita felt very lonely. She incredibly lacked that all-encompassing sense of security that her mother had so lavishly given her even during the trying times of Siberia. That was the major reason why she had given in to the temptation to get married. Ligita did not hide from her mother that she was not totally certain that she loves her fiancé, but she was tired of returning each day to her unheated hole in the wall, tired of scrimping each and every kopeck in order to make ends meet without knowing what tomorrow would bring. He offered shelter, and Ligita needed shelter. In accepting the proposal Ligita tried not to think that marriage meant more than shared walks and a few kisses. Emilija was very upset about her daughter's impulsive decision. Since her own wedding the world had changed, and Emilija did not wish that her own child should experience the anxiety and uncertainty that she remembered experiencing in the early days of her marriage. Being aware of Ligita's stubborn nature, her mother did still try to attempt to gently influence her daughter. It's most unlikely that my grandmother's shy objections would have had any positive result, if yet another turn of fate had not terminated the planned odd marriage. At the time neither Emilija nor Ligita would have known that in the State Security Ministry instructions were being prepared for the next wave of repression that would also touch Ligita.

Emilija's heart was starved for love and warmth, which she sought with people who knew and liked her daughter. Despite the prohibition of the Commandant's office, she occasionally sneaked off to Kolpashevo, in order to help take care of Andrītis, Aina's baby boy. Hugging the little boy close to her, she allowed herself the illusion that he was her grandson Andrītis, whom she had never seen. However, she felt the best with her daughter's other friend Māra, who lived in Togur and visited Emilija frequently. When they together read and reread Ligita's letters, they gave themselves over to reminiscences of the experienced joys and sadness, dreaming of the expected return home to Latvia. My grandmother gave part of her overflowing love to Māra, which the young woman gladly accepted because her mother had died in the first year of deportation, and Emilija's kindness helped to compensate for this immeasurable loss. These were very human moments of contact that warmed both of them and helped Emilija to forget for a moment her loneliness and separation from her own daughter. But soon Māra had to head home, and my grandmother with renewed pain felt how all the attempts to lessen her longing were only illusory. It was tormenting. No matter what she did, no matter where she went, this longing never left her. Now and then it washed over Emilija like a sudden physical wave of pain – her heart grew weak, and her knees buckled. With gritted teeth she moaned, but the despair that rent her soul and flesh, did not abate. Emptied and worn out, she had to return to her hard daily life, until the pain collected again and had to be cried out.

The Togur Latvians felt sorry for Mrs Dreifelde. They tried to comfort and entertain her. Without their support my grandmother's life would have been even more dismal. Knowing that she was old and unprotected, her landlady threw her out in the autumn and hired a younger and stronger person to do the work. It was an unexpected blow for Emilija, because to find new employment as a maidservant and a roof over her head in the poverty-stricken village just prior to winter was almost impossible. Thus in the dark and rain my grandmother in despair stood beside her small heap of belongings knowing that she had nowhere to go. The villagers would not help, while all the Latvians were themselves living in terribly cramped circumstances in rented hovels. How could she impose another burden on them? If it had not been for Ligita, Emilija would have remained outside, regardless of what would happen. Perhaps finally the end would come to this irrational and undeserved torment and humiliation. But her dear daughter was in Latvia, and she soon would be reunited with her child.

Emilija swallowed her despair and knocked on the door of some friends. In sympathy they invited her to stay with them, gave her some hot tea and made up a bed for her for the night. Emilija was grateful for being saved and sheltered. She realised that she could in no way repay them for the morsels of food that she ate and the roof over her head, because the only wealth she could claim were the 18 pails of potatoes she had been given for her work in the autumn, not even enough for her to survive the winter. She tried to prepare food, wash laundry, bring water, but her benefactors could do all of these things themselves. It was so distressing to live off the pity of others, because she could not find work. Only as spring approached, a local teacher hired Emilija as a maidservant. In order not to lose this long-searched-for work, my grandmother worked from six in the morning to eleven o'clock at night: milked a cow, scraped the unpainted floor, washed the laundry for five people, looked after two children, cleaned the house and suffered the tyranny of her landlady's mother, in exchange for all this getting the corner of the kitchen as her place to live. As well as nominal pay – 50 roubles per month, a set of used clothing once a year and just enough food daily to survive.

Day followed day, all exactly the same, and slowly Emilija grew tired of believing that soon she would be reunited with her daughter in Latvia. During the first summer after Ligita had returned to Latvia, Emilija had handed in a petition to the Commandant's office in Kolpashevo that in the name of family reunification she be given permission to live with her daughter, who was her only means of support. Emilija never received a response to her petition. As time passed, she gave in to hopelessness and depression, which can be sensed throughout her letters: "I'm here, but my heart is with you, my dearest. Soon a year will have passed, but my longing for you grows all the time."[177] In her darkest hours of despair it seemed to Emilija on occasion that everyone – her sister, brothers and even her daughter – had forgotten her, but then another letter of Ligita's arrived and the world again regained some of the pale light of hope, which was extinguished as time progressed, and once more Emilija's heart was heavy. In her thoughts Emilija was even jealous of Mrs. Emersone, who had the unearned fortune of listening to Ligita's troubles and joys, while Emilija was so hardheartedly torn away from her child. After having recovered from a heavy bout of pneumonia, she wrote to Ligita: "Oh, my dear child, how terrible that there is no tender hand when one is helpless. I regretted nothing in this world any more. Only you, how you would cry. I lay in bed ill and had nightmares about you."[178] To encourage her mother, Ligita promised that next spring she would come to visit, but Emilija rejected the offer: "I don't want that. I don't want to part from you again. Just come and get me."[179]

The first signs that the surveillance regime of persons in administrative settlement had become more stringent appeared in the summer of 1948. From Emilija's letter I learn: the Commandant's office has prescribed that no longer people are allowed to go to the nearest town Kolpashevo without a permit. In July, to delay moves to cities, passports were taken away from those locals to whom these had been issued after the war.[180] In March the next year, the deportees had to sign a paper that wilful leaving of the place of settlement would be subject to a prison term of up to two years.[181] Emilija did not dare to write to Ligita openly about the great consternation that she and the rest of the deportees in Siberia had felt when they saw cattle cars with thousands of deportees arrive from Latvia in May 1949. In the letters there are only vague implications that "among the visitors there is a high death rate. Especially among the children and the old people,"[182] or "there is much tattletale talk that of those that came to visit, many remained halfway. Especially the young and the old have not reached their destination."[183] Ligita's mother's enigmatic language was immediately understood, and it vividly recalled to memory their own dreadful journey to Siberia full of uncertainty and torment. Strange as it seems, the extensive deportations of March 25, 1949, did not frighten Ligita, because she did not feel threatened. She had her release paper on hand. In addition, my mother was still relatively naïve to believe that the first deportation was a horrendous error, which now had been clarified and would not be repeated again. But Emilija did not allow herself to have Ligita's illusions, because the stories told by the newly deported coincided with what she herself had experienced. Precisely the same as the Dreifelds family, they had been dragged away in the middle of the night from their homes, crammed into cattle cars and without any explanation driven for weeks into some unknown direction. Therefore, her dear daughter also was not safe; she could be arrested any moment and deported again. Emilija never did find out that among those deported on March 25 also was her future son-in-law, Aivars, who was settled with his mother Milda right here on the other side of Ob, in Sokhta village, some hundred kilometres from Togur.

In September, Ligita wrote that her purse with all her documents had been stolen on the train. Emilija's heart grew faint from fear, because the loss of a passport was considered a serious crime, which could threaten her daughter's right to remain in Latvia. Since this mishap Emilija lived with an alarming evil premonition in her chest. In December, rumours spread that various people, who like Ligita had been permitted to return to Latvia, had been transported from prison to prison back to Siberia. In January, Emilija learned that Hortenze Strazdiņa had returned to Kolpashevo. Her transport had arrived in Tomsk prison after the end of the navigation season. There was no place to put the arrested persons; therefore the prison administration decided to drive them on foot to their imprisonment or forced settlement places. As one of the many in the guarded column of prisoners, Hortenze was forced to limp without proper shoes several hundred kilometres that separated Tomsk from Kolpashevo. Emilija gazed at the tortured Hortenze, listened to her horrendous story and, with her heart frozen with fear, thought – what if Ligita too!?

The unfortunate news reached Emilija on January 15. Ligita begged her not to write to her any more, because she was going to change her place of residence shortly or possibly even come to live with her mother. It had happened! Her child, her daughter like a criminal was now being driven to walk on foot through Siberian snows back to the places of torture. Without warm clothing or proper shoes. How would she survive? How would she avoid freezing? Mrs. Dreifelde's despair was so abysmal, so immense, that her deportee friends started to worry about the state of her mind. To everyone who tried to comfort her, Emilija feverishly repeated: "She has nothing on her back or her feet. It's so cold. Where is my little girl now?"[184] The words of comfort did not quite reach Emilija's conscious mind, because all the time a vision loomed in front of her eyes – her daughter's frail body in an endless field of snow. As if in a trance, she continued to do her maidservant's work – scrubbing the floors, preparing food and taking care of the animals. On the 4th of February at about ten in the evening, Emilija took a milking pail and headed out to the barn. There, after several hours, the landlady found her – collapsed and unconscious.

My grandmother Emilija died alone. In an airless, smelly barn, her head pressed against the scrawny flank of a cow. Her hand had slowly slid away from the warm udder. The cow in surprise turned her head and let out a surly moo. And then indifferently continued to chew her cud. A pain as sharp as a knife stabbed her heart. Her body swayed, and, with her eyes open wide, my grandmother fell into the manure-soaked straw. Outside a February snowstorm was raging. Emilija did not hear it. Nothing hurt any more. Gathering the remaining force of her fading consciousness she hurried to help her daughter. Emilija had to make certain that her child was not being driven barefoot across snow and ice. With the speed of light her soul conquered the many hundreds of kilometres that separated the stuffy barn in Togur from the Tomsk prison. Rushing on, Emilija's soul searched every bush and every hill, each winding path and road. She lingered for an infinitesimal thousandth of a second at each column of convicts and looked into the covered up, tortured face of each prisoner. Ligita was not there! Now Emilija knew that her daughter had been spared this trial. Relieved and grateful, Emilija Dreifelde sighed, and handed her soul over to the Lord.

The next day the Latvians respectfully buried my grandmother. She was dressed in a dark dress sewn especially for this solemn occasion provided by Mrs. Dzenis. She also thought of inviting the local photographer, who took photographs of Emilija, so that when Ligita would arrive she would have something to remember her mother. Emilija looked dignified and at peace in her coffin. As if she had found release. The coffin was driven by a horse-drawn sleigh to the nearest graveyard, which was located a kilometre and a half beyond the village. The farewell ceremony was simple and heartfelt – someone said a short speech, then several Latvian songs were sung. After the burial, as is the custom, friends shared their memories about Emilija as they sat round a modestly laid table.

I remember my grandmother's grave, because in my childhood I often went there with my mother. I was there for the last time in the spring of 1957. Snow had already melted, and on the unpretentious grave mound the wind was bending half-broken long grasses. My mother was crying hunched over on her knees, and I felt terribly sorry for her. These were our farewells to grandmother Emilija, because after a few days our family finally headed home. To Latvia.

Family Member of a Bandit

Some time on or after the twentieth of March 1949, rumours started to spread in Latvia that something horrendous, something similar to the 14th of June 1941, was about to happen. Railway personnel had access to information that at the freight stations cattle cars were again being "equipped" and strung into trains. Three years had passed since the arrest and trial of my grandfather Aleksandrs, but each time my father's mother Milda heard stories about missing people and arrests, she felt as if a cold hand had grasped her heart.[185] Up to now they had been left in peace. After the arrest of her husband, their flat had been searched; Milda had been called in several times for questioning, but afterward none of the official "organs" had expressed any further interest in the family. Acquaintances, wanting the best, advised Milda to divorce her husband, because they felt that by doing so she could save herself and the boys from the horror of repression. My grandmother's mother Matilde, too, tried to persuade her daughter – a divorce would underline that Milda was in no way linked to "the bandit and enemy of the Soviet power." Milda, however, was not able to do this. Aleksandrs had harmed her so often that the thought of a divorce had been raised more than once, but during the chaos of war there had not been time to attend to the matter. Now, when misfortune had befallen her husband, Milda considered such an action as betrayal, even if she knew that she was jeopardising her children and her own safety.

As the rumours about further deportation intensified, on the morning of March 25, Milda decided to send her youngest son Arnis to her mother in Sigulda. Aivars had to go to the factory; hence my grandmother did not share her worries with him. What if the rumours turned out to be unfounded; then for missing work without justification her son could have major problems. Even trial and imprisonment.[186] How much Milda regretted keeping silent later! It would have been better for him to sit a hundred times in prison in Latvia, rather than she should helplessly watch as Siberia destroyed her son's youth and health.

That spring Aivars was feeling wonderful. The hard winter had ended, and, bathed in spring sunshine, the world had acquired a yet inexperienced appeal. He had a girl of his own with whom to go for walks or to the movies in the evening, and he was preoccupied with his youthful dreams, future plans, work and studies. Aivars was a fourth-year student in the technical college and was working at the State Electrical Factory, where for the first time he had begun to earn something. Milda dared to hope that the poverty, in which they had lived for many years, would be alleviated. Before Aivars started to earn some money, the nurse's pay my grandmother earned was the only source of income for the family. They lived from hand to mouth, surviving on pea soup, in which, on rare occasion, floated a small speck of bacon. For the first time in his life my father felt well dressed, and that increased his self-confidence. In the black market he had bartered new pants and had had two modern windbreakers sewn with large shoulder pads and metal zippers, as well as acquired decent shoes and an overcoat.

March 25 did not differ from other workdays. Aivars' work colleagues also had alluded to some vague rumours, but no one knew anything specific. In addition, people were afraid of talking about such matters. My father did not think the gossip he heard pertained to him. He and his mother lived an unpretentious and inconspicuous life, in which there was nothing that would draw the attention of the militia or Cheka. There were thousands like them. Could they really deport everyone? And why? In this Aivars was mistaken, because the cause and effect of the horrendous events of the first year of occupation had not settled in his child's mind with as much force as the war, in particular, the debacle at its end, which, seen through the eyes of a teenager and compared to his past experience, overshadowed everything else and for the rest of his life was remembered as the apogee of fear – the air raids, the wounded, and the refugees streaming by. All of this now was past, and he wanted to live! Only a few years had been spent under Stalin's sun, and at that time no one, certainly not Aivars, had a realistic perspective of the true extent of the terror that the Cheka was inflicting. This lack of information and his youth protected my father from a constant feeling of insecurity and from being overly cautious. For the older generation, who had lived through the shock of the Year of Terror, insecurity had become an integral part of their lives. In the evening of March 25, Aivars headed home, weary but without a care. He and his mother ate supper, then Aivars sat down to study. Milda had somewhat calmed down, because there had been no news of any sort of mass detentions. Perhaps all of it was simply rumour, she tried to convince herself. There was a knock at the door ...

"It was a Friday. Around nine that evening two men dressed in civilian clothes entered the flat, ordered us to get organised and come along with them. We, my mother and I, in shock, did not know what to do. Neither my mother nor I could carry anything heavy, thus, in the excitement, we took only what was absolutely necessary. Then one of the intruders pulled down a rug tacked on the wall, threw bedding and some other things in it. They did not ask about my brother. [...] In the stairwell stood another guard, while in the courtyard stood a fourth. Down in the street we took our places in a car. We were driven to the corner of Red Army Street and Valdemāra iela. [...] There were already many people in the assembly hall. More and more people were brought in. Here we were informed that, based on a government decision, we were being deported as family members of a bourgeois nationalist. During the night we were transferred to a small bus that took us to the Ropaži railway station. At about two or three am at night, we were moved into a railroad wagon. [...] It was a large cattle car with built-in wooden two-story bunks covered with straw. In the middle of the wagon was an iron stove. There also stood a *parasha* – a crude slop bucket used as a toilet, which was later concealed by a blanket. [...] There were many fellow sufferers. Almost all were farm people from the area. I think there were about 50–60 people in the wagon, mainly middle-aged, but there were also old people. The worst surprise was a family with two small children, one only a baby. Later I heard that both the children had died."[187] This is what my father remembers of the shock of deportation.

On Saturday, the train moved from Ropaži to Sigulda, where other "organised" wagons were linked up. During the day Milda and Aivars stared fixedly through the small wagon window, hoping to see Arnis. Later they learned from my grandmother Matilde's letter that Arnis had in fact been at the station, but had paced along the rows of wagons in vain. At dusk on Sunday, pulled by two locomotives, the train started to move. Sigulda was the last stop in Latvia. Aivars recalls: "In Cēsis the train reduced its speed. We saw people on the platform wiping their eyes. Nearing the border, someone started to sing a farewell refrain to Vidzeme, but no one joined in. Thus we, with very heavy hearts, left Latvia, moving through Valka in the dark.[188]

In Aivars' written down recollections a presumption appears that the deportation had taken place because of a denunciation by a neighbour. When one learns of the top secret decisions taken at the beginning of 1949 by the USSR Council of Ministers[189] and the State Ministry of Security,[190] it is immediately clear that the fate of Milda and her sons Aivars and Arnis was decided on 13 November, 1945 when the Chekists arrested my grandfather Aleksandrs and sentenced him as a bandit and bourgeois nationalist to ten years in a high security prison camp. Even Milda's divorce from her husband would not have changed their status – all three of them were for eternity labelled family members of a bandit. I, too, was branded already when I was still inside my mother's body. Born as the granddaughter of the "socially dangerous element" Jānis Dreifelds and "bandit" Aleksandrs Kalnietis, according to the criteria of the Stalinist era, nothing could erase this shameful stain from my biography. The order of deportation for Milda, Aivars and Arnis was written on February 26, a month prior to their actual detention. If Milda, led by her mother's instincts, had not sent her youngest son to the countryside, Arnis would have been together with them in the cattle car as well. Rattling along the interminable 6000 kilometres of rail to their place of forced settlement, their destination known only to the Chekists, my grandmother and father finally grasped the true extent of the deportation. As their train made its interim stops at stations, they almost always saw on the rails beside them another train with deportees. Immediately conversations were struck up through the window about who they were and where they come from. There were Estonians, Lithuanians and Latvians. It seemed as if the Baltic States were being emptied of their entire population.

The March 1949 deportation was much more efficiently organised than the first one in 1941. During the earlier deportation, the occupation regime and army did not have to worry about the "forest brethren," who continued their resistance movement from the Baltic forests after the war. They could have attempted to interfere with the deportation of people by organising armed raids. The USSR State Minister of Security approved the top secret operation plan, called "Coastal Surf" (*Krasta banga*) on 28 February 1949. Through this extensive deportation the USSR leaders wished to intimidate farmers negatively disposed toward collectivisation and force them to join the kolkhozes, as well as reduce the number of forest brethren. The greatest secrecy was observed in the preparation of this second wave of mass deportation. The territory of Latvia was divided into operative sectors with a commander in each sector and adjunct operative group under his command. On March 18, the top brass of the operation were briefed and the day following – the supervisors heading up all the trains.[191] The combat forces and the local Communist Party activists received the order to begin executing their assignment only six to ten hours before the beginning of the operation. In order to misinform residents, the relocation of armed forces of the interior and other specialised units was done in the name of spring manoeuvres. The operation was co-ordinated by 812 secret transmitting stations. At the borders of Latvia, Estonia and Lithuania, 8422 lorries were concentrated, which, in the morning of March 25, headed out to the 118 railway stations where 4437 cattle cars were already stationed.[192] From the 25th to the 29th of March 1949, 43,000 persons or 2.28 % of the population of Latvia were deported in 33 trains. Of this number, 4941 persons, or 12% of all the deportees, died during the deportation.[193] It was true genocide that the Soviet Union executed in Latvia, Estonia and Lithuania. 69,071 persons or 72.9% of the deportees from the Baltic States were women and children.[194]

The Operation "Coastal Surf" bore witness to how much Stalin and his emissaries had learned from the Grand Masters of mass extermination – the leaders of the Third Reich. In terms of the secrecy and precision, planning details as well as execution, the operation of the March 1949 deportations from the Baltic States was in no way inferior to the "perfect system" that the Nazis employed when deporting inhabitants, especially Jews, from countries occupied by the Reich to the large death camps of Europe. The Nazi and Soviet approach only differed in their "final solution" phase. The greatest concern of the Reich was to intensify the effectiveness of its death machine so that, in the shortest time possible, more people would be exterminated, while the Soviet regime had the luxury of experimenting to see how long the "class enemy" could survive in extreme circumstances. Moreover, such an experiment cost the state virtually nothing. On the contrary – it even generated a profit, because while the "contingent" was alive, it had to work. Yes, geography is a powerful factor! It limited the scope of the Nazis in an overpopulated Europe, while for the Soviets it afforded the possibility of stretching out into the vast expanses of Siberia without interference. The solitary risk – a portion of those who had been forced to settle managed to survive, despite the inhumane conditions that the Soviet regime "magnanimously" granted them. Hence people had to be forced to settle for life.

The implementers of the Operation "Coastal Surf" received high honours from the USSR for their "demonstration of courage and heroism." The most bitter pill to swallow was the sad fact that almost 30,000 local Latvian residents participated in the realisation of the mass deportations of March: heads of regional and municipal deportation headquarters, their deputies, staff on duty, compilers of operative information, chauffeurs, etc.[195]

In the same way that my mother Ligita and grandmother Emilija were only adjuncts in the security agency's family record or deportation case of the "socially dangerous element" Jānis Dreifelds, Aivars and Milda did not exist on their own. Investigation Case No. 8485 was created for the family of "bandit sympathiser" Kalnietis Aleksandrs Janovičs, not specifically for Aivars Kalnietis or Milda Kalniete.[196] I should not be as distressed as I am about such disregard for the identity of human beings, because it is the logical outcome of the class-oriented approach. Nonetheless, each time I see it, it makes me angry that tens of thousands of decent people were classified according to some sort of generalised criteria of class struggle, not as individuals, while every criminal had the right to his name, surname and personal case file. Even in the formulation of Aivars' and Milda's release documents, not a word is said that would make one sense that the release is an acknowledgement that the repressions of the Stalin era had been exaggerated and my father and grandmother had been innocent victims. The rationale for the recommendation to repeal the forced settlement order supplied by the LSSR prosecutor Juris Sproģis is the death of Aleksandrs Kalnietis, which provided sufficient reason to conclude that "there is no basis for keeping his family members in settlement."[197] This attitude very clearly reveals Soviet duplicity and priorities.

The deportation case file of the Kalnietis' family was begun March 25. It contains 35 pages. Included in the case file are the orders written at the end of February for the detention of Milda, Aivars and Arnis, information regarding Aleksandrs' criminal record and a statement by the War Commissariat – "that in the family of A. Kalnietis there is no one who is serving or has served at an earlier date in the Soviet Army, or has received any decorations or medals, nor has anyone been a member of [the Soviet] partisan movement."[198] A surprising factor is the erroneously indicated place of residence for the Kalnietis' family. Might it be that some official of the executive committee, who had been assigned the task of putting together the list of places of residence for the detained, knowingly tried to confuse the search party, or was it simply an accidental coincidence created by absent-mindedness or sloppiness? When the blunder was discovered at the militia, the 205th Housing Supervisor Porietis fearfully made a notation, according to which the Kalnietis' family had at least five places of residence. Nonetheless the real address Mēness iela still was not mentioned.[199] Therefore on the 25th of March the "operative unit" knocked on at least five doors, in each instance scaring the inhabitants to death. Unfortunately the materials in the case file do not indicate how the Chekists succeeded in finding Mēness iela 18, for the address is not mentioned in the documents of the preparatory phase of the campaign.

The second error concerns Milda's and Aivars' place of forced settlement. According to the "contingent" consignment documents it is obvious that the head of the convoy had to deliver the two to Belaya station in the Amur region. However, my father and grandmother were "loaded" into another train and on the 20th of April arrived in the Tomsk region, where they were immediately added to the register at the commandant's office. No one paid any attention to so insignificant an error, and in their documents they continued to be registered in Amur region, confirmed once more in the decision taken by the Special Commission of the USSR State Security Ministry 16 June 1949.[200] Surely this mistake was uncovered at a much later date, but it seemed insignificant. Amur or Tomsk region – what was essential was that both were "transferred to distant USSR regions."

In the findings of the State Security Ministry regarding the deportation, a third family member, Arnis Kalnietis, is also mentioned. After the conclusion of the operation, a report was sent to the Minister regarding the fact that Arnis was not arrested, and a request was made for an order to change the record. In responding to this "top secret" notice, the LSSR State Security Minister Alfreds Noviks approved a new deportation finding on April 26, in which there are only two family members mentioned – Milda and Aivars. It is possible that a similar action was taken also in other instances when the person to be detained could not be immediately located. The operation had to begin and end on time. Every item or detail not carried out tarnished the brilliant progress of the operation "Coastal Surf" and the chances for awards to people involved in its implementation; hence the Chekists were not interested in a thorough search for the persons not detained. On a corner of the signed deportation finding is a hastily handwritten reference to the USSR Prosecutor's order not to provide information regarding the real cause of death. Did this mean that for the sake of more convenient internal GULAG bookkeeping Arnis Kalnietis was considered dead? Perhaps because of this Arnis was left in peace, unlike the children who returned to Latvia from deportation in 1946 and again were hunted down in 1950 and sent back to Siberia "for the sake of family reunification."

In the case file of the Kalnietis' family alone three blunders in Cheka work are to be found.

Similar mistakes probably can be found in the files of other deportees, which indicates how little the righteous knights fighting on behalf of the proletariat were really interested in executing their assignment in substance. Like all the intimidated officials of Stalin's regime, they only took care of themselves. So that they themselves would not be accused of negligence and become victims of the system, they had to implement the decisions of the USSR supreme leadership to the letter. They could not deport fewer people than indicated in the order; therefore it was better to exceed the numbers and take others in the place of those not located, even if they were not mentioned in the lists. Often the "kulak" lists were falsified, "poor" farmers being listed in order to deliver the numbers shown in the deportation order. The Chekists also violated the instruction not to deport ex-servicemen who had served at the front, people serving or having served in the Soviet Army, those awarded USSR decorations or medals and Red partisans or their family members.[201] Moreover, they did not care if the deportees were old, sick or nursing babies. The old were carried onto the trucks, while the babies or small children were left to be taken care of by their parents. Those deported as a result of an error or excessive zeal later attempted to prove that they or their relatives did not belong to the "contingent." It took years, because, as it is usual with officials, the people implementing the deportations did not want to admit their errors and did everything to subvert the "re-examination of the case" by tying it up it in bureaucratic red tape.

Therefore, it is the surprising to learn that during the 1950s there were instances of people sent into forced settlement "in error" being allowed to return and even having their confiscated property restituted.[202] A few of the deportees succeeded in returning to Latvia illegally, employing a certificate from their town or rural council, which served as identification on their way back to Latvia, instead of the passport that had been taken away from them. In order to curtail such soft-heartedness, the Latvian SSR Council of Ministers approved an order threatening that " based on the November 26, 1948, decision of the USSR Supreme Council Presidium, those who issue any forms of certificates and references for persons deported from the territory of Latvian SSR, will be liable to criminal prosecution for encouraging escape." Across a corner of the document is a Russian language note in the handwriting of the Prime Minister of the Latvian SSR Vilis Lācis: "To be explained *orally* [original emphasis] to the chairmen of the Executive Committees for passing on to township councils."[203]

Reading the memoirs of the deportees, the road to Siberia seems like a gradual descent into hell that deadened the soul of human beings and made them realise that the calamity of today was less harsh than the one expected tomorrow. With the monotonous rattle of the train wheels, hopelessness and submission to fate slowly took over the body and spirit of human beings. "The end is here; life is over,"[204] my father thought at seventeen years of age, as the train carried them further and further into an unknown land – the vast, poverty-stricken and unkempt Russia. There were only a few families from the city in the wagon, who, the same as Milda and Aivars, subsisted only on their daily ration – 500 grams of bread, hot water and, on occasion, a thin broth. The majority of their neighbours in the wagon were from the country and had managed to bring some food with them for the journey.[205] Embarrassed in front of their poor fellow sufferers, they turned away, trying to eat their food in secret. Nonetheless the heavenly fragrance of dark rye bread and smoked bacon wafted in the air, overcoming the stench of the toilet and the odour of unbathed bodies. Sensing the enticing food smells was pure torment for Milda and Aivars: a light whiff that first touched a cheek, immediately afterward hitting the mouth and forcefully eliciting insatiable hunger pangs. Even though during the war and post-war years the family rarely ate its fill, my father had never before experienced so sharp a hunger. With each day of deportation, their hunger grew. In the beginning Aivars tried to fool his stomach, slowly nibbling his bread, crumb by crumb, but such self-control was beyond his strength, and after a short while his daily ration vanished in a few bites as if it had never existed. Milda always left a slice of her rye "brick" bread, making the excuse that it was enough for her to have a smoke.

My grandmother often stood at the open wagon doors, looking out into the distance, smoking, one after the other, cigarettes she had rolled herself. Sharp smoke stung her eyes, bitterness scalded her mouth, but the harsh taste for the moment appeased the hunger worm gnawing her flesh. But the hunger seemed nothing in comparison to the despair that tore at her soul. Milda felt as if life had betrayed her. She did not understand why her fate should be so dreadful. She leafed through her life over and over, in which, as a result of the bleak events of the last few days, now only dark pages could be seen. At birth, she had greeted her firstborn son with the words: "Is the boy normal?" Having cried so much after the premature death of her first husband, the twenty-three year old Milda worried that her tears would have weakened or even crippled her baby. How her second husband Aleksandrs had tyrannised her with his fits of jealousy and then left her with both boys to face the poverty and destruction of war alone! She never had had a man's shoulder to lean on. Except for her father, who had been already in his grave for many years. She had always struggled on her own. How she had worked! What had she not done in order to survive! Now only to end up in Siberia. For life! Her own and her son's lives were now finished forever. Her heart was also terribly heavy because she did not know the fate of her youngest son. What if the boy had also been caught and was being deported by himself in some other train? If that was so, it would have been better if all of them had been taken together, rather than the child suffer the dreadful journey to

Siberia by himself. She also thought of her mother Matilde, who now was left alone without the support of her daughter. How was she to survive in the future?

The general depression was somewhat relieved by the surrounding nature. My father very much wished to see the Volga, the longest river in Europe, but the train crossed it at night. They reached the Ural Mountains during daytime, however, and Aivars marvelled as he gazed at the snowy mountain peaks. The majority of the deportees saw mountains for the first time, and they made an indelible impression on the people raised in the flatlands of Latvia. As soon as the mountains were crossed, the endless Siberian forests or large plains began, where neither clusters of houses nor any sign of life could be discerned. It was depressing. Having experienced June 14, 1941, people knew where they were being taken and what to expect at the end of their journey. Gazing at the impenetrable thick forests, Aivars reverently felt the insignificance of human beings when compared to the mightiness of nature. Somewhere in the same sort of forest he would be fated to eke out his existence. How could one survive in such isolation from the world? Perhaps therefore, when, after a few days of train ride, my father again glimpsed houses and people, they made so vivid an impression on his memory. "Once in the early morning we arrived in some city. Judging from the many smoking chimneys, a large industrial centre. I was surprised to see a whole "platoon" of young girls dressed in grey padded jackets and red kerchiefs. They were going to work singing! Thus, even here a human spirit could survive and delight in song."[206] The scene was encouraging, and it cheered up Aivars somewhat. How little does a human being need to find sustenance in despair!

Around the 20th of April, Milda's and Aivars' train No. 97329 reached Tomsk. The military convoy handed over their "transport" to the local guards. For the temporary housing of the deportees, a transfer prison camp for criminals had been cleared in great haste. It bore a striking resemblance to black and white documentary film sequences about Nazi concentration camps that my father had seen in Soviet post-war films. Never could he have imagined that similar prison gates would close behind him. Surrounded by a high fence and barbed wire, five or six gigantic barracks were located in a territory divided into two sections. Here the two trainloads, approximately 6000 people, were settled.[207] The barracks were modelled after the classical GULAG architectural style, each containing two-story bunks, a narrow passageway, a "*parasha* " and an iron stove in the centre. Milda and Aivars succeeded in getting a place to sleep, while in neighbouring barracks people had to sleep in shifts. In the narrow passageway there was no place to store belongings, thus they had to be left outside under an open sky. So that nothing would be stolen, the deportees took turns guarding them. Milda and Aivars had so few belongings that they slept on top of them. Already the first night the curse of the camp – lice and bedbugs – arrived. There was one bathhouse for the entire large crowd of people. At a cold-water tap one could at least wet down and wash the thick layer of dirt accumulated during the long journey. The bathhouse was also used as a temporary morgue, where the corpses of people who died in the camp were stored. In such conditions the deportees from all parts of Latvia had to wait until the ice would melt in the River Ob and they could be transferred by boat to their permanent places of forced settlement.

Milda had her Latvian passport taken away in the camp. Aivars had not yet come of age; therefore he did not have a passport. From then on until 1957 his single identity document became the registration certificate, in which, twice a month, it was noted that the deportee had not wilfully left the place of forced settlement. The commandant of the transfer camp informed them that both of them as family members of a bandit were deported for life, and they were ordered to sign a printed form with the notation:

> I, the deportee, have been informed that, by order of the USSR supreme governing bodies, I am deported for life without right to return to my previous place of residence. I have also been informed that without a permit from the local authorities of the Ministry of Interior I do not have the right to leave this place and to change place of residence and workplace even temporarily. I also am aware that in case of violation of this signed agreement, according to the 26 November 1948 decision of the Presidium of the Supreme Council of the USSR, I will be considered liable and be sentenced to 20 years of hard labour. I have been familiarised with the 26 November 1948 decision.[208]

Even though some of their fellow sufferers had already signed this document, nonetheless, in doing so, Milda felt that a heavy door slammed behind her and would never open again. Aivars put his arm around his mother's shoulders and tried to swallow the lump that had caught in his throat: he thought he would never again see Rīga, his brother or grandmother.

Days in the camp dragged. Monotonously. The young people somehow passed the time playing games, trying to lose themselves in pretended merriment. Now and then some of them were sent to do some work outside the camp, which was a reprieve of sorts. Once Aivars volunteered for such work. He had wanted to see what the city looked like and what kind of people lived there. He did not anticipate that the hoped for amusement would become one of the bleakest of his memories: he had to move the first people who had died in the camp. My father records what he remembers: "They were twelve-year-old children. Relatives had sewn the corpses in white sheets because there were no coffins. We took them from the room leading into the bathhouse, where rats had already managed to feast on their faces. One of the children was brought from a barrack by a man who had slung his body like firewood over his shoulder. The corpse had not yet stiffened with rigor mortis. We also had to put an old, very heavy man, about fifty years of age, without any covering, in the lorry. Thus in an open lorry we drove to Tomsk University to hand over the dead to the anatomy department. It was a sad journey. We did not know where to look or how to behave. Even the guard carrying a rifle with a bayonet felt bad. We left the deceased at the university. The people taking them in asked what to do with the clothes of the dead. We told them to leave them there. Later, when it was very hard without boots, I recalled the dead old man's sturdy boots – how useful they could have been! But it's good that I did not take them. That sin would like a stone have pressed on my chest for the rest of my life."[209] Aivars had come face-to-face with death early. He had seen the mass graves of Jews in Rumbula, soldiers who had fallen in battle, Rīgans killed in air raids during the last days of war, but never had death seemed to him so undeserved and unjust as on that day when he accompanied the first victims of deportation on their last sad journey.

On May 1, the ice broke and started to move in the Ob. First, one heard something like cracking, as if frost were snapping at a tree trunk or house corner, but much, much louder. Gradually the sounds grew louder and more frequent, until the ice exploded. With immense force pieces of ice pressed at the yet immobile ice mass from behind, creating mound upon mound and filling the air with threatening crashes and thunderous sound. With the noise increasing in intensity, at one moment the ice dam in the river was broken and the river, roaring its supreme might, rushed forward with uncontrollable power. That spring Milda and Aivars did not see this grandiose sight, because the high fence around the camp isolated them from the world. After a few years, living on the shore of the Ob, my father experienced the ice breaking up for five springs, wishing and hoping that perhaps the next year would bring news of freedom and release, that he would finally board a ship to return to his homeland. In the sixth spring his hopes were fulfilled. My parents had received a certificate of release and impatiently waited for the ice to leave the river and for the much-wished-for boat to arrive to take my family home.

After the ice was gone, the camp was gradually vacated. Accompanied by guards, the deportees were moved to barges in large groups. The gigantic, shallow big boat was pulled downstream by a small tugboat, which operated with the help of an ancient paddle wheel. Now and then the barge stopped, and groups of people were transferred from it to shore, where they continued further to their planned places of forced settlement. All around them stretched an infinite, water-flooded plain, from which in places appeared some clumps of trees or a village finding shelter on higher ground. It was depressing to see how wasted the land was. For their entire long journey they had not seen such poverty. On the barge Aivars met the kind farmer's wife of the homestead where he had worked as a shepherd. She had been taken with both her two small daughters. On the sixth day, Milda and Aivars were ordered to transfer to a smaller barge, which continued the voyage along Korshan, a tributary of Ob, up to the point where it no longer could be sailed. The last barge stop was called the "Thirtieth Kilometre." There they were met by the heads of the surrounding kolkhozes with their horse carts. My father writes: "Everything happened as if at Jurģi.[210] Each of the kolkhoz chairmen – *predsedatel's* – attempted to obtain for himself the best labourers, the youngest and the ones with the most belongings. [...] We were assigned to the furthest village Sokhta, which, as we saw later, was also the poorest."[211] After the long arduous journey and poor nourishment, the young man who limped and the frail woman as slight as a teenager, would not have appeared promising labourers. When the rest of the *predsedatel's* had chosen their workers, all that was left for Milda and Aivars was the last remaining and furthest kolkhoz in the region. They still had to walk for thirty kilometres to their village from the "Thirtieth Kilometre" stop. Their belongings were driven by horse cart, and Milda was also allowed to sit in the cart.

Sohta village was founded by order of Stalin during the 1930s and populated by "kulaks" deported from the Altai and the Eastern slopes of the Urals. Their escort had left them at the edge of a swamp in the uninhabited taiga, not even providing the most elementary of shelters, nor leaving any food reserves. In their desperate struggle with nature almost all the old people and children had died. Only the strongest had survived. Now at least the deportees had a roof over their heads, their own potato field and a pig or a cow, from which to supply the state with its prescribed quota of butter and meat. Although grain crops were sown, the people who lived in the kolkhoz did not get the grain, because the meagre harvest also went to the state. They had to content themselves with subsisting from potatoes, pea meal bread and skim milk, supplementing these, now and then, with a bird or animal they could snare in the forest or fish they could catch. When Aivars became more familiar with life in this far corner of the world abandoned by God and people, he could not help but marvel how modestly the locals lived: they had accepted their grey and miserable daily existence and knew so little about the world outside that they had slowly started to believe that their life was really not so bad. They no longer were considered the class enemy, because during the last stage of the war, when Stalin lacked people at the front, the army started to call into service men from the deported "kulak" villages of Siberia. That freed the mobilised men and their relatives of the dreadful label "class enemy," but did not give them the right to leave Siberia. They were kolkhozniks, who, in compliance with Soviet legislation, were bonded to the soil like serfs of Czarist times without passports.[212] The young had fallen in the war; the old had died off. The more enterprising had either married and moved off to the city or had not returned from service in the army. In Sokhta and the neighbouring villages the majority that remained were either old people or women, who worked very hard, receiving almost no recompense for their labour. In 1949, for one day of work, the people in the Sohta kolkhoz received 300 grams of grain![213]

Although many locals had lost relatives in the war, they did not treat the deportees badly. Only once an old man, who had lost both sons in the war, threw himself at Aivars with his hoe, screaming: "*Fashist, ty moikh synovey ubil!*"[214]

Much that was strange and incomprehensible in the life of the locals. The fields had to be sown at a specific time, regardless of rainy or slushy weather. They did not care if something grew or not. The main concern was that the regional centre could be informed that the fields had been sown. The locals treated their animals cruelly, beating and cursing them. That differed so greatly from the sincere closeness that united the Latvian farm women with their cherished brown cows, whom they called by name, or Latvian men folk with their beloved bays or greys. The local children seemed to grow up on their own. The smaller ones wore pants with the seams of their seats left unsewn, so that those places where something falls out would always be open. Thus they ran around half-dressed, fly and mosquito bitten. It was a cruel natural selection of the fittest, where only the strongest survived. Marriage relationships, too, were somewhat loose, especially after the war, when in the small Siberian villages there were many more women than men. Pavel Ivanovich, the local Don Juan had a child out of wedlock in almost every homestead, and all knew about it. If some regional official, who had the power to either pardon or cause misfortune by pronouncing as malfeasant anyone who did not know how to keep his favour, visited the village, the *predsedatel'* would himself organise food and home brew, as well as a better looking woman for the official to sleep with.

Aivars felt repulsed by the primitive relationships between men and women, which contrasted so sharply with the reserved, strait-laced attitude that was the norm in Latvia. Before he had mastered Russian, he did not understand vulgar words or double entendre obscenities, which were an integral part of the wooing ritual here.

Later, when the sense of what was said no longer was a secret, Aivars tried not to listen, because he did not want to tarnish with such filth the memories of his first shy love that had blossomed in the spring prior to deportation. There was such shortage of men in the kolkhoz that even the emaciated Latvian boys seamed appealing to the kolkhoz women. Our family archive contains a photo, which shows two sisters, milkmaids – corpulent, generous of build, with round and bland faces. Laughing and being horror-struck at the same time, my grandmother told me that the sisters had tried to persuade her to give her son to them. The sisters were ready to share their husband and to keep him well fed. And they promised also to take care of their mother-in-law. "I would much rather have seen Aivars dead," said my grandmother as she finished her story. Even though I was still a child, even I, gazing at the pie-like faces of the strange women, sensed what my grandmother had felt then.

Nearly all the Latvians who settled in Sokhta happened to be city people not accustomed to farm work. Milda at least had helped her parents, when they had moved from Rīga to the countryside in the 1930s and started to lease land. She knew something about hoeing, threshing and harvesting. Aivars was a true city boy, who knew how to work skilfully with electrical wires and connections, knew how to build a radio receiver or to haggle for a better price for some item on the black market. These skills did not help him in ploughing, sowing or harvesting, which now became his daily work. The first job that Aivars had to master was ploughing with four oxen that were harnessed to a large, cumbersome plough. So that the animals would walk a straight row, a woman or a teenager would lead them holding head reins. The ploughman had to know how to follow the harnessed oxen and how to plough a deep furrow. Much deeper than the ones ploughed in Latvia. That required the strength and body of a man, but Aivars had grown very thin. In recalling his first ploughing day, my father says he was continuously dizzy, as he, hanging onto the plough, had tried to stop himself

First photo of Aivars Kalnietis taken
in Siberian exile 1949.

from fainting. He was not the one who guided the plough: it was the plough that pulled him and led the dance.

He had developed scurvy, with unhealthy suppurating boils on his legs due to poor nourishment and lack of vitamins. Milda's legs too were covered with boils, but she ignored them for the most part. More than anything, her own powerlessness hurt: in front of her very eyes her son was failing, and the only thing she could do was to tear a few mouthfuls of food away from herself! As a nurse Milda had worked all her life trying to ease the suffering of others. She, who had cared for the sick and wounded, now had to look on helplessly as Aivars suffered. From my childhood I remember my grandmother's horrifying story, when she, putting a finger to her cheek, showed me how in Siberia my father's teeth had slid back and forth in his mouth; "I'd press on one side, and they, knick, knack, would move, I'd press to the other side and they, knick, knack, would jump back." The locals combated avitaminosis and scurvy with the help of a wild garlic called *kolba.* Many deportees mention this wonder cure as a saving grace in their memoirs. In the summer they ate *kolba* leaves while in the fall they collected and pickled them for the winter. *Kolba* raised the body's resistance to disease being a rich source of vitamins. Although the wild garlic helped Aivars, it did not lessen his hunger. No matter how frail a worker my father had been, after the sowing was done, he received a bonus for his good work – 15 roubles! Now Milda could buy soap.

Kolba alone would not have cured my father. Skim milk and potatoes saved him. The chairman of the kolkhoz was a decent man and, seeing how quickly the Latvian boys and girls were getting weaker, in the middle of July he dispatched them to some distant fields to mow hay. Aivars had become so emaciated that he could not climb on a horse. His head felt dizzy, and he did not have enough strength to keep a hold of the reins. The rider and the skeletally thin horse were well suited to each other: the horse's ribs were clearly visible, bow-fashion pressing out at the skin, while his backbones jutted upward like the teeth of a saw. They travelled through the taiga and swamps via a barely discernible path. Aivars saw with dread, how, in traversing the swamps, the horse slowly sank deeper and deeper, until only his neck and head remained above the quagmire. Mosquitoes and small biting flies in droves descended upon the travellers. The bugs ate at the flesh till it was raw. They crawled into eyes and fed behind the ears, until a face started to look as if it was covered with red patched, bumpy cobbles. Someone who did not know any better, would have thought that they had contacted erysipelas – a red, inflamed streptococcal skin infection, commonly known as "rose."

After a two-day ride, they finally reached the kolkhoz fields, where very soon the hardships of the journey were forgotten because they were adequately fed there. Mowing hay was hard work;

hence they were fed better than other workers from the kolkhoz. Each of them received a half a kilogram of pea bread per day, as well as all the potatoes and skim milk they could eat or drink. The skim milk was sometimes left to curdle and occasionally warmed to make cottage cheese. For one meal Aivars and his friend Kārlis used to clean up a full pail of potatoes, which they then boiled and mashed. Adding skim milk, they voraciously demolished all of it. They were so insatiable that they could have eaten another portion the same size. They also had to learn how to mow hay. Several days passed before the city-bred boys finally mastered an even stroke with a scythe. For the first few weeks, their frailty did not allow them to keep up with the locals, but later the Latvians became good workers, fulfilling their quotas and then some. Living this regimen, strength returned not only to the human beings, but also to the horses and oxen, whose flanks grew rounded and shiny. With a feeling of well-being from a body well fed, the beasts on occasion were even playful – racing across the field, throwing their back legs in the air and butting haystacks.

At the beginning of October, when the Korshan River started to ice over and the earth began to freeze, the field people headed back to the village. On the way back, swimming across the river on the back of his horse, Aivars fell into the icy water. There was no place to dry his clothing, so he had to ride in wet clothes. After a short while these froze and rattled like flintstone. Aivars was terribly cold, and he worriedly foresaw that after the icy journey he would without doubt fall ill again. He was never to forget that he had lain in the fields with tonsillitis and high fever. Without medication and without help until one night his swollen, festering tonsils had so constricted his breathing passages that Aivars had started to smother. Afraid and in despair, he had with his own hands torn open the pus-filled tonsils, and air with its power to refresh had flooded into his body. Never again did he want to experience such feelings of panic. Surprisingly Aivars did not fall ill after the icy swim, which is proof positive that the hard work and the primitive but more or less adequate food had made him more resilient.

Aivars' recovery gave my grandmother back something of the previous, seemingly inexhaustible joy for living. She straightened her shoulders, lifted her head and once again became independent Milda, who knew how to encourage others with a witty joke or how to calm a despondent person by laying out a game of patience or telling fortunes with cards. My grandmother was no fortune-teller, but in reading cards, which she started to do in Siberia, there was a necessary ritual, a psychotherapeutic séance, that gave her the strength to fight life's tribulations and adversities. Milda's card cure also helped other Latvians regain hope, as well as relieve their hearts: by examining the six of diamonds, the nine of clubs or the lovely Queen of hearts, one could talk over one's hopes and try to decipher something from an inscrutable future. The terminology created by grandmother also reflected the daily concerns of everyone. "Crown news" – a summons to the Commandant's office; "good news at lunchtime" – a letter from home; "King of clubs bringing ill fortune" – any of the officials of the regime; "a long crown journey at dawn" – transfer or some trouble. My grandmother also taught me how to play patience and do fortune telling, which I did during my school years, telling fortunes for girls from my class, precociously repeating the same terminology. But in response to new and changed conditions and the needs of my clients, the content was different. "King of clubs bringing ill fortune" meant the teacher who had caught someone in their usual mischief or because of some other violation, while "good news at lunchtime" had changed to a note from some boy with an invitation to meet after school. I had such grand success that the girls from the more senior classes on occasion honoured me with a request to share my clairvoyance with them.

At the beginning the local mighty men – the chairman of the kolkhoz and the brigadier, as his executive was called, did not take my grandmother seriously and, as it was customary in Siberia, tried to demonstrate their supreme power tormenting her with brutal orders and curses. Matters were made worse by the fact that Milda was slight of build – only a metre and forty-three centimetres tall and very thin. She looked frail and moved slowly, which only increased the managers' baiting. Once, at the winnowing machine, when the chairman had particularly overachieved with his tirade of rich curses attempting to make the "lazy cow and slut" move more quickly, my grandmother's patience had reached its limit and the dam broke. After the repeated – pour faster, string of curses, pour faster, curses – Milda threw herself at the *predsedatel'* brandishing her grain shovel. The huge lout of a man jumped back and fearfully stared at the small, frail woman, in whose eyes burned such anger, that the curses ready to spill from his mouth froze on his lips. Mumbling something about mad and crazy hags, in order to save face, he skulked away from the winnowing. From that moment on everyone left Milda in peace.

At the end of July, the first letter arrived from mother Matilde. With great relief, Milda learned that Arnis had not been taken captive. Her son was living in the country with Matilde, who now was the single supporter and caregiver for him. My grandmother had sent Arnis in such a hurry to Sigulda on the morning of March 25 that she had not even managed to send a change of clothing with him. From the letter she learned that her mother had not been able to get any of their poor belongings. All of them had been pilfered. Milda felt her heart constrict, understanding from the letter in what poverty her mother and Arnis now had to live: "…we have to eat every day, but we never have enough to eat. I am sad that we all are not together; there would be enough room and bread for all. It seems to me that this is just a dreadful dream from which I must wake. […] From all that I've experienced, there is a constantly bleeding wound in my chest, which only the grave will heal."[215]

In 1949, my great grandmother Matilde was already seventy years old. Behind her was a life spent at hard work, bones destroyed by rheumatism, her eyes half-blind, but the tenacity and spiritual strength that she had inherited from her ancestors allowed her not to collapse from repeated blows of fate. She put her trust in God Almighty, that He would not allow injustice to triumph and would protect her daughter and both grandsons, not allowing them to be destroyed. She saw herself as a tool in the hands of God, and that she was meant in some miraculous fashion to raise Arnis, who had been saved, until he would be able to fend for himself and help his mother and brother in far away Siberia. Her daughter had written that the two of them had been deported for life, but Matilde's life experience had taught her that no regime had power forever: what was decided by human beings could be changed by human beings. Matilde's letters contain an inspiring story of survival when every success in the struggle for basics – food, some item of clothing for Arnis, a planted row of potatoes or a handful of hay for the cow – is a great victory that allows her and Arnis to survive one more winter and to recover health in the summer. She herself had almost nothing to send to her dear Milda and Aivars, but she took care that some of the many relatives would give something so she could send a small package to her children. From what the relatives gave, she kept nothing for herself; everything – knitted socks and mittens, a piece of bacon or flour – was sent to her daughter. Milda accepted her mother's sacrifice with pangs of conscience, but she herself was a mother, and Aivars had to have boots and food to survive. Tearfully she read Matilde's letters: "Since July I no longer have any flour or barley. Today Vilma visited me and brought a litre of barley and material for a pair of pants for Arnis. [...] For the holidays we are left without bread."[216] Or else: "My strength diminishes with each day, but I'm as hungry as a horse."[217]

The first year after her daughter's deportation, she was sustained by the hope that as soon as son Voldemārs would be freed from prison, he would take the heavy burden from her bent shoulders and help his mother and sister keep going. Her son was no criminal. Things simply had not gone his way. In one of the regular militia forays to the black market in 1945, Voldemārs was arrested and sentenced to five years in prison for "speculating." How could this be called speculation – almost everyone attempted to sell or exchange something on the black market after the war.

Very soon Voldemārs himself wrote to Siberia from prison: "After I'm released, I'll help change everything for the better, as much as it is within my power to do so. [...] When we are all together again, we'll help each other to get settled as best we can, because I think my professional skills and experience, as well as my proficiency in languages will allow me to earn our daily bread and subsistence anywhere."[218] Milda deeply loved her brother. In her memory, nothing could tarnish the harmonious and love-filled period of her childhood when she felt safe and secure under the protection of her brother, because as the responsible older brother he had always defended and cherished her. Voldis had inherited from his father his stately build and handsome, Italianesque dark complexion with burning, brown eyes. He was witty and sociable – qualities, which made him much loved by women. As a result, Voldemārs had married substantially above his station, more than a son of the humble Kaimiņi family could have hoped for. He had an agricultural degree and was a member of a student fraternity, but, as it often happens with talented people for whom everything seems to be falling in their lap, her brother could not resist temptation, and slowly his life that had held so much promise was drowned in vodka. The high society marriage fell apart, and the subsequent path Voldemārs took was a slow, but irreversible descent downward, creating bitter disillusionment for his parents, who had taken so much pride in their son. Even though Milda knew that she no longer could depend on her brother, like anyone who is put in an impossible situation she hung onto her brother's promise to support her mother and the two of them in Siberia. Because of this, Milda's and Matilde's disappointment was the greater, when Voldemārs, after his release from prison and spending a few days at his mother's home, vanished for a long time. Then he showed up again, promised all sorts of marvellous things and vanished again. Now and then, Matilde received news that Voldis had been seen in Jelgava, Lielstraupe or even had left to go to Russia, but the son never seemed to find time to visit his mother. Much less – send her a rouble or two.

Troubled by poverty, Matilde and Arnis were forced to move several times. When Matilde died in 1952, there was no one to fulfil her wish to have her final resting place beside her husband Pēteris in Rīga's Forest Cemetery. Matilde was buried by total strangers in the cemetery of Bērze, and the thirteen-year old Arnis was left to struggle on in life on his own. My grandmother never forgave Voldemārs this betrayal, and after her return to Latvia she did not look for her brother. Only in the last years of her life, sensing death to be near, she wrote to her brother, asking to meet him. Voldemārs came. He was a very old, shrivelled-up man, almost blind, but even in this pitiful form, I, a foolish teenage girl, could discern traces of his previous appeal. When Voldemārs died, it was Aivars who took care that his remains were buried properly in the Forest Cemetery beside his father and sister.

Matilde's letters were filled with constant worry and complaints about Arnis, who was disobedient, did not study and did not behave as she thought he should. This really upset Milda, because she could not know how much of what her mother wrote was subjective exaggeration. Arnis was neither lazy nor bad. His naughtiness was no worse than that of other boys his age. He did, however, lack self-control and, on occasion, was rude, but the reasons for this were deeper. In the raising of her grandson, Matilde referred to the precepts of obedience developed in the previous century. She herself had the fortune to have stability and security provided by the large and

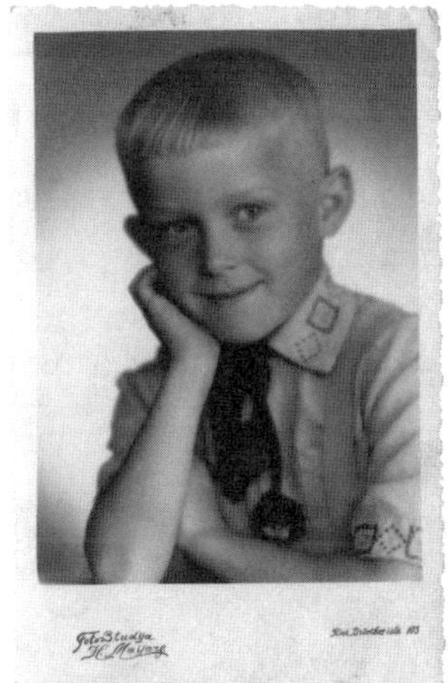

Arnis Kalnietis.

friendly Eglītis family. She was too old to be able to judge how much the eleven-year-old Arnis had been traumatised by the negative impressions of the war, especially the last trauma – the deportation of his mother and brother. Like a vicious circle, the fate of the boy was to be a repetition of his father Aleksandrs' unhappy childhood, whose parents had been taken from him by the First World War. The only difference was that Arnis was an orphan of living parents, because his father was imprisoned in the GULAG and his mother was deported to Siberia. Arnis was deeply unhappy and, like the majority of children, did not understand his own contradictory feelings and did not know how to express the sense of undeserved injustice that had become magnified in his subconscious, until it broke loose in some inappropriate, uncontrolled action that hurt Matilde deeply. Afterwards, having calmed down, Arnis blamed himself – why had he again been bad? Why had he done his dear grandmother wrong? Full of contrition, the boy hurried to embrace her.

The letters Arnis wrote to his mother were unusually mature and clearly expressed for a fifth and sixth grader. The letters calmed Milda. She no longer was so afraid that her son would go astray. If

Arnis was doing well in school, took part in sports, earned awards and still managed to help in farm chores, Matilde's complaints must be exaggerated. At least this burden had become somewhat lighter. Milda applied the same criteria for Arnis that she had developed during the first year in Siberia as a result of Aivars' and her own struggle for physical survival. Barley and potatoes on Arnis' plate seemed more important than the state of his soul. Only after some time did she begin to realise how unhappy her little boy felt. Not being able to describe in his own words his sadness, the boy had carefully copied to his mother a long poem in his letter. Its first lines burned Milda with their implicit pain:

If only once more in my life
I could meet my parents.[219]

Oh, if only once more in her life she could meet her Arnis and comfort him.

Arnis very much missed his mother. More than his father because, due to the war and the disagreements between his parents, they had spent little time together. He also sensed that Aleksandrs in some way was to blame for his mother's and brother's deportation. At least that is what Matilde asserted. To make matters worse, in school he had to learn about the struggle with bourgeois bandits who wanted to drown Latvia in blood and hand it over to the imperialists. Arnis had no one he could talk to, because people kept silent about these "things," hence the boy had to struggle and guess what was the actual nature of Aleksandrs' crime. Who was his father – a criminal or an innocent victim, the same as his mother and brother? His father's rare letters did not provide an answer. Contradictory feelings fought inside Arnis. He wanted to be a good son, hence he fulfilled his duty and wrote to Aleksandrs in the prison camp, but in his heart he felt hurt and bitter that his father had abandoned him and, even worse, taken away his mother. With a totally different fervour Arnis thought of Milda, with whom his only contact was also through letters, for which he waited so much that it seemed that they came too rarely and were too short: "Dear mamma, please write longer letters. I still have to write a letter to papa. Papa also expects some news from our homeland. Dear, dear mama, we haven't forgotten you. You'll still receive a lot of happy and sad news from your native land. Dear mama, please send your photos."[220] It seemed that with time the sadness diminished, but in reality, to protect himself, Arnis had hidden the sadness deep, deep in his heart. At the time he still was not aware that the sadness would be there forever, no matter where he went or what he did. Gradually the shadow of this deeply buried sadness also impressed itself in his features and in the expression in his eyes. Even I recall this: my uncle could be roaring with laughter or, face flushed, be telling funny jokes, but the minute he fell silent, immediately his face assumed an aloofness – as if joy and laughter had never existed.

The next blow that reinforced the boy's protective armour was the death of Matilde in the summer of 1952. Arnis was only thirteen at the time, when, not even having lived his teens, he was forced to begin the life of an adult. Now he was alone in the world. If the Bogdanovs' family of nearby Bērze had not taken the boy in, Arnis would have been put into an orphanage. Thanks to the care of his kind patrons, Arnis got more nourishment and a home to return to during school holidays. He had to give up his dream of becoming a sailor and go and learn in the dreaded vocational school. There he was given a free lunch, a change of clothing and a uniform coat made of rough blue wool. Exactly the same as for his father Aleksandrs, Arnis' life did not give him many options. My uncle always carried this bitterness buried deep inside him.

Milda never succeeded in healing the rift between her son and herself created by the injustices of fate. It would be more appropriate to call it a rift between her son and the world, to which he now

Arnis visiting his mother in Siberia 1954.

also relegated his mother and brother. Although she did not want to admit it, she sensed this when Arnis came to visit them in Siberia in 1954. Without taking her eyes of the so familiar yet strange face of her son, Milda listened to his stories about the past years, but it seemed as if there was a fine veil that separated them, which allowed them to feel the warmth and to look at each other, but there was no real contact. After returning to Latvia they both tried to overcome this estrangement, but they did not succeed in doing so fully. Milda had not been given the right to be with her son when his need for a mother was the greatest. Later Arnis had learned how to endure his solitude.

The first summer in Siberia was very short. They had hardly drawn breath and recovered before winter had arrived. Snow fell already in October. "I never have later in my life been so cold as I was that first winter in Siberia. On occasion it seemed that even my soul froze, but I did not fall ill," my father recalls.[221] Before deportation, some of Aivars' wages had remained unpaid, which his colleagues sent to him in Siberia. For this money he was able to obtain a quilted jacket, a winter hat and quilted pants. It was very crowded in the hut where the deportees lived, but even this did not save them from the cold. My grandmother, as the oldest and most experienced, decided that what they needed was a stove. Knowing nothing about its operating principles, just seeing what the locals did, Milda built a small stove from cow manure, which surprisingly did not smoke too much and still heated. One night Aivars shoved his feet too close to the stove, and his only footwear, the galoshes he had acquired in the summer, burned. He did not have money for purchasing new felt boots or *valenki*, hence he had to do with locally made leather moccasins – *chirki* – to these he added canvas tops. When the moccasins were stuffed full with the rough swamp grass and the legs bound with cloth, they were warm enough. In the first package that arrived from Latvia in October there was a sheepskin vest that served my father well all the years spent in Siberia, although the sheep wool in places became worn through to the shiny naked pelt.

The kolkhoz chairman commandeered the youngest Latvians to work in the forest that stretched for 30 kilometres around the village. All the woodsmen, the deportees as well as the locals, and people who had come from neighbouring villages to earn some money, lived in a gigantic barrack, at the centre of which was located a large, constantly lit iron stove. At one end of the barrack was a primitive grocery shop, where one could "chalk up" two kilograms of bread per day, as well as buy cream of wheat, sugar and even an occasional small piece of meat. Now and then they were lucky enough to snare a rabbit, which was then boiled with the cream of wheat and eaten as a tasty stew. For dessert they drank hot water with sugar. He was less fortunate with the potatoes, because Aivars had not thought ahead. They froze and, as a result, had to be eaten just the same, even though they were blue in colour. He now understood why the locals cooked the potatoes first, then mashed them and made round balls, which could be frozen. Thus they could keep in the cold for the entire winter the same as sauerkraut and be easily transported. In the future he did the same. There were many other things to be learned from the Siberians, who had developed their own methods for survival in these harsh conditions and how to compensate for the lack of vitamins and the monotonous, poor food. Afraid of again falling ill with scurvy, overcoming his revulsion, Aivars drank a pine needle brew – an acrid-smelling, brownish-green liquid that turned out to be an effective cure. The work was hard, and without the support of experienced men my father would not have been able to deliver his daily quotas. He had to pull logs out of the forest to the riverbank, where in the summer they were floated downward to sawmills. Even if it was not possible to save anything, Aivars at least was fed and could help his mother.

In December, news reached Aivars in the forest that his mother had broken a leg and had been taken to the hospital in Kolpashevo. The hospital stay was organised by one of the deported nurses, who had so persistently corralled the kolkhoz chairman that he finally had gone to the nearest post office in the neighbouring village to call out an air-ambulance. Milda lay in the hospital for the remaining winter months. At the minimum she was frugally fed in a warm place. I'm afraid to even think what would have happened to my grandmother if she had remained in the village. Fragile bones were Milda's curse: it was the fourth and by no means the last break in her life. In Siberia she was to experience another break, as well as two more later on in Latvia. Finally the Rīga Traumatology Institute arrived at the diagnosis that she had a rare bone disease that made her bones crystallise and become stone hard but at the same time very fragile. They broke at the slightest impact. After her return from Siberia, the mysterious "marble bone" disease put a stop to her work at the hospital, where her previous colleagues had welcomed her with open arms. My grandmother had only worked for two months at her much wished-for nurse's job, when she slipped on a discarded apple core on the street and fell. This time the break was so complicated, that the doctors spent several years trying to get the bones to mend, but after a long time of being bedridden and several operations the broken leg no longer bent at the knee. My grandmother had become an incapacitated invalid unfit for work, a very humiliating state psychologically. To the end of her life she could not reconcile herself with the thought that she had to depend on others.

Only now, after having experienced life, am I able to appreciate my grandmother's unique personality. She had moved ahead of her time by a whole generation, because she did not believe that a woman's objective in life could only be realised together with a man and through marriage. Work for Milda was an essential means of affirmation of her personality, rounding out the content of her life, not an enforced interim state to be suffered through until the time she would successfully marry or otherwise better organise her life. She had extraordinary will power that made brutality retreat and be controlled, because she was a free and independent spirit. No one had succeeded in bending her to their will – neither her husband Aleksandrs nor the Cheka goons. Only her own body betrayed her, but even then she did not submit easily. With immeasurable patience she suffered being bedridden for years on end, during which with great persistence she exercised her stiff joints, firmly believing that she would succeed in walking. Again! Until the next bone break put a stop to what she had achieved. Even in the hospital, where grandmother had to return again and again, she knew how to gain the empathy and good-will of all with her witty conversation and inexhaustible ability to suffer great pain.

My grandmother maintained an extensive correspondence with friends from her youth and Siberia, as well as relatives and people she had met in the hospital. Her letters were an example of perfected writing skill that in our modern age of hurried communication makes us realise more acutely that an essential form of human contact is now history and will never again return. Once in a letter from Siberia Milda had described how an intemperate and voracious calf had dragged my grandmother's dress from the anteroom of the sauna and started to munch on it. My grandmother, dressed as the biblical Eve, had hurried after the malicious beast to retrieve her clothing. In this fashion they had kicked up their heels across the snowy field – an angered, naked woman and a petrified calf, until the chewed and slobbered on dress had finally been taken away from the beast. The story had so inspired her friend that in the next letter she sent illustrations of the incident! Not trusting her fragile legs, for the last ten years of her life my grandmother was literally forced to become a prisoner in her flat, but even that did not stop her from living her life to the fullest and to be intensely interested in world events. With what fervour she followed sports events – her cheeks flushed, she shouted encouragement to her beloved basketball team. With the self-righteous insensitivity of youth, I often was unjust to her. I was not able to imagine how a free spirit imprisoned in a frail body could feel. How much she had to suffer!

After being released from hospital, Milda was no longer capable of doing the hard kolkhoz work. She and Aivars now had to survive exclusively on Aivars' earnings, which were just sufficient enough for them not to be subjected to the same helpless starvation as they had experienced the previous year. Grandmother helplessly lay in an old, rusted "Warsaw bed" – as metal beds with cone-shaped caps at all four corners were called in Russia. She smoked heavily, so that blue smoke billowed from the bed. Andrejs Upīts' thick novel *Green Land* that had been somehow snatched along from Latvia was the only source of paper for rolling up the so called "goat's leg" and had now been almost all used for her smokes. Usually the cat Briska sat on one of the poles of the headboard, while at the foot of the bed perched the chicken Cipa that had been saved from freezing. In recounting what she remembered, my grandmother called this scene the "witch's bed." The name was so conducive to imagination, that in my childhood I had to immediately think of fairytales, where exactly the same things happened – smoke billowed, evil old hags bewitched people and turned them into beasts. The only difference was that my grandmother was not evil. She was the incarnation of love and always saved me from my parents upset about some mischief I had managed to get into.

During the second summer of deportation, hearts did not ache as much from homesickness. Aivars' work in the forest, the ploughing, sowing and mowing, was done more easily, because now he was accustomed to it. He had also planted a couple of pails of potatoes so that at the minimum they would not have to be bought the coming winter. At the beginning of June he was sent to Inkino, the nearest mooring place for the big boats, where he had to load grain onto the smallest of the barges. Returning from Inkino was difficult, because they had to row against the current to go upstream on River Korshan. "We sat two men per oar. Altogether twelve men and a steersman. It looked like an ancient galley was sailing with slaves at its oars. We moved slowly, because the river had many twists and turns and in places was very swift. Sometimes we had to go ashore and pull the boat by a rope. We waded through deep, freezing spring water. Thus we travelled for three or four days."[222] How similar the fate of my parents – both, only each in their own time, had starved, worked beyond their strength in the fields and the forest and pulled large barges! There, in Inkino, while loading the bags of grain, my father had so strained his leg, which had been wounded during the war, that the bone deformation process had begun again. This could have been averted, but Aivars could not evade doing hard work and lifting heavy weights – such "laziness" was incomprehensible in Siberia. Thus from excessive stress his leg became shorter and for many years afterward hurt terribly.

Initially, the kolkhoz chairman viewed the deported Latvians with disdain, because, according to him, they were ignorant and lazy oafs, but, even emaciated, the Latvians quickly mastered farm work and became proficient labourers. That softened the chairman's heart, and afterward he got along well with his charges and, given the poverty of the kolkhoz, was understanding and responsive as much as he could. He felt sorry for Aivars, whose aching leg no longer allowed him to be any kind of a worker. Therefore after the fields had been sown and the completed work properly celebrated, the chairman persuaded the commandant to allow the young man to come along with him to the departmental centre of Kolpashevo. At the same time they planned to go and see a doctor. The trip was a great adventure for Aivars, because for more than a year he had not been in a city. Regardless of how poor Kolpashevo looked, it still was the capital city of a department as large as Latvia. All the institutions of the department, the schools, hospitals, the airport and the departmental manufacturing concerns were located there. The surprising thing was that all the buildings were made of wood. Only the general store "White" was built from bricks. The taller buildings were two stories high, also made from logs. The window frames of some of the older buildings stood out because of their lovely wooden carvings. The houses sat on round poles that were dug into the earth. The poles were covered by wooden boxes filled with earth or sawdust."[223] My father no longer recalls if the visit to the doctor helped any, but this trip was fateful in another fashion – it changed his and grandmother's life.

Some eight or ten kilometres from Kolpashevo was the village of Togur, where the Sokhta deportees Rasma and Kārlis Melbārzdis had been allowed to move. Aivars so much wished to visit his friends that he decided to risk it and headed out without a permit from the commandant's office. Would the commandant, after all, be roaming about on Sunday? – he hoped that he would get there without being caught. In observing and talking about life in Togur, my father understood that food was more substantial and the working conditions better for a worker there than in the kolkhoz. At the time he humbly wished: "… it would be good, to move and work here. Perhaps it would be possible to earn even 60 roubles a month; then it would be possible to buy a real loaf of bread and perhaps even a little bit of oil to enrich the meal."[224] It just happened that on his return Aivars ran into the Togur commandant at the bus stop, who immediately saw him as a person who did not belong in his supervised territory. "*Kto takoy? Pokazat bumagi!*"[225] My father was detained and taken to the Kolpashevo Militia Division, where he was thoroughly questioned. It was good that Aivars had learned to talk Russian to such a degree that he could coherently explain how he had managed to be in Togur, about his aching leg and sick mother in the kolkhoz. Having reached the end of his story, driven by despair, Aivars gathered courage and begged for a permit to transfer to Togur. The Commandant yelled angrily: What was he thinking of! After violating the settlement regimen how could he voice such a request! In reality he merited punishment and should be sitting in prison. Each sentence was followed by a string of invectives. Having yelled his fill, the man calmed down and dryly concluded that Aivars should come back in a couple of days. With much trepidation Aivars waited for the arranged meeting, for he was not convinced of a happy ending. He already imagined himself in a prison camp. But a miracle had happened: the commandant gave Aivars and Milda permission to move to Togur. Perhaps the radio that stood in his office had made the major's heart more compassionate. Aivars had told him that the radio was manufactured in a factory in which he had worked prior to being deported and in the fourth year of whose technical college he had been studying. "*Khoroshoye radio,*"[226] the mayor had grumbled and had looked, it seemed, more carefully at my father. Perhaps with the word "*khoroshoye*" he was also referring to Aivars and even to the Latvians as a group, who, though they were fascists, never caused him any concern, worked well and were peace loving.

Thus, at the end of summer 1950, Milda and Aivars were fortunate enough to pull themselves out of Sokhta swamps and taiga and move to Togur. My father started to work in local sawmill. They were assigned a small room with a stove in the new workers' barracks. The same room where after a year Aivars' newly wedded wife Ligita Dreifelde would enter, to be joined after another year by their daughter Sandra.

"My mother will wash my hair in rainwater"

I am together with my mother and father on Brīvības laukums – the Freedom Square in Tukums. For many years now there has been water fountain in the square replacing Lenin's sculpture that vanished. The square used to be called the Red Square during the Soviet period, but now it has regained its earlier name. I ask someone to take a photograph of the three of us. All around the square are stores that, in the hope of returning prosperity in Latvia, have sparkling windows offering goods that ten years ago seemed totally unattainable. In place of what used to be the Tukums Consumer Cooperative, where my mother worked after returning to Latvia in 1948, now stands a toy store. Only the militia building is where it used to be, but now it has been converted to the police precinct. Everything has changed to the point of being non-recognisable from that time long ago on December 7, 1949, when Ligita Dreifelde's life was again severed. I listen to my mama recounting what she remembers, and I physically feel the stress she had to live through after she found out that one of the freed Siberia deportees had been arrested again. This arrest was followed by another, and with each new arrest Ligita knew that her turn was near at hand. The door of the militia building was clearly visible from the second story window where my mother worked. Each time the door opened, Ligita lifted her head and examined the person coming out, sighing with relief or freezing in fear if it was a militiaman crossing the square in the direction of the Consumer Association. This continued for days and weeks, hope that perhaps the misfortune would pass her by alternating with despair about the inevitable. The stress was unbearable, and there was no escape anywhere, because the freed deportees were found no matter where they were. Neither a change in residence nor assuming the name of a husband at marriage helped. Nonetheless, my mother did not see "her militiaman" coming. She had gone to the market to shop. When she returned, he was sitting in her office at her desk waiting for her.

Ligita was led across the street to the militia precinct and locked in a cell. On the same day the first interrogation took place. Junior militia lieutenant Pumpe accused her of illegally leaving her place of settlement. It was useless to defend oneself and explain that she had had a permit to leave the Tomsk region, which, together with other documents, had been stolen in the train. A fragment from the interrogation protocol follows:

> Answer: On August 29, 1949, I lost my passport and other documents in the train.
> Question: Where is your permit to leave the Tomsk region?
> Answer: I lost it together with the other documents. I did explain that I had shown it at the passport office of the Tukums District Interior Division, and I received a passport on April 26, 1949.
> Question: How can you prove your testimony?
> Answer: I can't. Please take into account that I have received a passport and to get it I had to show my permit to leave the Tomsk region.[227]

As can be seen from the protocol, the junior lieutenant paid no attention to what was said by the woman being interrogated. He must have known that without a permit to leave, Ligita Dreifelde would not have been issued a passport, and that without a passport she would not have been registered in Tukums, nor would she have been able to get employment. Moreover, it would have been an easy matter to check, because the passport office was located in the same militia precinct. Most certainly copies of all the submitted documents, including the release document, were stored in the archive.

But Pumpe was not interested in doing a search because absence of documents was a wonderful excuse to fill in papers "correctly," as well as a justification for the detention.[228] He had completed his assignment and anything beyond that did not interest him, as it did not interest all the other "Pumpes" in Latvia and throughout the Soviet Union. After a few days Ligita, under guard of a militiaman, was taken to her home, where she was ordered to quickly get together necessary items for the trip. Then she was transferred to the Transit Prison near the Brasa railway station in Rīga.

For the moment, it is not clear why in 1948 a small segment of the deported people, primarily the young, were allowed to return to Latvia. Perhaps it happened in compliance with some unknown USSR Ministry of the Interior or some other agency's top-secret decision. Not to be ruled out is the possibility that an internal department instruction or verbal order from Moscow had been received by the surveillance system authorities of Tomsk and some other forced settlement regions, which was then disseminated throughout the surveillance agencies and, like all the orders of a totalitarian system, diligently executed. It is possible that the young people were freed because they had been under age at the time of deportation and in the chaos of war an order had not been received that after attaining sixteen years of age they should be included in the surveillance list. Hence, not knowing what to do with the "unlisted," the regional or district officials authorised by the Ministry of Interior had issued leave permits from the Tomsk region. One is led to think so because of Major-General Eglītis' and Prosecutor Mishutin's stated opinion that "the Kolpashevo City Internal Division permit issued to Ligita Dreifelde, daughter of Jānis, was issued illegally."[229] Just as likely the opinion could have been a falsification, done to comply with the USSR State Security Ministry's new requirements. Until 1948, all the "specially settled" persons were carried on the list of the First Special Division of the Ministry of the Interior. Afterward they were taken over by the

USSR State Security Ministry, which started a re-registration of the specially settled deportees in 1949. In the process, great "irregularities" were discovered: deaths had not been registered, young people who had come of age had not been listed, people who had escaped had not been located and some, for no stated reason, had been freed. The dead were "written off," while a search was begun for the missing, among them those who had attained sixteen years of age. Initially a local search was announced, followed by an announcement of an All Union search.

Ligita continued to live without care in Tukums, not being aware that on the 10th May 1949 an All Union search for her had been announced. Due to the slow and grinding operation of the Soviet bureaucratic machine, my mother was fortunate enough to spend the loveliest summer of her young life in Latvia: strolling along the seaside, dancing, wearing lovely dresses and shoes, visiting relatives, meeting with friends and even falling in love and getting engaged. She was "found" on October 8, when Lieutenant-Colonel Gailis, the person in authority at the Tukums District Militia Division, had responded positively to a Tomsk enquiry requesting the location of Ligita Dreifelde.[230] On October 25 a letter arrived from the USSR Ministry of Interior, in which it was specified that "on attaining sixteen years of age, the children of the settled people have to be registered in the list of administratively settled persons to ensure their surveillance," with the request: "In compliance with the above announcement, you are asked to transport Ligita Dreifelde, born 1926, daughter of Jānis, whom you have located, to her previous place of settlement in the Kolpashevo department of the Tomsk region, where her mother, the settled deportee Ilze Emilija Dreifelde, daughter of Indriķis is stationed."[231]

When I started to work on my book, I went through our meagre family archive together with my parents. There we found unique documents and letters that had been forgotten with the passage of time. Among these, also a small greenish coloured notebook – my mother's diary that was written during the second journey to Siberia. Mamma immediately took it, as if not wanting to show it to anyone. I understood her because I too would find it difficult to allow even people closest to me to look into my most intimate emotional experiences. I did not try to intrude on my mother's privacy with tactless curiosity, even though I knew that the content of this document was needed for my book. A few days later, one evening, my mother read the diary to my father and me. It was an emotional experience the like of which will never be repeated for me – to listen to the words coming from a distant past in my mother's voice that now and then choked up or drowned in tears and sometimes sparkled with satisfaction or even laughter. In some places she added some detail revived in her memory by the text or made a striking comment. I have included this reading in my book, as valuable in its own right, something of the past that continues to live today. After lengthy hesitation, my mother agreed to the inclusion of the diary fragments in my book. Convinced by me, she overcame her shyness understanding that the diary is a document that no longer belongs just to her but to history, because it provides an authentic proof of the evil the Soviet regime inflicted on innocent people.

I have read the diary again and again, each time finding new nuances, intimations and facts that I find deeply disturbing and searing because of the repeated cruelty that my mother had to suffer. Like a criminal she was transferred from prison to prison. Humiliated and without any rights, she spent almost five months in prison, during which time her initial despair was gradually replaced by total apathy, the only means of self-protection at her disposal against new emotional traumas inflicted in the abnormal criminal world she had been thrown into. The document consists of a few yellowed pages covered with writing in pencil, in which her emotional experiences have been saved: her humiliation, physical fear, depression, hope, stubbornness, initiative and helplessness. No one will ever be able to erase these and other traumas from my mother's as well as from the other deportee's conscious or subconscious mind. At present there has been virtually no research in Latvia into the consequences and influence of deportation on the continued lives of the deportees, nor what effect it has on the next generation that had not experienced deportation but whose life developed in direct contact with those who had to go the painful path to Siberia.[232] The deportation has certainly left its traces in me and in the psychological and value system orientation of my generation.

The diary is written as imaginary letters to Ligita's fiancé, which were never sent to him. Writing these letters was a substitute for contact with the world outside the prison, because she was forbidden to write or receive letters. The diary helped her to survive and hope, to feel like a full-fledged human being not just a defenceless prisoner.

January 19, 1950.

Today for the first time I write to you. I already wanted to write to you yesterday because my heart was so full. Last night I reread all your letters that I had brought with me. I feel like crying about my terrible fate. [...] Today I also received the package you sent. I am, of course, very happy about it, but I don't need anything, and I don't want you to send me anything here. In my imagination I saw you standing and waiting by the prison, yet you were unreachable. I sometimes dare to believe that you really will come to me in Kolpashevo. But only sometimes.

January 25, 1950.

I had climbed up to the window to look at what is happening outside the prison. Just at that moment a trolley bus passed by, jogging my memory again. Do you remember how in the summer I had time to spare before the train and how we, out of boredom, boarded a trolley bus to go for a ride and you said, let's not ride to the last stop because that's where the prison is. Now I again saw a trolley bus, perhaps the same one that we, being so carefree, boarded that time. As a result I stepped back from the window and lay down in my wooden cot to cry, to slowly cry out all the collected hurt. How terrible it is that I'm here! Sometimes I manage to be totally calm – that's when I make my mind go blank. But the frequent moments of thought have made me totally apathetic. I have no wish to walk outside – I don't even know why. Perhaps the prison walls deaden everyone, and now I won't have to wonder about people who have suffered all of this and who have been freed, why they are so cautious, always expecting new humiliation.

January 27, 1950.

I leave today. I don't know what lies ahead of me. I don't have to think because others are thinking in my place. That's better, because I'm not able to do anything on a sustained basis. Now we will be separated by such a great distance. Up to now we were only separated by prison walls and a few minutes ride in a trolley bus. Now we will be separated by great distance and prison walls until spring.

January 28, 1950

Yesterday evening all of us who had been called to be deported were transported to the railway station near the prison. I was going down this road for the first time but, of course, not the last. Our belongings were put on a sleigh, which we had to pull ourselves. Of course, I again felt terribly tormented by the moral humiliation. I wish I could become so deadened that I no longer hurt. Just now we drove by Velikie Luki. If you come to visit me this summer, you'll have to travel by here and then please remember that I also have looked at all of this, only through bars.

February 1, 1950.

Right now I'm in Kuybishev prison and I'm thinking about how unusual it is for a totally innocent person to sit in a prison among thieves and bandits. I want to tell you everything from the beginning. In Moscow we, that is I and another girl, Ilga, were put off the train and transferred to a different wagon, where we were seventeen people in one compartment. I think that you'll not be able to understand how seventeen people can be put in one compartment. [My mother explains to me: "It was an ordinary train compartment, equipped with three-story sleeping berths. The topmost berth was closed off so that five people could sleep in it. I cried nearly all the time."] I'm sure you can't imagine how it is to be thirsty but instead to have to lie in dreadful heat – one on top of each other. You can cry and think that you won't survive, but it's unbelievable how much a human being can bear.

When we were let out of our cage to go "on order" to take care of our bodily functions, I was unimaginably happy that I could get a jug of water, which I fell to and drank dry. It's impossible to describe how dreadful the feeling is when you're so thirsty. [My mother interrupts her reading and says: "I remember that water. It was in a pail that stood in the toilet. It was infinitely repulsive. Probably obtained from some ditch. A few pieces of ice floated in the greenish-grey water, but I was so terribly thirsty and I drank the water."]

The second most dreadful thing is that you have to lie there all the time in horror and fear that someone will shortly start to scream all sorts of obscenities! [Again, an explanation: "Yes, we were being transported together with all sorts of female criminals who didn't even know how to talk normally. Only curse. In the next compartment there were German women. They talked in German. They, the same as we, weren't criminals."] In the first few days I wanted to die, because it seemed that I wouldn't be able to survive till the end. But it's possible to adapt to all conditions. In the following days I could already respond sharply to ironic questions from the guards. One day I was called out from the compartment and ordered to wash the floor, and the guard felt very disappointed that I, instead of an unhappy face, showed a happy and smiling face. When he still wanted to bait me and asked how I liked to wash floors, I answered smiling that I secretly had always wanted to do so, because washing floors was my favourite work. [Remembering their dialogue, my mother laughs with the satisfaction of a winner: "He asks me: *Naverno hata i korova u tebya byla?* What a standard for riches! No, I snap back: *Pianino bylo.*[234] He surely did not know what that was. The guard tried in all kinds of ways to pick on me. Once he decided to check my small suitcase to see if there was anything illegal hidden in it. What could have been in it after all – some clothing and other trivia."]

[…] People have to become abnormal travelling in such conditions. I was horribly unhappy that I had so many belongings with me, because I could not carry them, but I still had to carry them from the train to the lorry, which took an eternity; on the way, I was near fainting when one of the militiamen took my burdensome belongings and gave them to some men to carry. [My mother sighs: "He probably saw that I was staggering from lack of strength. A German had to carry the suitcase. He had brought an accordion with him. He had bound his hands with rags so they would not freeze, because otherwise he wouldn't have been able to play. Later, in the lorry I had to sit on his lap, because there wasn't even place to stand.] […] I didn't want to faint, because seeing how weak I was, would have given them satisfaction. In the lorry we again had to sit crowded one on top of each other. Thus we were transported to the prison, and now, as if in a dream, I remember the prison in Rīga that, compared to this, is like a castle, and, of course, the society in Rīga and the one here, which never hears anything but the most vulgar expletives. You can't even imagine how it is. ["How dreadful," my mother shivered momentarily in disgust. "In Rīga the deportees shared a cell. All of them were decent people. There we were among thieves and bandits."]

February 3, 1950.

I'm in total despair, because to be in the midst of such people, who feel at home here, who only know how to swear, steal etc. – is simply impossible. I can't write a letter to you because the minute that this gang will see that I have paper they'll surround me and pull me in all directions. I now feel as if I'll go insane if something doesn't happen. It's only to be expected that everything will be stolen, that Ilga and I will be killed etc! We never leave the spot we've taken without one of us left to guard it. Even though all the gang members are just waiting for the moment when no one will be near my belongings to pilfer them. But they won't wait too long before they will steal them while we're right there. I went to the prison administrator and begged him to transfer us to the deportee cell. He promised he would do it. So, if I survive till they put me into another cell perhaps then I'll stay alive. It's impossible to describe how I feel right now. [...] That such people exist in this world as the ones in my cell I never could have imagined, and if I'd been told about them I would not have been able to comprehend it. I live in constant fear and emotional stress.

February 4, 1950.

I'm still here, and there's not even the least of hope that we'll soon leave. Ilga and I have to do everything with the greatest of secrecy, because the minute that someone sees us eating they all surround us. [...] Right now Kolpashevo and everything associated with it seems to me like a fairy tale; all of it seems so incredibly far, that I can't imagine I'll ever get there.

February 5, 1950.

It's Sunday today and the eighth day since I've left Rīga. If I had still been in Rīga, today was the day you promised to come and visit me. Again in my thoughts I imagine that the trolley bus is passing by the prison in Rīga and that you are on it. Now the only satisfaction in my trivial life is the hoped for meeting with you in Kolpashevo, a thought that perhaps always will remain only a fantasy, because it's possible that soon you'll have forgotten me.

February 7, 1950

Yesterday evening I glimpsed the Kuybishev houses through the prison window. Since the prison is surrounded on four sides by mountains, it's very easy to see the houses on the mountain. They are beautiful three and four story brick buildings, where happy people must live. [My mother's look becomes dreamy: "In comparison to us they surely were happy. I didn't see any people, just lights shining like small stars. I kept thinking: people are eating supper, living normal lives. How normally could people have lived in the Russia of that time, but compared to us that was a different life."

February 22, 1950.

[...] Yesterday was such a day that I'm not even able to describe it. In my cell there are people exactly the same as me and only seven of the gang of thieves. [My mother explains: "All the people like me were put in one cell. I can't remember how many of us there were, but we were many because there wasn't enough room for sleeping. We also were afraid to go near the thieving women, who were sleeping in the middle of the cell. We settled by the wall on the floor."] Behind the wall some 170 "boychiks," 12–18 years of age, had been put. They started to wreck the wall in the morning, and some of them were put into the isolation cell. That incited them so much that they broke down the door, and all the guards took off. Thus we were left to fate. [My mother relives the shock of that day: "They tore down the wall. Having broken out pieces of the wooden bunks, they pounded at the wall so long that finally it collapsed. It was fortunate that it did not fall on anyone. But it did flatten the *parasha* [the toilet bucket]. The intruders were primarily young boys dressed in totally unsuitable clothing too large for them. The older ladies, Russian actresses, advised us, the younger ones, to smear our faces and to bind our heads in rags. Which we did."] Finally a guard unlocked the door and told us to leave quickly. All of us were still sleeping so you can imagine what sort of panic developed. My hands were trembling, and I could do nothing. Of course, half of us ran outside and the other half stayed, and so the boychiks, armed with wooden sticks broken off from their bunks, were able to surprise us! They didn't touch us, because it was enough for them to rape the seven thieving women, but I still was scared. We finally were able to escape safe and sound. ["We slept on the upper bunk. When the break-in happened, all of us hid in the neighbouring cell. The thieving women were abused so thoroughly that they couldn't even walk."]

February 26, 1950.

I'm still in here. Yesterday, early in the morning, I saw you in a dream. I hadn't dreamt of you for a long time – probably you never think of me any more. You so very lovingly bent over me and said: "Liguci, I think it would be better if the two of us lived in the country." I kept silent, thinking about how that would be, and having arrived at the conclusion that I would be very satisfied, I happily said: "Yes, I also think so." [...]

March 8, 1950.

Today is my second day in Novosibirsk. I travelled for five days. This time the trip was not so horrendous, because we were only ten people in a compartment. Of course, also this time I could not do without tears, even though I have hardened myself to such a degree that I don't know how to cry any more. [Mama falls silent: "Every time I was put on a transport, I had to cry a lot. Among the people who were being transported there was a Russian actress. She tried to console me, patting my head: everything will be all right, everything will be all right ... What exactly could be all right!"] If someone offends me, I reply so sharply that they fall silent. I arrived in Novosibirsk around six in the evening. It was so painful to see the beautiful station through bars, the station from which I departed less than two years ago full of hope and happiness with the conviction that I would never return. [My mother is crying.] Of course, I haven't lost hope even now, that this station will someday see me happy once again ... Now I'll be in prison and I so terribly miss my mama. ["My mama had by then already been dead for more than a month," my mother sobs.] I'm only 600 kilometres away from her. In Kuybishev I didn't find it so hard, because I had accepted the fact that my mama was far away. Here it is different. Each day I wait to be called to go to Tomsk, and from there I don't know how I will get farther, because the boat only starts sailing the middle of April. I so want to write a letter to my mama; I don't want to tell her that I'm here, but I would like to write an entire page full with the word "mama." It's the 8th of March today.[235] Last year my workplace organised a party – this year only memories remain – that's also good! Perhaps everything that I hope for will change finally for me like this – into memories.

The diary stops here. After three months of forced confinement in the company of bandits and thieves, my mother had become apathetic. She no longer wrote in her diary, because after all she had experienced, Latvia and everything that was associated with it, including her fiancé, seemed like an unattainable dream that no longer had any relevance to her life at the moment. Only the thought that she soon would be with her mother gave Ligita the strength to survive. It was very hard in the Novosibirsk prison, but it was even harder in the Tomsk prison, when only some three hundred kilometres separated Ligita from her mother. Ligita's world increasingly was limited to the prison cell, in which two incompatible societies – the civilised, cultured and the criminal one – now lived side by side. Several times in moments of sadness Ligita had written in Russian in her notebook some of the poem lines she had heard in the cell. How much the prison environment had traumatised my mother, can be sensed from the noted down banal Russian prisoner's rhyme:

> Now that I'm in prison
> everyone sits and so do I,
> because without a prison
> you're neither here nor there.
>
> Interrogation comes first
> then camps and camps forever.

These verses are on the same page as Alexander Pushkin's wonderful love poem:

> I loved you: I wonder if in my heart
> years from now this love shall burn …

At the end of April, the ice had finally left River Ob and the navigation season began. The transported persons were put on a boat to be taken to their places of settlement or prison. For the first time since her arrest on December 7, an armed guard no longer was watching her. She and the other deportees could walk on the deck of the boat, stand at the railing or sit down in a free place of her choice. Ligita gazed into the water and without thinking observed the passing villages. Each sailed kilometre drew her nearer to her mother. She so wanted to wash herself because it was a week since she had been in the bathhouse in the prison, but she consoled herself with a wonderful image: her mother had collected rainwater and was washing her hair. "My mother will wash my hair in rainwater, my mother will wash my hair in rainwater ...," Ligita sang to herself. Only one day separated her from Emilija and shelter.

The boat arrived in Kolpashevo in the afternoon. Ligita was ordered to debark. For a while she stood confused on the pier, waiting for the convoy to take her farther. It did not arrive! Then my mother braved walking back and forth in order to check if anyone would scream "*Na mesto!*"[236] No one did. She finally could walk along a street unguarded. Of course, the first trip was to the Kolpashevo Commandant's Office to register that she had arrived at her place of forced settlement. Having examined the papers and written something in his record book, the Commandant announced as if it were a self-explanatory thing that Ligita Dreifelde had to live in Kolpashevo. "Why Kolpashevo?" she exclaimed, "I want to go to my mother in Togur." There was a moment of silence. Then the Commandant, as if feeling embarrassed, laughed and said: "Don't you know that your mother has died?" Ligita did not understand. The Commandant repeated it again, now in an impatient tone: "Your mother Emilija Dreifelde died on the 5th of February."

Ligita staggered out into the street. Her mama was no more. She had been left totally alone.

After several months, during the last half of summer, Ligita went again for her regular visit to the graveyard. She visited there frequently. As was her custom on Sundays, she had put on her best dress and was carrying a bouquet of flowers she had picked at the edge of the woods to put on her mother's grave. A group of Latvian young people she knew were heading toward her, and Ligita noticed that among them was someone new. It was Aivars Kalnietis, who had recently moved to Togur with his mother. Aivars wished to somehow attract the beautiful girl's attention, because he had heard of her tragic fate from friends. He innocently joked: "Is the lady with the flowers going to a rendezvous?" Ligita snapped back: "No, to my mother's grave." She turned and left. That is how my parents met on a Togur street

"We won't give birth to any more slaves"

The village of Togur was located on a steep cliff above the Ob. Some thousand people lived there, approximately half of whom worked at the sawmill. The governing body was the Village Soviet, which was located in the same building as the militia. The agency of greatest importance for the deportees was the Commandant's Office, which they were forced to visit more than they liked: twice a month they had to register there. Moreover, every time they had to go to nearest city Kolpashevo or somewhere else they had to get written

Togur in spring mud. Ligita and Sandra 1956.

permission from the Commandant's Office to leave their place of settlement. The local families that had settled in the village in earlier times lived in detached log houses with windows decorated with beautiful wood carvings, while the newly arrived people, including the deportees, were crowded into barracks belonging to the sawmill. In a square in the centre of the village a radio transmitter and loudspeakers had been installed, from which the inhabitants were frequently reminded how fortunate they were to live under the leadership of

Great Stalin, and in his honour joyful Soviet songs were broadcast continuously. From the square, star-fashion, radiated streets, a name they quite did not deserve, because in the fall and spring the driveable portion became riddled with a series of mud ruts, in which now and then a load of saw dust was dumped. This sawdust was available from the sawmill in large quantities because, having collected over the years, it had formed a layer several metres thick. Once the collected sawdust caught fire, and for several weeks people tried unsuccessfully to extinguish it. It was very much the same as with peat bogs: getting rid of the flames at the surface was easy, but the fire turned into slow internal smouldering, burning away large holes in the layers of sawdust that subsequently collapsed, dragging a few of the fire fighters into its depths as if into a bottomless abyss. The main street of Togur left an almost orderly impression, because along its side stretched a sidewalk made of wooden boards. In the spring, when the snow started to melt, all the streets turned into water arteries, navigable only with the help of planks balanced on wooden blocks.

In contrast to the kolkhoz villages, barracks belonging to the sawmill, as well as the village centre, had electricity, which in the dark, cold winter evenings made life more bearable. It was possible then to read or to listen to the radio, whose reception Aivars had managed to improve. Every time Latvia or Rīga was mentioned in a Moscow radio broadcast, or a Latvian melody sounded, my parents and Milda listened, feeling very moved, wishing that this indirect contact with their native land would never end. Knowing full well that it was not possible to pick up Rīga, sometimes in moments of sadness Aivars twisted the radio knob back and forth, hoping that a miracle would occur and through the static, the distant: "Radio Rīga speaking." would be heard.

The second item of great importance, surrounded by an aura of wishful thinking and hope, was the post office, where packages and letters arrived from Latvia, the one and only real source of reliable news. After the ration card system was abolished, goods not previously seen started to appear in stores: footwear, clothing, metal dishes, and later, even some bolts of fabric.[237] The few who had some money in the 1950s could even order goods by mail, selecting them from the "*Posiltorg*" catalogue.[238] By this means, my mother obtained a sewing machine that still sews today. The local store also carried "bricks" of rye bread, somewhat tart in taste, and cookies covered with a sweet sugar glaze called *pryaniki* baked at the local bakery. The latter were the greatest delicacy of my childhood.

The village hospital was my grandmother's most wished and hoped for place. It had an operating theatre and a maternity ward, several doctors, paramedics and nurses. Milda very much wanted to work as a nurse, but there were no vacant positions, and even if there had been, priority in hiring would have been given to local people, not the deportees. Later, when nurses was sent for qualification upgrading courses to the department centre, Milda was fortunate enough to get one or two months work in the hospital a few times. During this working period my grandmother managed to earn the total confidence of the doctors and the friendship of the other nurses.

The socially most prominent place in Togur was the Sawmill Club. For October Revolution and May Day celebrations festive meetings took place there and the inhabitants were reminded of the untiring concern that Stalin and the Communist Party he led had for their well-being. On holidays, cultural events and young people's dances were scheduled in the club, with the customary flirting in local style and drinking from a bootlegged bottle of home brew or moonshine vodka. The young Latvians rarely went to the dances but organised their own gatherings in their homes. There were regular showings of Soviet films at the club, because the Communist Party considered movies an ideal mass-oriented brainwashing device and made certain that travel films would be accessible even in the farthest corners of the Soviet Union. Each showing was preceded by a newsreel showing political news that usually were at least six months old. This was followed by the much-awaited film, a Soviet version of the "Hollywood dream": wonderfully dressed, beautifully coifed kolkhoz and working women with manicured fingernails, whose exemplary achievements opened a door to Moscow, appreciation and a better life.

Ligita, Aivars and Milda 1952.

Ligita and Aivars were married in Togur in May 1951. The bride wore a fine wool crepe suit sewn earlier in Latvia. The bridegroom was dressed more modestly – in the pants and zippered windbreaker he had traded on the black market in Latvia. The wedding feast they thought was splendid enough for kings: fried potatoes followed by cream-of-wheat porridge with sugar. Instead of wedding champagne they drank beer and egg punch. There were no guests, because the wedding day had been kept secret from the local Latvian community. In the evening, as it got dark, Aivars and Ligita went to fetch the bride's meagre dowry: two sheets, a blanket, two stools, a teapot and a kettle. On their wedding night the bridegroom's mother slept at the foot of the newlyweds' bed. Milda would have happily left the young people alone, but she had no place to go.

Remembering their wedding ceremony is always cause for great merriment for my parents. When the two of them had shyly expressed their request to marry to the Village Soviet secretary, she asked them to wait because she first needed to register some old woman's goat in a domestic animal register. Having done that, she turned her attention to the marriage of the Latvians. The secretary was somewhat ruffled, because her supervisor had gone away leaving the seal locked up, and she was not experienced enough yet to know how an important document, such as a marriage certificate, should be written up. At the least, she did understand that a marriage should not be registered in the same place as a goat, and she did invite the young people into the supervisor's office. Even though the marriage of Ligita Dreifelde and Aivars Kalnietis was written into a book, they were not issued a certificate that confirmed this fact. The pompous words " *Ot imeni Soyuza Sovetskikh Socialisticheskikh Respublik ya vas obyavlyayu muzhom i zhenoy* ..."[239] were forgotten, as was the traditional kiss. When my parents finally rushed out into the street, they collapsed in a fit of laughter that continued right up to their small room in the barracks, where Milda was waiting for them in a solemn mood. After the first few words of the story about the goat and the seal, she joined in their laughter, adding her own witty comments. In accordance with the law, all newlyweds in the Soviet Union had the right to take three days of vacation, but Aivars was not granted these, thus Ligita spent their wedding vacation alone.

After the first unsuccessful meeting with Ligita in the summer, Aivars had approached her again in the fall at a Latvian house party. From that time onward they started to go together, and the local

Latvian community followed the development of their love story with baited breath. Ligita's and Aivars' wooing brought romantic intrigue into the monotonous lives in Togur, and for a while their relationship dominated conversations. Girlfriends discussed the real or imagined details of the love story; they were enjoyed like desert at family mealtimes and Latvian Sunday gatherings. News of what was happening in Togur also reached Kolpashevo, where the Latvians did their part in sifting the good and bad character traits of Aivars and Ligita. The person who suffered the most from this collective creative process was my grandmother, to whom women friends brought the most conflicting news, both praise and condemnation for her son's fiancée. Finally Milda decided to have a talk with her son in order to save what was still salvageable or to help what could still be helped. From her son's passionate words Milda understood that Aivars was experiencing the first deep feelings of his life, and thus, having repressed a worried sigh about the compatibility of characters and her son's youth, my grandmother readied herself to get to know Ligita and to accept her.

Six months passed from the first time my parents saw each other and their wedding, a period that was an intensely romantic time spent in great spiritual elation by both of them. They were as if intoxicated seeing their future in each other, trying to push out of their consciousness the insurmountability and inescapability of the dreadful words "deported for life." Love made Aivars and Ligita free, even though they were deprived of any other freedom. Perhaps because of this, they almost never mentioned Siberia in their courtship revelations to each other, but again and again returned to the happiest period of their lives, before THAT had happened. During this orgy of recalled bright moments, Ligita's disjointed stories about starvation, hard work and her mother's death crept in now and then like a bleak dissonance. On hearing this, Aivars understood that Milda's and his own calamity, which they had had such a tough time surviving, had been relatively easy when compared to the intolerable torment suffered by Ligita and the others who had been deported in 1941. At the time my father was much too young to be able to comprehend how this inhuman suffering had psychologically traumatised Ligita and what an indelible impression it had left on her personality and character. He could not take his eyes off his sparkling, wilful, appealing, capricious and joyful Ligita, nor stop listening to her, and kept thinking of how fortune had smiled on him endowing him with this wondrous being. Aivars was not aware, nor could he be aware, how really fragile and in need of support my mother would be for the rest of her life. Ligita would live the life of an adult, but she would never attain the strength and integrity of a mature person's character. These qualities had been left behind in Siberia.

In looking back, it seems to me that all the negative circumstances had compounded in my parents life, so that the adaptation and adjustment period in their first year of marriage was made harder, almost impossible. The three of them, the newlyweds and Milda, lived in one tiny room in the barracks, where there was space for nothing else besides the two beds and the table. Aivars and Ligita had almost no time on their own, because Milda could not find work. How often could she go out to visit? So she was always right there – during the day sitting on the bed or at the table, at night, sleeping in the nearby bed. Moreover, their work schedules did not allow them to be together. Aivars had to work three shifts; Ligita worked two. When one was leaving for the factory, the other was coming back. They both did physically hard, exhausting work at the sawmill. My mother suffered especially. After lifting heavy wooden boards for ten hours, her face had a greenish hue and she could hardly stay on her feet at the end of her shift. When she got to their room at the barracks, her only wish was that someone would take pity and comfort her like Emilija had done. But no one, not even the kind-hearted and easy-going Milda was able to do so, and Ligita's need for unquestioning love remained unfulfilled. On occasion it seemed to her that even Aivars was not caring enough, which my mother never hesitated to let him know. Perhaps subconsciously she was jealous of Milda: the fact that Aivars had a mother and she did not.

In turn, Aivars was tormented by inner insecurity. Though he was married, he did not feel like a real husband or the head of a family. Secretly he was very proud that he had become a married man, but he was too young to be able to respond unabashedly to the traditional suggestive jokes that were directed at him at work after the wedding. Married relationships in Togur very much differed from what they were in the Latvian society. The locals did not show any respect or love to their wives in social contexts. On the contrary, they tried to underline their "old lady's" insignificance in front of each other, which the wives did not object to because they knew very well that their "big mouth" would sing a different tune at home within four walls. While my parents were among Latvians, Aivars behaved as he should have if he were in Latvia. The minute they got into local contexts, a strange shyness took hold of my father, and he became taciturn and reserved in the presence of his wife. This offended Ligita and made her angry, because she did not understand why her husband was behaving so "stupidly" instead of showing the uncouth *muzhiks* what it meant to be a real man. During that time my parents quarrelled a lot, but they always made up and, with the sweetness of making up, they progressively grew closer to each other, until "me" was more and more often replaced by "we." Perhaps in other, more favourable circumstances, where they would have had more options, this solidifying of "we" would not have taken place. Aivars and Ligita would have remained each with their own truth, not seeking to find a compromise or understanding. But they were "settled for life," and this common fate strengthened the love and value of close people, because it was only the family that could provide strength to survive deportation and lack of rights.

Ligita wished fervently for a little daughter, because it seemed to her that she would thus finally have someone who would belong exclusively to her and for whom she would be the one and only and irreplaceable person. Perhaps her desire for a daughter had developed after Emilija's death. Aivars agreed that a little daughter would be better than a son, even though secretly he was not so convinced about this. The idea of a child, too, seemed like something abstract and distant, but if his wife so fervently wished for one, then let it be so. Finally the doctor confirmed that their hopes had been fulfilled and that at the end of December Ligita would be a mother. Her husband was at work, and she had to wait for several hours before she could tell him the great news. Like their first meeting, also this life-changing event reached Aivars on the main street of Togur – while one of them was going to, the other coming from work. On hearing the news, Aivars did not even manage to say something loving to his wife, but, totally stunned, continued to walk home. He felt he should feel joy and excitement, but it seemed as if in their place a heavy burden had descended on him. He was horrified by the thought that after less than a year he would have to assume responsibility for another human being. My father did not feel ready for this – everything was happening too fast.

In her dreams my mother had seen lovely images of a beautifully dressed little baby in a bright room. The child smiled and stretched its chubby little arms toward its mother. She imagined that her pregnancy would be a period of gentle feelings of well-being, when she, with a radiant countenance, could let her husband and mother-in-law care for her – a time of soft footsteps and loving words. The reality was totally different. She had to go to the sawmill each day and continue to lift the heavy wooden boards, because pregnancy was not enough of a reason to be excused from doing hard work. The family did try to spoil her, as much as was within their power, by buying delicacies and whatever would give her strength, but a heavy feeling of nausea took away her appetite, making Ligita disinterested in food. My mother was troubled by an increasing feebleness. Earlier, she had barely held out till the end of her shift, but after coming home and resting somewhat, she had recouped quickly. Now Ligita no longer felt that she could work her full shift and, arriving back home, collapsed on her bed into apathetic sleep. Several times she fainted at work until the local nurse took pity of her and recommended that the manager find easier work for Ligita.

Milda watched worriedly how her daughter-in-law's health deteriorated, growing progressively weaker, but she tried to console herself that after the first few months Ligita's organism would adjust and she would recoup. But the opposite happened: the weakness did not diminish, and in July Ligita's deteriorated state was so acute that she no longer could go out on her own. My mother's cheeks were flushed, and on occasion she burned with fever. The first time that Milda had an inkling that this might be tuberculosis she quickly suppressed the thought. That would be too unjust and undeserved but, again and again, she felt Ligita's forehead, took her temperature and measured her pulse. She knew this disease much too well, because it had also weakened her husband Aleksandrs. She did not say anything to her son about her suspicions. Finally Milda no longer could ignore the symptoms and understood that Ligita had to be taken to the hospital in Kolpashevo immediately. My mother was so weak that she could not sit up in the public bus; hence my father requested and got a horse and wagon from the factory. Having laid his wife in the wagon, depressed by dark thoughts, he headed for the hospital.

Fortunately it was not tuberculosis, just a neglected pleurisy that was successfully cured. In order to get well, the doctor prescribed a calorie-rich diet for Ligita: butter, meat and sugar that could already be bought in the Togur store in 1952. In order to put aside the necessary roubles for obtaining the much-needed products, Aivars and Milda again reverted to a diet of potatoes. In the beginning, as if fulfilling a heavy assignment, Ligita ate without enthusiasm or appetite, secretly wondering to herself how it could be that, because of her illness, she was totally indifferent to and even repulsed by the delicacies she had craved for so long. But her sense of taste slowly returned and, with it, her lost strength In the last months of her

Ligita after work.

pregnancy, my mother already felt so well that her body no longer troubled the dreams of the child, who now energetically kicked in her womb. She did not doubt for a moment that it would be a girl. What would she have done with a boy? She had already chosen a girl's name. Sandra. She had found it in Theodore Dreiser's novel *An American Tragedy*, one of the few foreign books published in translation in Latvia, which was passed from hand to hand among the local Latvian community. My mother read and reread it, and in her imagination she was propelled back into the world where women wore lovely dresses, drove in cars and lived a normal life. Sondra! That sounded so sublime, so unattainable! Aivars objected that this name seemed strange to him. Finally the two of them found a compromise: the cold, distanced "o" was changed to an "a" that made the name "Sandra" more Latvian. I like the name, because it seems to me that its rhythm and resoluteness suits my firm and determined character.

In 1952 seven years had passed since the end of the war. Even though, in the name of the victory of communism over imperialism, Stalin continued the terror against his people; even though already a second generation after the Bolshevik Revolution was enslaved in subhuman work and deprived of all hope to ever live in conditions suitable for human beings, nevertheless some improvements had reached even Togur. My parents no longer suffered starvation and were fed now. They were even paid for their work on a more regular basis. Aivars had begun to work as an electrician, which, at that time, was a responsible and relatively well-paid job. Concerned about Arnis and Matilde, who had been left in Latvia in miserable circumstances, my father was even able to put aside a couple of hundred roubles to send to them. The majority of the deportees were able to come to terms with the thought that they would still have to spend many years in this part of the world and tried to settle as best they could in these circumstances. People around them managed to obtain a goat or a pig, planted potatoes and cabbage, all of this to ensure survival in their meagre existence. But the dream of everyone was to get a house of their own, because the sawmill had started to assign building lots to its workers. Aivars, too, handed in a request for land to the factory. My parents realised that this was a singular opportunity for them to get away from the unbearable barracks and live surrounded by their own family without the smell and noise of their neighbours behind the wall. It was a hard decision for my father, because in the construction of his home he could rely only on the help of some of his friends. My parents did not have enough money to hire a builder.

Milda listened to Aivars' and Ligita's dreams and could only discreetly shake her head. Was her son overestimating his ability? What did he know about building a house? But Aivars was determined, and in the autumn before I was born the foundation for the house had been put down. My father had planned to reach the roof-building stage before the start of winter, but he had overestimated what he could do. The long day in the factory exhausted his energy, and the snows came sooner than expected. He had to stop building. Having regained her health, Ligita used to walk to the construction site and look over the work done to date. Four rows of logs, whose construction Ligita had followed happily, already protruded above the snow. After so many years of living in all kinds of desolate corners, finally she was going to have her own home. Compared to the crowded barracks the planned twenty-five square metres seemed like an enormous area. Everything had been thought out. There was a tiny room for her mother-in-law, a kitchen and an entry hall. In her imagination my mother already saw the building completed. In the room she would hang starched white gauze curtains and Milda's flowered Moldavian carpet on the wall. She would put the table by the window, while in the corner would be her

House built by Sandra's father in Togur.

baby's crib. The house being a tangible thing overshadowed memories of her ancestral home that had remained in Ligita's consciousness as something unattainable and unreal belonging to some earlier incarnation. She did not want to look back, because she was here where she had to live from now on.

My mother's great moment arrived shortly before midnight while she was by herself in the barracks. That week Aivars was working the night shift, and also Milda was not at home, because she had been hired to do a month of work at the hospital. By fateful coincidence, it was the last night my grandmother was on duty. Feeling the first sharp pains, my mother became scared. It seemed to her that it should not hurt so much and that something dreadful was happening. How much she wished for her mother at that moment! Emilija would have known how to help her. "Dear mama! Mama!" she cried out loudly. If only there were someone to help and console her, to tell her what to do. The pain intensified, and a sticky liquid started to flow down her legs. Seeing the latter, Ligita totally lost her head, because she thought it was blood and that soon, very soon she would die. She started to scream loudly, but it was totally useless, because there was no one to hear and no one to come to help her. Suddenly her scream broke; my mother fell silent, collapsed on the bed and for a while sat there hunched. There was no point in waiting, she had to summon her strength and get to the hospital herself. Somehow managing to get dressed, she stumbled there through the snow. She only had to walk some hundred metres, but they seemed to take an eternity. In the reception area, the nurse questioned her about why she had come, but after looking at Ligita, she understood and immediately led the crying woman to the maternity ward, got her dressed in a hospital gown and left her to be alone in the pre-delivery room. It was midnight.

The next morning, having returned from night duty and not finding her daughter-in-law, Milda, distressed, hurried back to work. She was almost convinced that she would be greeted there with the joyful news of the birth of a grandchild. But no – the birth was still in progress. My grandmother begged to be allowed into the maternity ward, which, for fear of infection, had been isolated. Already in the corridor she could hear her daughter-in-law's shrill screams. The doctor tried to calm down the distressed Milda Petrovna: everything would end well. But no matter how accustomed my grandmother was to the pain of others, she found Ligita's changed, wild voice to difficult to bear. She rushed out into the street, to meet her son coming from the sawmill. In an excited and incoherent voice Milda recounted to Aivars that all had begun at midnight, that they did not know when it would be over, and what a terrible time Ligita was having. The two of them literally ran back to the hospital. Hours passed, and still there was no change. In terrible agitation, my father, as if obsessed, circled the hospital. It was unbearable to think that there behind the log wall his beloved Ligita was suffering, and there was nothing he could do, not even hold his wife's hand nor say loving words. He was not even allowed to comfort her. During this stressful time, he imagined that he heard Ligita's screams, but it was only the echo of his own excited imagination that reverberated in his ears. Again and again, my father knocked at the maternity ward window, but the answer was always the same: not yet, he must wait.

The birth continued throughout the night and until midday the next day. Between two waves of pain, my mother managed to sleep for a moment before she had to get up again, because the painful contractions returned and they were easier to bear while walking. Also screaming helped, because her body tensed to such a degree while screaming that it seemingly subdued the pain. This will never end, thought Ligita. Now and then she asked what time it was. Eight hours had already passed! Then ten. And nothing had changed! Only the pain had intensified until she no longer had the strength to stand up. My mother hung onto the bed board, black rings flashing before her eyes. Even her voice had turned hoarse from screaming, and all the following screams more closely resembled harsh wheezing. The doctor was explaining something about narrow, underdeveloped hips that did not allow the baby to come into this world, but the words did not really reach Ligita's consciousness.[240] She had already begun to lose strength and, now and then, slipped into unconsciousness. The midwife did try to wake her, slapping her forcefully, but this only helped for a short while. The doctor understood that the progress of the birth had slowed down to a dangerous level and that she had to act quickly. She immediately cut into the birth canal in several places with a scalpel and with a forceful movement of her arms, forced the child out. Thus, on December 22 at 13:30, I arrived in this world. On hearing my cry, my mother had feebly asked: "Is it a boy or a girl?" Finding out that it was a daughter, happy and satisfied, my mother fell asleep right there on the delivery table.

Ligita woke up in her bed. "I have a daughter! A little daughter!" she thought with a smile and impatiently longed to be together with her baby as soon as possible. She wanted to look at her child carefully, because she had not been able to examine her thoroughly during the brief look she had had at little Sandra at her entry into the world. The midwife came in asking how the new mother was doing. Ligita felt fine, as if the pains she had suffered had never existed. My mother learned from the midwife that the baby would be brought to her at midnight to be fed. Finally, this first meeting took place, and

"I've got a daughter!" 1954.

a tiny little parcel wrapped in white swaddling from which a tiny red face peeked was put into Ligita's bed. "Sandra, my little sweetie" murmured the mother, drowning in my blue eyes. "What black hair you have! I don't like it at all," she said anxiously. Even though I was wrapped very securely, I had managed to push my chubby little hand out of the wrapping. My mother touched my hand gently with one finger, which I instantly grabbed with surprising strength. After six days, my mother was released from the hospital.

On that day, besides me, two boys were born in the Togur village – a Russian and a German. My mother often thinks about the fate of these children. Probably the German family now is living in Germany, where the son has obtained good education and work. If the Russian lad stayed in Togur or its vicinity, his life is probably just as pitiful as it was in the 1950s. While creating a film about the fate of the deported children of 1941, a filming group recently visited the places where Latvians had been deported. The filmed sequences are shocking. They mercilessly reveal the obscurantism and misery in which generation after generation continues to live. Exactly the same as during the boom days of Stalinism, the people made fools by propaganda still firmly believe that their life is the best and that the imperialists of the world, who still live at the expense of Mother Russia, are to blame for the misfortunes in their life.

When his wife left the hospital, my father went to the Village Soviet to get my birth certificate. After taking care of all the formalities, the Commandant said: "Aivar Aleksandrovich, in the future on the 15th and the 30th of each month you have to register your daughter," and, bursting into laughter, he continued, "so that we can make certain that she has not fled her place of settlement." My father was stunned. While expecting me, neither he nor my mother had been aware of the harsh truth that their child, from the moment of her birth, was "deported for life." With a heavy heart, my father walked back slowly to the barracks. He blamed himself for being so thoughtless as to allow himself to fall prey to the illusion of happiness, in whose name he had destined his daughter for Siberia. "Carrion crows! Cretins! Bastards!" my father screamed soundlessly. Returning home, he looked at my mother, his eyes dark, and snapped: "We won't give birth to any more slaves!" I have no brothers or sisters.

The Long Way Home

My parents' house is the only place I remember living in Siberia. In the fall of 1953, when its construction was completed, I was big enough to step over its doorstep by myself, just holding onto my mother's hand. My mother remembers this moment with pride. The house had been built with my mother's and father's own hands, not distinguishing what was woman's and what man's work. They even made the bricks from clay dug right there in the garden, which they mixed with sand for the stove and the hearth. For insulation they used moss gathered in the swamp, dried and then stuffed in the crevices between the logs. My mother plastered the inner walls with a mixture of cow dung and clay, and when it dried, she whitewashed the walls. All the furniture – a table, two chairs, stools, beds and a cupboard – were handmade by my father. He used his "connections" in the sawmill electrical plant very skilfully to get electricity drawn to the house located in a non-electrified district. All the other residents of this distant corner of Togur also benefited from this, because they used the newly installed electrical connections to extend electricity to their own homes illegally. My parents dug a well in the yard so that water would not have to be carried in pails from a distance. The well froze in the winter; thus the only source of water then was snow, which was collected in pails, carried into the warm entry hall and piled into a large barrel to melt. While the snow was fresh, the water was clear, but with the approach of spring, the chimney soot from the local factories and houses that collected on the snow stained it grey, and gradually a thick layer of dirt settled at the bottom of the water barrel.

In contrast to the other neighbouring houses, in the summer there were boxes of flowers at the windows of ours, grown from seeds sent by friends from Latvia. Also the path from the gate to the entryway was bordered with flowerbeds, which was the cause for great amazement for the locals. They could not understand why so much energy should be expended on such non-edible and useless things as flowers. Near the house was a small garden, in which my parents grew vegetables and potatoes. The earth in this part of Siberia was unusually fertile; even after the short summer, five tonnes of potatoes could be dug up in the fall from a planting of 150 kilograms. This amount was enough to satisfy not only our own needs but also feed a decent size pig, which, after slaughter, could provide us with meat almost every day. The second most important food for us was sauerkraut, which my parents prepared in a gigantic 15-pail barrel. The barrel stood in the cold entryway, and in the winter, whenever they wanted to cook sauerkraut, they hacked a chunk from its frozen mass. They kept fresh meat in the same way, its odour being a source of unending temptation and suffering for our tomcat. With consummate optimism, he scratched with his thin nails at the ice block, never earning more than a few small icy slivers smelling of meat for his efforts. So that I would always have fresh milk, my parents kept a goat.

Our house has remained in my memory as being white, warm and sunny. These impressions reflect the secure and love-filled world that I lived in and ruled. My day started with a loud cry "Oma-a-ma-a!" that announced to the household that its goddess had woken. Because my mother and father were at work most of the time, my call was usually answered by my grandmother and the cat that immediately rushed to do my bidding. Kitty, being the swiftest, always managed to jump into my bed, which was strictly forbidden, to purr and lean against me to be patted. When my grandmother touched the white curtains around my bed, the cat bounded out and, purring soulfully, rolled on the ground, right by. My grandmother shook her finger in the direction of the cat, which he totally ignored, knowing who really was the favourite of the house. My grandmother handed a cup of warm, freshly milked goat's milk to me, which I drank with great pleasure, enjoying the white whiskers the milk left above my lips, about which my grandmother teased me good-naturedly. When the morning ablutions had been finished and breakfast had been eaten, then it was time for "good deeds." "Missy" had breadcrumbs and cut-up bits of cheese rind poured into her palm, which I then doled out to the neighbour's hens. On hearing my loud voice, the owner of the hens, Andreyevna, crossed the street to chat with my grandmother. She was a kindly, toothless old woman, whose life had been a series of trials and tribulations. Having got married to a drunk of a husband at the age of fifteen, she had let sixteen children into the world, only one of whom had survived, and he, due to his father's alcoholism, was born half-witted.

When the morning visit was finished, my grandmother got me dressed, and we headed out to the store. Along the way I talked to all the passers-by, who all had to smile at my precocious behaviour and outspokenness. My grandmother shone with pride at every one of my "witticisms." I particularly liked the store, because one could look at all sorts of interesting things there and get a hard candy from the kind saleslady Darya. In the mornings, when my mother did not go to work early because she was on afternoon shift, she lifted me into her bed, and we both spent a lazy time telling each other fairy tales we invented. In mine, the chief protagonist was Cinderella, who danced a tango or boogie-woogie with a prince. Now and then a little bird brought her fine nylon stockings, candies or some other goodies in his beak. At the end of my fairy tale Cinderella always was allowed to return to the land of her dreams, Latvia, which I had come to know from what my parents had told me and from the children's books sent to me.

My mother refused to accept Siberia. With the first changes in the life of the deportees she uncompromisingly fought for trivia, which in her opinion were symbolic of a normal life: resisting depar-

Ligita in her work clothes.

tures from European social norms and dressing style imposed on us by poverty. Even if one had to drink from a tin cup, a saucer was put under it. Even though it was tin, it was still a saucer, for "It was unimaginable to drink from a cup without a saucer in the Dreifelds family." As conditions of life improved, at least for Sunday lunch, a dessert was served after the sauerkraut or potatoes: "heavenly manna" (cream-of-wheat beaten with cranberries to fluffy lightness), a thickened berry sauce or a "sweet bread soup" cooked from chunks of rye brick bread. My mother despised the repulsive quilted pants and the "*pufaika*" – quilted shapeless jacket, the thick shawls and felt leggings over boots, in which she had to imprison her femininity. As soon as the workday was finished, she unpeeled herself from this enforced shell and changed into one of the dresses she had sewn herself, put on shoes she had brought from Latvia, so she could once again feel like a woman. My mother had learned to sew when she had received the first package mailed from Latvia. The articles of clothing that came seemed unbelievably extravagant to Emilija and Ligita, who had barely survived starvation, and for the sake of economising they undid the linings from the clothes to sew blouses, jackets and other necessary things to wear. At the time Ligita knew nothing about sewing, but she was determined and had imagination. After making her friend Māra lie down on the floor and drawing the contours of her body, my mother "created" a pattern. Slowly her proficiency improved, so that she even started to sew for others.

No matter how poor my mother's possibilities were, she never gave in. She also dressed me in the style of dresses, coats with a fur collar and a muff to warm hands that she remembered from her childhood. In looking at the photos of those days, it's hard to imagine that I am wearing a party dress sewn from a pair of recycled old, dyed pants of my father, while the fancy furs are the scraps of the past glory obtained from some fellow countrywoman, which my mother had carefully patched together to form a hat. In contrast to the local children, I wore diapers. That amazed the Togur doctor and nurse: finally someone had put into practise the recommendations set out in all the intelligent books about a child's hygiene. Every night I was washed in a little bathtub, something that was particularly hard to do within the confined space of the barracks, not even mentioning the hardship of obtaining hot water from melting snow. My clothes were always clean and pressed. When in 1956 the first package arrived from my mother's brothers in Canada, my mother accepted the beautiful clothes and shoes as the most natural thing in the world. She was not daunted by the fact that the only place where she could wear these was the main street of Togur or on a visit to the city of Kolpashevo. Having dressed herself and me in elegant Western overcoats, my mother, her head held high, and I set out for walks along the barracks, the log houses and wooden fences, stunning every passer-by and curious onlookers glued to their windows with our appearance. I can just imagine what effect an article of clothing that had scarcely reached Europe left on the villagers – a snow suit, in which the practical Canadians dressed their children to protect them from the cold.

My mother's belief in a civilised life and the miracle of returning to it was irrational, because nothing in the real world around us bore witness to the fact that these hopes had any sort of basis. The negation of Siberia had rooted deeply in her subconscious, intuitively expressing itself in actions and words that contradicted the acceptance dictated by her rational mind. I have always been moved to tears by an episode that bears dramatic testimony to the strength of my mother's faith. When it was time for my first smallpox immunisation, she would not allow the serum to be scratched on my upper arm, but insisted that the scratches be made on my leg. In explanation, my mother said to the surprised Russian nurse: "My daughter will need to have beautiful shoulders, because one day she'll have to wear evening gowns!"

My upbringing lay squarely on my grandmother's shoulders, because my mother and my father did shift work, moreover, at different times. Holidays were rare, and even these rarely coincided. As all Soviet factories, the Togur sawmill participated in a socialist competition on plan fulfilment. Since it had been awarded first place in an All-Union contest, by administrative decision, the workers often "volunteered" to work on holidays in order not to lose the honour they had won. In my mother's opinion, my grandmother spoiled me too much, and with my "Little Sandra wants; Sandra needs," I was twisting her round my little finger. My power over my grandmother was so great that for my sake she voluntarily gave up

Sandra and Milda 1954.

her only weakness – smoking. When I, with comic seriousness, had repeated the comment I had heard from my mother that my head hurt from the smoke, my omama put out her lit cigarette. Smiling slightly, she said that she would no longer smoke because she did not want to ruin the health of her little kissable darling. She lived up to her word and never smoked again.

I had a terribly stubborn nature that my mother, wishing the best for me, tried to break. She did not succeed, because, even after a spanking or being put to stand in a corner, I still maintained I was right. Today I'm convinced that these dramatic modes of punishment had the contrary effect: they strengthened my will power and prepared me to stand up for myself and for my opinions in life. They also hardened me to run head first into walls. Even if I got bumps on my head, occasionally the wall collapsed. My grandmother taught me to print letters, which I knew how to do quite well at the age of four. I so liked to write that once I filled all of my father's notebooks with my scrawls. Instead of the expected praise for helping him in his night school "lessons," I was properly scolded, because he had to rewrite everything from scratch. Besides that, notebooks were hard to get.

With Christmas approaching, my grandmother taught me in the Latvian tradition to recite simple verses at the Christmas tree. She sternly reminded me not to divulge this to my parents so that I could surprise them at Christmas. I couldn't help but brag about my accomplishments, of course, but that did not stop my father and mother from being "surprised" and totally delighted about how bright I was. The first Christmas that I remember ended sadly for me. I very much offended Santa Claus, who came precisely during the time my grandmother had gone to feed the piglet in the barn. When Santa Claus had been invited to step from the entryway into our living room, the light lit up his face. It seemed surprisingly similar to my grandmother, and I impulsively rushed to him, pulled his

Christmas. 1956.

beard, saying: "Omama, why have you pushed all that straw into your mouth?" Santa Claus was very hurt about this nasty behaviour of mine and, not saying a word, hurried out, in his confusion, however, leaving his bag of gifts. My excuses and tears did not help any, because Santa Claus never forgave me the offence and never came to see me again. For many years I waited for the miracle to be repeated again, having fervently resolved to be good, but the suspicious resemblance to my grandmother troubled me. However, for practical reasons I kept quiet about my suspicions. The next time I met Santa Claus was after many years in Latvia when he had come to visit my own son Jānis with a bag of gifts. Therefore, he must have forgiven me …

I grew up almost without any playmates, because my parents considered it dangerous to let me roam around without adult supervision as the local children did. The minute they had learned to walk they vanished with their peers for the whole day. In one of the most exciting of my childhood days in Siberia, I too sneaked away from my grandmother and once ran off with a group of children. We

Sandra's playground in Togur.

played along the edges of the swamp, threw sticks and had a competition in who could pee further. There I noticed for the first time that boys were much more suited to this type of sport than girls, because nature has given them a wonderful tool for achieving top results. It seemed unfair to me. On the way back we fooled around a bit near the overpopulated barracks, where I forgot my shoes, which had been obtained with such difficulty. Nearing my house I started to realise how I had overstepped my bounds and what a terrible scolding I was going to receive. My grandmother was very happy to see me, but she could not conceal the loss of my only pair of shoes from my parents, and therefore I did not get away without a scolding. At the time I could not have known that my parents were trying to limit my contacts with local children because they feared that I would become "Russianised," which, if nothing changed, would be inevitable anyway. They watched worriedly how I talked Russian as well as Latvian. In my child's Latvian the phonetic influence Russian could not yet be sensed, but now and then a Latvianised Russian word appeared. The very thought that I would have to go to Russian school and that my Latvian identity would be threatened troubled my parents like a recurring nightmare. Even for me, when I look into the past, the loss of Latvian identity seems to be the most dreadful thing that could have happened to me.

My Siberian memories contain no black spots, because my world was bounded and sheltered by my parents' love. I could not know what they felt when they thought about our future. According to local standards, our family could have even been considered well to do. My parents finally had reasonably good earnings, we had our own house, warm clothing and were well fed; but precisely because their total energy was not consumed just for physical survival, my mother and father felt more acutely the enforced lack of liberty and the terribly shallow monotony of their everyday life. My parents were young and longed to learn, travel and see the world, but they were tied to their provincial and distant village, from which, without a permit from the Commandant's Office, they were not even permitted to travel to the nearest city, no matter how wretched it was. Their only outside contact was the radio, while their only form of entertainment was through movies or the library. The movies they saw were prettified Soviet films overflowing with infantile optimism, but at the minimum they could see another life there: in Moscow and Leningrad. Even though all the books in the library were in Russian and also carefully chosen to inculcate Soviet people with fundamental Communist ideas, my parents read a great deal because that helped them to survive their mundane existence. Newspapers reached Togur with several days delay, but this was of no significance, because everything that happened in the world seemed distant and unreal. What difference did it make what happened yesterday or even a week ago? This slow-paced life sucked one in, tied a person down. In the greyness of daily life the hope of returning to Latvia had diminished, as if ground down on a millstone, slowly turning into a pale-faced phantom shut up in the furthest corners of a soul, so that the heart protected by hardened armour of indifference would not be tormented by unfulfilled longing.

Stalin's death on March 5, 1953, did not raise any hope for my parents or the other deportees, because in their mind the terror was not connected with any concrete person but with the Communist regime in general. One individual's death did not change anything in the system, because others would replace him and just as cruelly continue their battle with the enemies of communism. Stalin's approaching death could be sensed. All day the radio broadcast sombre melodies, brought news bulletins about the leader's state of health and read letters from workers, kolkhozniks and socialist intelligentsia. The letters wished that dear comrade Stalin would get well and promised to study his last brilliant work "Economic Problems of Socialism in the SSR Union" with the greatest zeal.

In Togur the news of "the greatest loss to the party, Soviet land and all the proletariat of the world" was broadcast on the radio on the 6th of March. The announcement in the newspaper *Pravda*, bordered in black, arrived at the village as usual – with delay. The news was considered horrendous, because having listened for years to stories of the untiring concern of the Father of the People and his battle against internal enemies, most of the people felt as if they had been orphaned. In precisely the same way as the Russian peasants had believed in the good Czar, who seemingly knew nothing about the evil deeds of his officials, the majority of the Soviet people were naively convinced that it was the Leader alone whom they had to thank for not having been visited by greater evil. What did tomorrow have in store for them now that they had been left without protection and in the hands of the evil people that their Dear Father had so wisely unmasked. The local women cried and wailed aloud the Slavic mourning ritual words: "Why have you abandoned us, apple of our eye and eagle ... To whom would I, an orphan, now turn to ..." The intense theatricality of the wailing was a magnificent shelter wherein one could hide one's confusion and ignorance. Someone, after all, must be watching how sincerely a person mourned, and afterward everyone would have to answer for it. The faces of the deportees closed up and became inscrutable, which could be misinterpreted as the shock of sorrow. In public places one or two even wiped away a tear and for the sake of security tried not to express any sort of feelings. Everyone "mourned" and all knew well how it should be done.

In the afternoon of the same day, the first mourning meeting was called at the sawmill, at which the director read the official party and government notification of Stalin's death. Then the party secretary, union chief and some of the leading people in the party, as well as some shock workers stepped up to the rostrum, each trying to outdo the other in eloquence. They read from their crib sheets about the inconsolable sadness that had been thrust upon them and humanity in general since "the most eminent human being of our era," " luminary in the science of Marxism," "the great Generalissimo," " the most prominent war leader of all time," "the best friend of the workers of every country of the world," "the hope of repressed and poor unfortunates," has left this world. But no matter how consuming the mourning, one should not submit to it. One had to watch out for the evil designs of the world's imperialists, who wished to profit from the abysmal pain of the Soviet people to gain their own advantage. Therefore, everyone resolved to be as one with their native Communist Party, which like the fairy-tale tree sheltered the whole world under its branches and whose roots stretched deeply into the masses of people, the heart of humanity and inspired people to new victories in their work. It was the only way they could show comrade Stalin that he would live forever in everyone's heart. At the end of the mourning ceremony, all of them unanimously adopted a letter they would send to the Central Committee of the Communist Party of the USSR, the USSR Supreme Council Presidium and the USSR Council of Ministers, in which they promised their native party to fulfil their work plan before due date and to maintain their vigilance against the class enemy. Letters with similar content were approved everywhere, and these, without cease, flowed to Moscow. Since almost times immemorial, for first time the letters were no longer addressed to Yosif Vissarionovich Stalin; it almost seemed to be an unnatural occurrence.

After the meeting, my father was called to a special *tête-à-tête* with the director of the electrical plant. "Aivar Aleksandrovich," he said, " you have been entrusted with the responsible assignment of installing supplementary radio broadcasting loudspeakers in the central square in the village, so that every single word that is said in the memorial meeting in Moscow can be heard! If anything goes astray, you will be the first one to be blamed!" My father listened to his director's words with dreadful premonition, because he knew very well that even the smallest mistake in broadcasting the funeral ceremony would endanger him and his family. Why should it so happen that he specifically was to be burdened with this responsibility?

In following the propaganda patterns of class struggle, the choice of the director would have seemed somewhat odd, because my father was a politically unreliable deportee, for whom Stalin's funeral would be the precise time to reveal his hate and to get involved in sabotage. But in life things did not happen as they did in Soviet films or fiction "masterworks." Aivars was the most professional electrician at the sawmill. His skill seemed much more important than political vigilance to the director, who was very concerned that the task should be accomplished without any mishaps and that he himself would not get into any trouble. This insignificant episode illustrates perfectly the duplicity of the Soviet regime: to denounce in words and actions, but then suddenly turn a blind eye, when they had need of the class enemy.

Aivars attached sickle-shaped hooks to his feet, which like long claws, hooked into electrical poles, allowing him to crawl upward. Together with the other electricians, he stretched the electrical wires and installed the loudspeakers. Having made certain several times that everything was operating without problems, with a trembling heart, he waited for the afternoon of March 9, when the live broadcast of the Leader's funeral would be transmitted across the Soviet Union.[241]

Around two in the afternoon, all the villagers who could walk had gathered in the square round the Stalin monument. This was a standard plaster cast painted the colour of bronze, a typical example of a Soviet propaganda sculpture, which with minor variations – the hat either held in the hand or on the head, with an overcoat or without – could be found in every Soviet village and town. Its purpose was to make the leaders better known and loved by the populace. My father watched on at what was happening from an electrical pole, where he had positioned himself in order to avert any unforeseen mishap or accident. Live transmission from Moscow to Togur village was an unprecedented event, and everyone, holding their breath, listened to the sombre voice of the announcer Levitan,[242] as he described how the Red Square looked with its funeral decorations. The coffin with the remains of Stalin apparently had been placed on a cannon carriage. It was placed beside the Lenin Mausoleum and was drowning in red flowers. Of course, the announcer did not mention the dreadful tragedy that had happened on March 7, when the crowds wishing to bid farewell had swelled to such an improbable size that from the pressure from behind many people were trampled to death and injured.[243]

When the Politburo members had settled into their places on the platform above the Mausoleum, the meeting was ready to begin. The first speechmakers were "trusted comrades," Malenkov, Beria, Khrushchev and Molotov, followed by the "spontaneous" mourners, such as his "trusted disciples," workers and kolkhozniks, Moscovites, people from Leningrad, Gori – Stalin's native city – and various others. The ceremony continued for more than two hours, and even though it was cold, the villagers stood, almost without moving, understanding that the moment was too special, to allow any untoward weakness such as freezing to interfere. Finally Chopin's funeral march sounded, and the announcer explained that the trusted comrades-in-arms of the great leader, Malenkov, Beria and Molotov, had hoisted up the coffin and were carrying it into the

Mausoleum. At exactly twelve noon Moscow time, factory sirens were sounded all over the Soviet Union. The sirens heard through the loudspeakers were joined by the screeching sirens of the sawmill in Togur. When the hymn of Soviet Union died away, everything stopped for five minutes: trains, ships, worktables, cars and people. Only the Kremlin cannon shots were heard over the radio. "Now it is over – he's been buried," thought my father. Sitting at the top of an electrical pole he had the luxury of not having to make a sanctimoniously sombre face, or worry about people reading his thoughts. He felt unbelievably relieved: there would be no negative repercussions because the loudspeakers had worked without any problems. He could finally crawl down and head for home.

The day after Stalin's funeral Togur became the same as it had been for many previous days and would be for days that still were to come. Echoes of the cruel power struggle taking place among the "comrades," the "comrades-in-arms" and the "disciples" within the four walls of the Kremlin virtually did not reach their far corner of the Soviet Union. My parents did not even notice that Stalin's name was mentioned more and more rarely in newspapers, being replaced by Lenin and an emphasis on the leading role of the Communist Party. Stalin's most likely successor seemingly was Georgy Malenkov, but alongside him one always heard and read the names of Lavrenty Beria, Vyacheslav Molotov and Nikita Khruhchev, which meant that power no longer was concentrated in the hands of one leader but had to be shared. At the beginning of April, an article appeared in the newspaper *Pravda* about the termination of the "doctors' case,"[244] as well as the exoneration of some "falsely slandered" persons. The deportees followed these news with incredulous interest. Could that mean that their fate would also change?

The first great surprise was criticism of the villainous deeds committed by the all-powerful State Security Minister Lavrenty Beria expressed at the July plenary session of the Central Committee of the Communist Party, where he was labelled a "bourgeois degenerate" and "an agent of international imperialism."[245] The plenary session seemingly had revoked the prohibition to doubt the leaders' "infallibility" and when, at the end of December, Beria was shot, the lost hopes for change once entertained by my parents and others were forcefully revived. Other incidents as well indicated that something was about to happen. Rumours spread that the surveillance regimen was being relaxed and seemingly some of the prisoners in the prison camps were being allowed to move to settlement places. They heard that some people had been freed before they had served their terms and were permitted to live in nearby villages or cities, work there and even receive pay.[246]

A surprise awaited my parents in the Commandant's office on August 1, 1954: I no longer had to be registered.[247] I was freed until the age of sixteen! They too had been liberated from coming in for the semi-monthly registration: in the future they would only have to do it once a year; moreover, they were free to relocate anywhere within the boundaries of the Tomsk region. Someone knew enough to say that the edict about "deportation for life" had been revoked.[248] What was happening gave wings to hope. Almost every time the deportees met, their conversation began with the words: "Have you heard ...," followed by a recount of some new miracle that someone had heard from another person who had ... This is how preparation for the way back home started, continuing for three years, made longer by total ignorance about what was happening "up above."

Hearing about the changes, many had again gathered enough courage to write petitions with a request to be released from administrative settlement. My mother too decided that she would again try her luck and hand in a document addressed to the Supreme Council Presidium Chairman Kliment Voroshilov at the Commandant's office. In the request, written in June 1954, she explained in detail the circumstances of her deportation, in conclusion turning to the people determining her fate with the words: "In 1952 I gave birth to a daughter. [...] I humbly beg that you remove the cruel punishment from my daughter and me, which we are enduring because of my dead parents, and give me back the status of a free Soviet citizen."[249] In contrast to the petitions written during the initial years after the war this one has been saved in the Dreifelds' case file.[250] It can be seen that the investigator had examined it carefully, marking the parts he considered most important with a red pencil. It had seemed significant to him that my mother had already been removed from the special registration list in 1948. It had not passed the eagle-eyed Chekist that the surname "Dreifelds" had been spelled differently in different places; but, having ascertained that it was always one and the same person, he had decided to send the case file for review to the Latvian SSR. Attached to the file were also references from her employer and the Commandant's office. Both were positive, because the deported woman had "for the total time of settlement done socially useful work. She had obeyed all regime regulations."[251] However, the good references never did influence the Major from the Latvian SSR Ministry of Interior, who found more useful the erroneous observation by Tukums Militia Lieutenant Pumpe that the deported woman had illegally left her place of settlement in 1948. Having noted that "Ligita Janovna had not stated any arguments that would provide basis for revoking the special settlement order," the major recommended that the request should be rejected.[252] My mother was not the only one who received such a rejection. The generalised nature of the rejections shocked those receiving them, because it clearly demonstrated that the fate of the deportees would only be given cosmetic improvements and even if the decision about deportation for life would be revoked, there seemed no hope of returning to Latvia. It was a bitter realisation. In the summer of 1954 it was hard to imagine that only a year and a half later the Soviet Union would be shaken by the 20th Congress of the Communist Party of the Soviet Union that would open the way for the return of my family to Latvia.

They had to continue living in Togur and try to take advantage of the cracks that had opened in the dense wall of the regime creating an opportunity for some sort of improvement in their living conditions. Proof of a relaxation was demonstrated by the sawmill administration allowing Ligita Janovna to take professional improvement courses, which, on completion, allowed her to become a quality controller for wood products, a job that partially freed my mother from heavy physical labour. In turn, my father was promoted from a simple electrician to chief electrician of the electrical plant. After these promotions my parents started to earn decent wages and some Soviet luxury items started to appear in our house: a wristwatch, a photo camera and a fur coat. An unexpected turn of fate was an invitation for my father to join the Young Communist League.[253] Who could dare to refuse? He had to join. My father received a similar recommendation to join the Communist Party at the end of the 1950s, when he had already returned to Latvia. He skilfully used his "bandit family member" history to excuse himself, pretending he did not consider himself worthy to be at the "vanguard" of the people. Thus, without getting into trouble, he was able to escape the totally unacceptable collaboration with people who had ruined his life.

When the news reached Togur that some of the deportees would be accepted in the Tomsk Polytechnic Institute, my father decided to try, because at that time studying seemed the only way he could tear himself free and have a better life. He dreamt of becoming an engineer, of learning English and writing a radio construction handbook for amateur radio buffs. Before he was deported, he had managed to complete three years at the Technical College. It looked like one evening course at the local workers school would suffice for him to prepare for his studies, but he had forgotten much, and he also needed to learn how to write properly in Russian, otherwise he could not pass the entry exams of the Institute. My father's initiative and perseverance could only be admired because, in order to fit in his studies, he had to reduce his sleeping time to just four or five hours. He still had to work three shifts, but at least the length of his workday had been shortened to eight hours, and all the workers now were allowed one day off during the week. In two years he had finished the evening courses, and he was ready to go to Tomsk. We stayed at home, anxiously awaiting the news. In order to somewhat reduce the tension of not knowing, my omama and mama again turned to the psychotherapy of laying out patience, falling into despair each time that the cards did not fall right and drawing a breath of relief when they did. We already knew that father had passed all the tests with excellent marks; only the last most dreadful test was still to be taken – a composition in Russian, which could cancel out all the effort to date. Finally a telegram arrived: father had challenged fate and won!

My father managed to finish one year of studies in Siberia. When we returned to Latvia in 1957, it was a bitter disappointment to learn that the Rīga Polytechnic Institute would not allow him to continue his studies. The admission committee considered release from administrative settlement insufficient evidence of innocence and believed that such a "bandit family member" had no business being among upright Soviet students. Thus Khrushchev's "thaw" had not yet reached Latvia. On the other hand, the decision regarding reinstatement of class criteria for admission to Soviet Universities – had.[254] Only after a meeting with the dean of the faculty was Aivars Kalnietis allowed to continue his studies. Even though it was in a Russian group.

My father has always been able to rise above the embitterment about his war-crippled leg, his youth cut short by deportation and the difficult time trying to make ends meet after returning to Latvia. He always maintained his inner radiance, which everyone who comes in touch with him intuitively senses. Beside my sparkling but spiritually fragile mother, he always has been a tower of strength for our family. It is father who has made all the most important decisions without hesitation, at the same time leaving the family members with the impression that they were the decision makers. I have never understood how he has managed to do that without crude manipulation or long verbal tirades. The harshest word in his vocabulary of anger is "crow" or a long silent pause. He is the brightest and most even-tempered person I have ever met. He is also my best friend, who has accepted me as I am – wilful, capricious and uncontrollable. I can talk about anything with him from the most intimate experiences to existential problems, as I try to find way out from another dead end I've reached while pitting my

Aivars and Sandra 1955.

principles against reality. Tactfully my father has directed me through the hardest moments in my life, after each defeat helping me to regain strength through his understanding care. Only now, after many years, do I realise that the determined nature I have inherited from him has helped me to control myself. In my foolhardy youth I did not know where to go or what to grab so as not to allow the temptations of uniquely diverse life pass me by. Always in my mind's deepest recesses there was an image – the lit up profile of my father bending over his books, studying for many years to fulfil his dream. Whenever I have been afraid to make a major decision, take on work or responsibility, my father's presence in my subconscious has empowered me to make the right decision. That is how it will always be. Even when we will be separated for a short while by eternity.

The second messenger of serious changes that in the spring of 1955 buzzed through Togur village was the news that one of the deportees had received a letter from his relatives abroad. This news deeply affected my mother – perhaps finally she would find out what had happened to her brothers, with whom she had lost all contact since 1948. They had not even written to their relatives in Latvia, and no one knew in what country the brothers had finally found shelter. A letter arrived from Canada on November 3. On receiving the strange looking foreign envelope with a striped edge, my mother immediately recognised Viktors' handwriting. Her heart started to beat violently. Finally her brothers had found her! Finally! Crying, she hurried home, throwing her coat down at the door, as she, with trembling hands, impatiently tore the letter open. My dear, dear ones! It was incredible that after so many long years someone would call her "My dear little sister!" Voldemārs and Viktors were living in Canada, Arnolds was in England. The older brother Voldemārs, in addition to two sons, Juris and Jānis, also had twins Rūta and Pēteris. Viktors was married for a second time – to Austra, and they also had twins, Gunta and Daina. A year later, a son was also born to Viktors and his wife. At the time, only Arnolds had not remarried. A few years later he was married again – to Marta, and they had three daughters – Ligita, Marta and Zīle.

Having experienced her first deep emotions, my mother reread the letter several times to my father, grandmother and me. Being read out loud it took on new value. The words impressed themselves in our awareness; they mingled with the stories we had heard earlier from mother, imbuing them with a new, fleshed-out meaning that made them come alive. Since this first letter to my mother, her brothers' invisible presence shared all the joys and sorrows of our family. When I got older, I was even jealous about my uncles, for whose letters my mother waited with such great anticipation. Egoistically it seemed to me that there was not enough room in her heart for me. What could I have known of the depressing sadness of unfulfilled longing, which my mother had experienced for so many years, knowing that her love has to be fed only from bits and pieces of memories and letters.

I am not able to read the letter my mother wrote in response to her brothers without bursting into tears. They, too, cried when they read the indescribable pain that was woven through the few pages containing the compressed and fateful story of their parents' and sister's life.

> It hurts to think that so many years have passed and not once during this time have you tried to find me, even though it would have been much easier for you than for me. The last time I received your greetings was seven years ago. Then I was still living in Latvia, but now I am again in the Tomsk region. Mama did not live long enough to meet me when I returned for the second time. She died on February 5, 1950, from a heart attack. I was left alone, totally alone ... After all the hardships that I had suffered on my way back here I had fervently hoped to meet mama, but instead of this I was given an official death notice at the end of my journey. It was the greatest shock of my life, which to this day I still cannot quite take in.
>
> I often reread and know by heart your only letter, Viktor, the one written in 1947, that we, mama and I, read together at that time, crying all the while. I have been married now for four years. My married name is Kalnietis. We have a very dear little daughter Sandra, who at Christmas will be three years old. We both work at the sawmill. In the beginning I carried

wood boards, but now already for the second year I work as a sorter. My husband Aivars works and studies at night so that he may sometime in the future qualify as an engineer.

[…] Please, please write to me – you simply have no idea how happy it makes me to hold your letter in my hand. Write about your small "chicks," which mama so wished to hug – she had to die not seeing any of her grandchildren. I continue to see you as you were fifteen years ago. I already have many grey hairs at the age of twenty-eight, therefore, you must have more, because life has not spoiled us. Please, send some photo of yourself, so that I may have something to look at when I think of you.

[…] I cry as I write, remembering all that has happened, and I realise that never again will we relive any of it, not even this small detail – how proud I was to dance with you all in the Dubulti High School dance, which, I'm sure, you've forgotten. And now we have grown old. I could still dance at my age, but the grim day-to-day life has made me forget about dancing. Viktor, do you recall how you used to throw me up in the air and discovered that I became smaller? And how I hugged you that last evening, when you brought me the new shoes? As if you knew: for a long journey!

Please write to me and don't imagine that I could get into any sort of trouble. [...] I remember your name days and birthdays every year – I'm probably not remembered by anyone. […] In the next letter I'll send you a photo of mama in her coffin. Please write. […]"[255]

When ice left the Ob River in the spring and the navigation season started up again, the first package arrived from my mother's brothers. It was very much waited for, because the brothers had

Ligita and Sandra wearing overcoats sent
by Ligita's brothers.

written that several packages sent at different times were on the way. My father helped mother bring the heavy package home from Kolpashevo, but then he had to hurry to work. Thus he missed the great celebration and joy of opening the package. My grandmother and I had the privilege to enjoy the never-yet-experienced pleasure of undoing the box, with screams of delight greeting every piece of clothing that my mother pulled out laughing and threw in the air. Even today, when I have travelled almost half the world and seen so many lovely things, nothing can compare or overshadow the wonder of that first contact with the normal world outside, which I experienced that day looking at things never before seen that changed my mother into a fairy-tale queen. There were dresses and stretchy nylon stockings, lace trimmed lingerie and an elegant coat, white silk blouses and pleated skirts. "Is all this loveliness meant for me?" my mother marvelled, trying on the beautiful clothes, one after the other. All the other family members had not been forgotten either. I was the second in the number of gifts. When my father returned from his night shift early in the morning, my mother had already left for work, but I was still sleeping. My father silently, reverently, one after the other, touched all the beautiful things and then, carefully, as if gently caressing them, folded them all. "What things. What beautiful things," he thought. "Never ever will this stupid state be able to create anything like this!"

I doubt if at that moment my father fully realised how much these insignificant words, spoken while looking at the most common everyday things, which were the norm elsewhere in the world, reflected the unbridgeable abyss that separated the Soviet Union from the normal world. My father's life was too hard to spare the time and desire to debate the underlying logic of historical and social developments. His distrust of the Soviet system was instinctive and rooted in his own sad experiences. Even the shocking unmasking of Stalin's cult and crimes on February 25, 1956, by the 20th Congress of the Communist Party could not change it. Some others naively and hopefully interpreted this as putting an end to all evil and finally making possible the world of justice and equality, which the first communists had envisaged and which, because of the malice of a few individuals, had not been constructed after the Revolution. So much secrecy surrounded the congress events that, except for the delegates, the common Party members were not informed of anything that was happening.[256] Today it seems strange that in a world with universal literacy, where newspapers were issued in monstrous numbers and where there was access to the radio, Khrushchev's Secret Report was disseminated from mouth to mouth almost as if during Czarist times. At the beginning of March, local party committees received stringently controlled numbers of brochures with the notation "No release to press" and the order that they should be read collectively at meetings to party members, the Young Communist league and activists.[257] It was a shock to the Nomenclature and aparatchiks, the listed party workers, but they had grown accustomed to executing orders from above. Therefore, the Soviet Union was flooded with a wave of meetings that deeply shook up and divided the society into supporters of the unmasking Report and its opposition. Even in present day Russia there are people who are convinced that great Stalin had been unfairly accused. My father too was invited to a reading of the Report at the sawmill's joint meeting of the Party and activists.

The reading had already started when Aivars entered the Director's office. He remained standing at the door, half-hidden by the doorframe that shadowed his face and hid him from nosy looks. The Party secretary sat at his desk reading from the brochure words, which people would have been afraid even to think, certainly not voice aloud. A tense silence permeated the room. Everyone sat with their eyes lowered and faces blank. My father listened how the Partorg in a hoarse voice, from time to time licking dry lips, tore from his pedestal the "most eminent and most humane" man, who had for thirty years decided the fate of the people of this monstrous empire, killing hundreds of thousands of innocent victims. The pulse at my father's temple was beating violently, and occasionally his thoughts wandered, dwelling on what he himself had experienced. Yes, the fabricated cases of Latvian Communist leaders Eihe, Rudzutaks and Mežlauks also had not been omitted from the Report. These people had faithfully served the Soviet regime, until in 1937, together with many other Latvian political workers who had remained in the USSR, they had been eliminated. If the ruling clique had treated their own like this, what could class enemies without rights hope for? Aivars waited impatiently, whether the Report would mention the mass deportations and such unfortunates as him. More and more Communist surnames, statesmen, military leaders were mentioned and then finally, he heard: "… the gross violations of Lenin's national policies of the Soviet State. It concerns the deportation of whole nations from their native lands."[258] My father felt pressure in the pit of his stomach. "… how can whole nations, including women, children, old people be held liable for the hostile acts of one person or a group […] submitting them to mass repression, losses and suffering."[259] Chechens, Ingushins and Georgians were mentioned, but not a word was said about Latvians,

Lithuanians or Estonians. As if we did not exist – my father thought bitterly. He was even more deceived regarding the conclusions of the Report concerning what was to be done to overcome the consequences of the personality cult. These were generalizations so watered down that it was unclear whether the deportees were destined to be included in the planned "overcoming" actions. Perhaps the words "Renewal of the Soviet socialist legitimacy and the prevention of its violations" were a promise of sorts? Everything depended on what "they" would consider in the future to be Soviet socialist legitimacy.

The local Partorg finished reading, turned his flushed face toward the audience and posed the question required by discussion procedures: "Does anyone have any comments?" There were none, and there never could have been any, because discussion was not expected nor had anyone been given the task to make comments. Then he suggested: "There is a motion to support Nikita Sergeyevich Khrushchev's Report to the 20th Congress in its totality. Who votes for this …" Everyone voted for it unanimously. The people, not looking at each other, silently left the room.

Since the fall of communist regime in 1991, when historians have had access to the archives of the Communist Party, Khrushchev's "thaw" has been researched extensively. It was a contradictory process, wherein the struggle of individuals or groups for power within the governing cohort – Malenkov, Khruschev, Beria, Molotov, etc. – became intermingled with the premonition that the Soviet Union was nearing an economic catastrophe, which would sweep away the governing elite. The GULAG was no longer profitable, because the repressive system had reached such dimensions, that the cost to maintain it exceeded earnings from the non-productive work of slaves.[260] Also confrontations with the USA and its allies no longer were within Soviet abilities, because almost a third of the publicly known State budget was expended for military needs including involvement in conflicts in Korea and elsewhere. In fact, the expenditures were even greater because of a secret military budget.[261] Neither humanism nor concern about clarifying the historical truth moved Khruhschev and other Politburo members in the summer of 1955 as they were preparing to unmask Stalin's cult at the 20th Party Congress. This was a necessity dictated by a desperate situation, whose price was power. Characteristically, the "unmaskers," who for many years had themselves participated in Stalin's repressions and were, therefore, equally guilty, had arrived at a mutual unspoken agreement to circumvent the question of their own liability except, of course, in instances when it suited them for political reprisals. Such concealment of facts also gave the lower ranked members of the Nomenclature an opportunity to have the excuse that they knew nothing about the true extent of the repressions, thus escaping liability. On Khrushchev's conscience lay the many who had unjustly suffered and been made victims in Ukraine. On his initiative, the Presidium of the Supreme Council of the USSR made the secret decision regarding the mass deportations from Estonia, Latvia and Lithuania in 1949.[262]

However, already the first months of public debating the Report demonstrated that "the people were not conscientious enough," that they were posing uncomfortable questions, as well as daring to press for further democratisation. In June, therefore, the Central Committee of the Communist Party of the Soviet Union passed a resolution "Regarding the Personality Cult and Elimination of its Consequences."[263] In this resolution Stalin was named as the only person primarily guilty of all the misfortunes and crimes, thus taking away liability from his "comrades," "comrades-in-arms" and "disciples." But with this resolution the deleterious curiosity and dangerous ideas about establishing a true democracy did not subside amongst intellectuals. The Communist Party had to stop it, and in 1957 the first wave of post-Stalinist repressions were directed against the revisionists of the Party line.[264] It was specifically during Khrushchev's regime that a new form of repression was added to arrests and prison camps – psychiatric hospitals, wherein for many years courageous Soviet intellectuals and dissidents were kept captive.[265]

The expectations after the 20th Party Congress were high, and the wait for news was unbearable, because all decisions and regulations about release of various "specially settled" categories or relaxation of their regimen were made secretly and the deportees had no official information about what was happening.[266] Only rumours, guesswork and continuous coincidences, which, when added up, made one conclude that release was imminent. On the 7th of July my father wrote an emotional letter to Khrushchev, in which he employed all the Soviet clichés to be convincing about his innocence, but even these could not overshadow the reality of his experience: "There [in school] we were taught the humane ideas of Lenin and Gorky, which say that one must always look for the best in a person. Then why is it that the worst is always seen in me? [...] We have given birth to a little daughter, so small and chubby – I truly love her. A year ago she was removed from the registration list, but the dark stain of my stepfather that pursues me will also condemn his granddaughter. How am I a threat to the Soviet regime? What crime have I committed? Why have I been deported? These questions worry me every day, and I can't find a logical answer to them. I believe in justice, which my mother, the school and the Young Communist League have taught me. I, as a person who passionately believes in the victory of justice, beg you, Nikita Sergeyevich, please direct your attention to this letter."[267] A petition from my grandmother was sent together with my father's petition, first to Moscow and, after an examination of all the "facts," to Rīga. On my grandmother's petition was written the resolution: "Review the complaint of Milda Kalniete and prepare it for a final decision." After several months of meandering through several offices, the case file was ready, and on December 4, 1956, in a closed session the Criminal Case Board of the Latvian SSR Supreme

Court decided "Release Milda Kalniete, daughter of Pēteris, and Aivars Kalnietis, son of Aleksandrs, from further detention in forced settlement."[268]

With a few days delay, also my mother's case was reviewed, and, observing that Jānis Dreifelds died in Vyatlag on December 31, 1941, and Emilija Dreifelde, too, died in forced settlement, and taking into account that the deported woman is married to Aivars Kalnietis, who is in settlement for different reasons and regarding whom the LSSR Prosecutor has submitted a protest to the LSSR Supreme Court with the recommendation to have him freed from further detention in special settlement, the investigator recommends that Ligita Dreifelde-Kalniete should be removed from the special settlement registration list.[269] On the 25th of December, the investigation conclusions were approved by the LSSR Minister of the Interior and the LSSR prosecutor.

For unknown reasons the responses to my parents' petitions were delayed, and they, deeply depressed, looked on as the navigation season neared its end, with many of the deportees already having managed to depart. On November 10, my mother's closest friend, Māra Kramiņa, whom my mother had known since 1942, left by aeroplane to Rīga. The parting was one of mixed joy and sadness, because our family had not yet received an answer to their petitions. My mother wrote to her brother Viktors: "Because our friends are leaving, I feel terribly distraught and sad. We are the only ones remaining for the winter, and winter lasts until May. We'll probably calm down and accept it, but right now I dread the approach of winter."[270] Christmas arrived and the permit to return had still not been received. My parents were in despair. My father could not hide it when he wrote his Christmas greeting to my mother's brother Viktors: "Let's see what the New Year will bring. We hope for much, but surely it is going to be nothing. That's how we hope every year, because we so very much wish that all would end sooner. [...] My

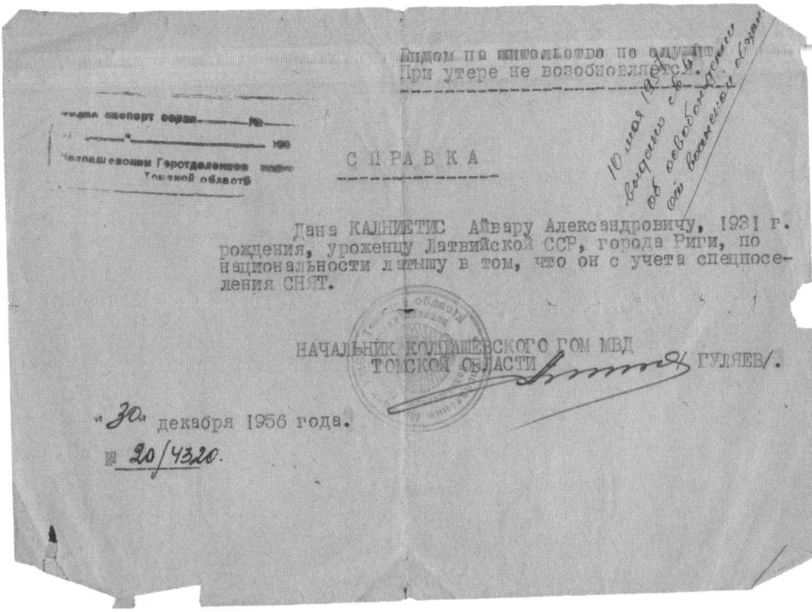

При утере не возобновляется.

СПРАВКА

Дана КАЛНИЕТИС Айвару Александровичу, 1931 г. рождения, уроженцу Латвийской ССР, города Риги, по национальности латышу в том, что он с учета спецпоселения СНЯТ.

НАЧАЛЬНИК КОЛПАШЁВСКОГО ГОМ МВД
ТОМСКОЙ ОБЛАСТИ /ГУЛЯЕВ/.

"30" декабря 1956 года.
№ 20/4320.

Notice of Aivars Kalnietis' removal from the special settlement registration list.

ladies in particular are hoping. I myself, however, am very sceptical about the very nature of the thing – but only on the surface. Very deep down some internal voice always makes me hope for a happy ending. I just don't want to show it [...] and if there is going to be disappointment, it won't hurt so much."[271]

My father and grandmother received their liberation certificates on December 30. My mother still did not have a response, and she waited, worrying and secretly asking herself: what if she alone had to remain? My father tried to calm her, but he himself did not feel convinced about what he was telling her. Everything could be expected of "them." Previously they had separated families, why should it be different now? Finally, on January 12, my mother was called out to the Commandant's Office. She was free!

How insignificant looking the release document appears! A small, yellowed half-page on which a few sentences are typed in

Ligita Kalniete. Last photo taken before returning to Latvia 1957.

stilted Russian: "Notification is given to Aivars Kalnietis, son of Aleksandrs, born in 1931, birthplace Rīga, Latvian SSR, that he has been removed from the special settlement registration list." In the top corner is noted: "Residential space not guaranteed. In the event of loss, certificate will not be reinstated."[272]

Aivars Kalnietis. Last photo taken before returning to Latvia 1957.

On May 20, 1957, we boarded a boat in Kolpashevo. The long way back home, which for my mother had lasted for sixteen years, for my father and grandmother – eight years and three months, for me – four years and five months – had begun.

Dear Voldiņ!

[...] finally I'm on a train going home. [...] The beginning of the journey was relatively good, but when we debarked from the boat, all sorts of misfortunes began. Now everything is over, and for the third day already we're sitting in the train. We are approaching the Asia–Europe border. We left Tomsk when there was still rain and snow there and nothing had turned green yet. Here everything is green, and the crab apple trees are in bloom – such beautiful scenery. We are entering the Ural Mountains, after which we'll soon be in Europe. Aivars remained in Tomsk, because his exams begin June 1.

It seems to me that I already wrote you that it's almost impossible to find a flat in Rīga. I had thought that during the time Aivars would take care of finding a flat and our registration, Sandra and I would go to Liepāja to visit aunty. Everything turned out differently. One of Aivars' old classmates has rented a flat – one room and a kitchen, so, at the moment we are heading straight for "our home." [...]

Now we are already in Europe. In the place where Europe begins there is a white post with the sign saying "Asia–Europe." The lilacs are in bloom. On the table in front of us is a bottle with a lilac sprig. Nature is so beautiful here that looking out of the window I can't get enough of it. Tomorrow we'll be in Moscow. The time is very strange. Here it is Moscow time, that is, four hours later than it is in Tomsk. There was virtually no night; all the time it was light. [...] If everything turns out all right tomorrow, we'll be able to head straight for Rīga. The express train gets there in only 19 hours. I'm travelling all the time in a sort of apathy, with no feelings of joy that only after a few days from now we will be in Rīga. Perhaps this will change, as we get closer.

May 29. [continuation] Voldiņ, I had intended to mail this letter in Moscow, but I didn't even have a moment of time. Yesterday at eleven in the evening we arrived in Moscow and had to rush head over heels to catch the Rīga train that left at one a.m. From the station where we arrived we had to get to the Rīga station. Even today I feel badly about that short trip. In the taxi there was a meter, according to which we had to pay five roubles, but the chauffeur asked that we pay 15 roubles. I eventually paid ten and regretted that I had done so, because he had no right to take more. To this day I resent this loathsome impudence. Similarly, the porter ripped us off for 20 roubles. [...] In the train again I had a dreadful feeling – the train is heading for Rīga, but we are the only Latvians on it. Tomorrow morning we will be home – in Rīga. How strange – it's snowing outside. Everything is green, and it doesn't make sense that snow is falling.

My friend Māra, who left in November for Rīga, is waiting for me with open arms. We have so much in common with her and the others who lived in Kolpashevo. Māra is counting the days when we'll finally arrive, because she has no one that she is close to. She has nothing in common with the local Rīgans. [...] I won't finish this letter yet, because I want to write down my impressions on crossing the border. This will be the fourth time that I cross the border. Hopefully it will be the last.

May 30. In Rīga. Voldiņ, we are in Rīga – and I'm incredibly happy! Right now I'm in my friend Māra's flat, which seems to me pure paradise. She has managed to rent a room in her parents' house and reclaim some of her mother's furniture, so she has made her flat very cosy. We were warmly welcomed at the train station. Māra had not slept for several nights before our arrival because she was so excited about seeing us again. Her friends have their own car, and all of them had come to meet us. We were given beautiful bouquets of flowers. Such a wonderful feeling travelling along Rīga streets. Māra had gone overboard and spent a lot to make us the best food to welcome us. It wasn't really necessary, but it is so nice that we have been met with such sincerity and warmth. In the afternoon, Māra, Sandra and I went for a walk, and upon seeing wonderful Rīga, I surely was one of the happiest people in the world at that moment. Now and then, passing by, we heard people talking in Latvian. In stores there are signs in Latvian, even on the radio one hears Latvian. I still have not been to the centre, because I have nothing to wear, our luggage not having yet arrived from Kolpashevo. It has to arrive some day now, and then we'll go to the centre, to Jūrmala, etc., which I will describe in my next letter. This morning I accompanied Māra on her way to work (she lives in Imanta); we walked beside the railway tracks, with a train speeding by every ten minutes. There is much that has been reconstructed in Rīga, as I saw through the car window on our drive from the train station, but to my eyes it looks even more beautiful than it was. [...] Your Ligita.[273]

My mother had three wishes: returning to Latvia, seeing her brothers and our family having a flat. All of these wishes have been fulfilled. But even today my mother wakes from a dreadful dream. Again it is night and someone is knocking at the door. Strange men enter and order her to get ready. The deportation nightmare begins, and my mother in despair thinks: "The last time it was a dream. Now it's real." On waking she gazes long into the empty night until she calms down and understands: she is home again. In Latvia.

Paris. August 23, 2001.

Notes

Prelude

1 "Vācu prese paziņo par Vācijas un Padomju Savienības neuzbrukšanas līgumu" [The German press announces Non-Agression Pact signed by Germany and the Soviet Union], *Jaunākās Ziņas* 22 August 1939.

2 "Vācijas ārlietu ministrija par Baltijas valstu drošību" [The German Ministry of Foreign Affairs on the security of the Baltic States] *Jaunākās Ziņas* 24 August 1939.

3 See Ansis Reinhards, ed., *Lettonie–Russie. Traités et Documents de Base in Extenso* (Rīga: Collection "Fontes" Bibliothèque Nationale de Lettonie, 1998) 117.

4 After the Locarno Conference (1925), Foreign Secretary Austen Chamberlain of Great Britain announced: "The Polish Corridor is not worth even a single bone of a British grenadier." The political lexicon in 1939 started to use a rephrased version of this quote. See Telford Taylor, *Munich: The Price of Peace* (New York: Vintage Books, 1980) 201.

5 As of autumn 1939, the Red Army garrison consisted of more than 21,000 soldiers. See Dzintra Vīksna, "Oktobra līgums" [October Agreement], *Lauku Avīze* 5 October 2000.

6 The Latvian Army was comprised of 27,000–29,000 men. Starting spring 1939, taking into account the tense situation, the army ommander, in several secret mobilizations called up several generations and categories of reservists into the Latvian Army. As a result, the numbers in the Latvian Army increased substantially. See Valdis Bērziņš and Ainars Bambals, *Latvijas armija* [Latvian Army] (Rīga: Zinātne, 1991) 87, 93.

7 The USSR and Germany agreed on the repatriation of the Baltic Germans in a secret protocol, which the two States signed on 28 September 1939.

8 Agrarian reforms were started in Latvia in 1920.

9 Edgars Andersons, *Latvijas Vēsture1920–1940. Ārpolitika* [History of Latvia. Foreign Affairs], vol. 2 (Stockholm: Daugava, 1984): 361.

10 The Deputy Commissar of State Security of the Peoples Commissariat for the Interior of the USSR, Ivan Serov's order No. 001223 "Par pretpadomju elementu deportācijas procedūru Lietuvā, Latvijā un Igaunijā" [On the Procedures for the Deportation of Anti-Soviet Elements from Lithuania, Latvia and Estonia], *Via Dolorosa: Staļinisma upuru liecības*. [Via Dolorosa: Testimony of Victims of Stalinism], vol. 1, (Rīga: *Liesma*, 1990): 32. Large-scale deportation plans were prepared for and implemented in the Soviet-occupied areas of Eastern Poland in 1939. The same plans were used for mass deportations from the Baltic States and Moldavia in 1941. See *Policy of Occupation Powers in Latvia*, ed. Elmārs Pelkaus (Rīga: *Nordik*, 1999) 155–61; Jānis Riekstiņš, "Deportation in Latvia on 14 June 1941," *Aizvestie* [The Deported], ed. Elmārs Pelkaus (Rīga: *LVA*, *Nordik*, 2001) 697–715.

11 In different time periods the KGB (State Security Committee) has been called by different names. Here and hereafter, the name used will correspond to the official Russian abbreviation used in Latvia in the relevant time period. NKVD (People's Commissariat of the

Interior) 17 June 1940–30 January 1941; NKGB (Peoples Commissariat of State Security) 31 January 1941–24 March 1946; MGB 25 March 1946–13 April 1953; for a brief period – 13 April 1953–10 April 1954 – MGB was amalgamated with the Ministry of the Interior; KGB (State Security Committee) 10 April 1954–7 September 1978.

12 Andersons 2: 322, 336.

Occupation

13 According to the 1935 census statistics, the population in Latvia was 1,950,502. Valsts statistiskā pārvalde [National Statistics Bureau], *Ceturtā tautas skaitīšana Latvijā 1935. gadā* [Fourth Population Census in Latvia 1935], eds. V. Salnitis and M.Skujenieks (Rīga, 1936) 12.

14 To date, a Latvian Commission co-operating with Russia has not succeeded in signing an intergovernmental co-operation agreement on historical and archival research.

15 Andrejs Feldmanis, "Avotos un literatūrā visbiežāk sastopamās kļūdas un neprecizātes, aprakstot uzbrukumu Masļenku sardzei 1940.gada 15. jūnijā" [The Most Frequently Found Errors and Imprecisions in Sources and Writings Describing the Attack on the Maslenki Border Post on June 15, 1940] *Masļenku traģēdija – Latvijas traģēdija* [Tragedy of Masļenki – Latvia's Tragedy] (Rīga: OMF, 2002) 279–87.

16 Jāvalda savstarpējai uzticībai" [There Must Be Mutual Trust], *Jaunākās Ziņas* 17 June, 1940.

17 In military bases in Latvia and its borders an armed force of 300,000–500,000 men, more than 1000 tanks and ca. 500 warplanes were stationed. Up to 2000 warplanes and more than 2500 tanks were battle ready beyond the border. See Andersons 2: 429.

18 *Valsts prezidents pieņēmis valdības demisiju* [The State President Has Accepted the Resignation of the Government], *Jaunākās Ziņas* 17 June 1940.

19 Ibid.

20 After the occupation of Latvia, Kārlis Ulmanis was deported and exiled to the USSR – to Orjonikidze, and later to Voroshilovsk (now Stavropol). When the war between the USSR and Germany began, he was imprisoned in Voroshilovsk. With the approach of the front, the prison was evacuated. Because of ill health, he was imprisoned in Krasnovodsk prison in Turkmenistan, where he died on 20 September 1942. The location of his grave is not known. See *Policy of Occupation Powers in Latvia* 151.

21 "Es palikšu savā vietā, jūs palieciet savās. Valsts prezidenta aicinājums tautai" [I will Stay in My Place, You Stay in Yours. An Appeal of the State President to the People], *Jaunākās* Ziņas 17 June 1940.

22 Ibid.

23 Ibid.

24 The USSR presented an ultimatum to Lithuania on June 14 and to Estonia on June 16. Both Lithuania and Estonia acceded to the ultimatum.

25 Several contemporaries of Ulmanis have confirmed this in their memoirs. See Alfreds Bērziņš, *Labie gadi* [The Good Years] (New York: Grāmatu Draugs, 1963) 290; Edgars Dunsdorfs, *Kārļa Ulmaņa dzīve* [Life of Kārlis Ulmanis) (Stockholm: Daugava, 1978) 442; Miķelis Valters, *Mana sarakste ar Kārli Ulmani un Vilhelmu Munteru Latvijas traģiskos gados* [My Correspondence with Kārlis Ulmanis and Vilhelms Munters during Latvia's Tragic Years] (Stockholm: Jaunā Latvija, 1957) 90–93, 122–25.

26 According to statistics, in the 1936–37 academic year in Latvia there were 30.4 university students per 10,000 inhabitants, which was more than in any other country in Europe. In France – 20.8; Great Britain – 16. See *Latvija citu valstu saimē. Kulturāli saimniecisks apskats* [Latvia in the Community of Nations. A Cultural and Economic Overview] (Rīga: Militārās literatūras apgādes fonds, 1939) 38.

27 Andersons 2: 483.

28 Kārlis Stradiņš, ed., *Latvijas PSR vēsture* [History of Latvian SSR], vol. 3. *No 1917. gada līdz 1950. gadam*. [From 1917 to 1950] (Rīga: LPSR ZA, 1959): 387.

29 Andersons 2: 484.

30 Declaration of the Saeima "Par Latvijas iestāšanos Padomju Sociālistisko Republiku Savienības sastāvā" [On Latvia Joining the Membership of the Union of Soviet Socialist Republics], *Sociālistiskās revolūcijas uzvara Latvijā 1940. gadā. Dokumenti un materiāli*. [Victory of the Socialist Revolution in Latvia in 1940. Documents and Materials] (Rīga: *LPSR ZA*, 1963) 296; *Policy of Occupation Powers in Latvia* 93.

31 In June, 1941, 5770 people were to be deported from Latvia to Yukhnovo, 1180 people to Beltbaltlag, 1000 people to Onega, 6850 people to Krasnoyarsk Territory. See "Plan for Deportation in Lithuania, Latvia, Estonia and Moldova Prepared by the USSR NKVD in June, 1941," *Policy of Occupation Powers in Latvia* 152.

32 Riekstiņš 703.

33 Jānis Stradiņš, "Atmiņai, atskārsmei un cerībai" [For Remembrance, Awareness and Hope], *Via dolorosa: Staļinisma upuru liecības* [*Via dolorosa*: Testimonies of Victims of Stalinism], ed. Anda Līce, vol. 1 (Rīga: Liesma, 1990): 9.

34 The figure is based on surveys carried out during the German occupation. It does not include Jewish deportees. Recent research suggests that the actual number may be lower. See Kārlis Kangeris, "Latvijas statistikas pārvaldes materiāli par *Baigo gadu* Hūvera institūta arhīvā"[Materials of the Latvian Statistical Office about the *Year of Terror* in the Archive of the Hoover Institute], *Latvijas arhīvi* 2 (1994): 87–90.

35 Indulis Zālīte and Sindija Dimante, "Četrdesmito gadu deportācijas. Struktūranalīze" [Deportations of the 1940's. A Structural Analysis], *Latvijas vēsture* 2 (1998): 78

Deportation

36 Latvijas Valsts Arhīvs (State Archive of Latvia, hereafter LVA), fonds 1987, ser. 1, file 20293, p. 12 (case file of Jānis Dreifelds deportation)

37 A political organization founded in 1930. Its ideology was similar to fascism, with a particular emphasis on anti-Semitism. President Ulmanis prohibited the organisation to operate in the territory of Latvia in 1934. The organisation resumed its activities in July, 1941, after the German occupation. *Latvju enciklopēdija*, ed. A. Švābe (Stockholm: Trīs Zvaigznes, 1952–53) 1896–97.

38 Text in italics in the pre-printed form.

39 LVA, fonds 1987, ser. 1, file 20293, p. 13.

40 Ibid. p.14.

41 In accordance with Peoples Deputy Commissar of the USSR State Security, Ivan Serov's, top secret 1941 "Instructions regarding the manner of conducting the deportation from the Lithuanian SSR, Latvian SSR and Estonian SSR" the operations should be conducted with-

out noise and panic, so as not to permit any demonstrations and other excesses not only by the deportees, but also by a certain part of the population inimically inclined toward the Soviet administration." *Policy of Occupation Powers in Latvia* 155.

42 Full statistics do not exist about murdered Army officers and soldiers of Latvia. The available numbers confirm that of the 30,843 men in the Latvian army, every sixth one suffered repression. In total, in 1940–41, 4665 military personnel suffered repression. Of these, 3395 are classified as missing and unaccounted for. See Ainars Bambals, "1940./41. gada represēto latviešu virsnieku piemiņai: Virsnieku Golgātas ceļš un liktenis GULAGa nometnēs (1941–1959) / In Memory of the Latvian Officers Repressed in 1940–1941: Their Road to Golgotha and Fate in the Stalinist GULAG Camps, 1941–1959" *Latvijas Okupācijas muzeja gadagrāmata / Yearbook of the Occupation Museum of Latvia 1999* (Rīga: OMF, 2000) 149.

43 In accordance with Peoples Deputy Commissar of the USSR State Security, Ivan Serov's: "Instructions regarding the manner of conducting the deportation from the Lithuanian SSR, Latvian SSR and Lithuanian SSR": "All persons entering the home of the deportees during the execution of the operations [...] must be detained until the conclusion the operations, and their relationship to the deportee should be ascertained. [...] After having [...] ascertained that they are persons in whom the contingent is not interested, they are liberated." *Policy of Occupation Powers in Latvia* 158.

44 LVA, fonds 1987, ser. 1, file 20293, p. 14

45 In accordance with the USSR NKVD deportation plan prepared in June 1941, "feeding of the deportees during the trip shall be carried out through railway buffets [...] based on this calculated cost – 3 roubles per person a day, including 600 grams bread." See *Policy of Occupation Powers in Latvia* 153.

46 Ibid 159. In accordance with the instructions regarding the procedures for the execution of the operation, the families were not to be informed about the impending separation. In the process, the head of the family had to be warned that personal male articles had to be packed separately, because a sanitary inspection would be conducted separate from women and children.

My Grandfather Jānis

47 Suzanne Champonnois and Francois de Labriole, *La Lettonie* (Paris: Editions Karthala, 1999) 176.

48 *Latvju enciklopēdija*, ed. Arveds Švābe, (Stockholm: *Trīs Zvaigznes*, 1950): 231.

49 Tatajana Bartele and Vitālijs Šalda, "Latviešu repatriācija no Padomju Krievijas 1918–1921" [Repatriation of Latvians from Soviet Russia], *Latvijas Vēsture* 4 (1998): 28.

50 Jānis Lismanis, *1915–1920. Kauju un kritušo karavīru piemiņai* [Commemorating the Battles and the Fallen Soldiers] (Rīga: *NIMS*, 1999) xii.

Vyatlag

51 *Latvijas valsts pasludināšana 1918. gada 18. novembrī.* [Declaration of Independence of Latvia on November 18, 1918.] (Rīga: Madris, 1998) 113.

52 Precise statistics are not available regarding the Latvians who were killed or suffered repression in the Soviet Union. The majority of sources state an approximate number: 70–80,000.

Effective January 1939, according to census statistics, 128,345 Latvians were residing in the USSR, 23,065 fewer than in 1926. See Aivars Beika, "Latvieši Padomju Savienībā – komunistiskā genocīda upuri (1929–1939) / Latvians in the Soviet Union: The Victims of Communist Terror, 1929–1939," *Latvijas Okupācijas muzeja gadagrāmata / Yearbook of the Occupation Museum of Latvia 1999* (Rīga: OMF, 2000) 89. In accordance with the Operative Order No. 00447 of USSR Interior Peoples Commissar N. Yezhov "On repression operation against former kulaks, criminals and other anti-Soviet elements," the first wave of repressions started on August 5, 1937, and it was planned to shoot 47,150 and imprison 140,950 persons, among them also Latvians. See *Policy of Occupation Powers in Latvia* 37–38.

53 "Peace Accord between Latvia and Russia of August 11, 1920, Rīga," *Likumu un valdības rīkojumu krājums* [Collection of Government Laws and Orders], 7 (18 September 1920): 21.

54 Reinhards 42.

55 *Reconnaissance "de jure" de la République de Lettonie le 26 Janvier 1921 par la Confé ence interaliée*. See *Reinhards* 42.

56 LVA, fonds 1987, ser. 1, file 20293, p. 5.

57 Ibid.

58 *Bēgļu reevakuācijas līgums starp Latviju un padomju Krieviju* [Refugee Re-Evacuation Agreement between Latvia and Soviet Russia] in *Likumu un valdības rīkojumu krājums* 7 (18 September 1920): 21.

59 In the majority of publications, 200,000 is the quoted number, however, according to the 1926 All-Union census there were 151,410 Latvians in the USSR. See Beika 46.

60 The top secret "Plan for deportation in Lithuania, Latvia, Estonia and Moldova" was prepared by V. Nasedkin, Head of the General Department of Camps of the NKVD, and approved by Lavrenty Beria on 14 June, when the deportation was already in progress. See *Policy of Occupation Powers in Latvia* 152–54; Riekstiņš 702.

61 Investigation Case No. 13 207 of Jānis Dreifelds Kristaps' son (the title and all documents in the case are in Russian). LVA, fonds 1987, ser.1, file 20293, p.51.

62 Vyatlag or Soviet Correction Work Institution K-231 was a complex of more than 20 prison camps. See Bambals 140.

63 LVA, fonds 1987, ser. 1, file 20293, p. 5.

64 Ibid, p.9.

65 Ibid, p.7.

66 Ibid.

67 The Special Commission (Meeting) of the USSR People's Commissariat of the Interior operated outside the existing institutions of the judicial system. It reviewed cases of the accused and arrived at decisions in camera – without the accused being present. Thus the USSR operated for 35 years, and the decisions made were not subject to appeal. See Jacques Rossi, *Le manuel du GOULAG* (Paris: Cherche Midi Editeur, 1997) 95.

68 The Latvian Popular Front (1988) was a democratic popular movement created as an alternative to the Communist Party, with its main objective being the renewal of independence for Latvia. On March 18, 1990, in the elections of the Supreme Council of Latvian SSR, the LPF obtained the necessary majority of deputies to realize its mandate and adopted The Declaration of the Restoration of Independence of the Republic of Latvia on May 4, 1990. After restoration of independence and development of a multiple political party system, LPF gradually lost its significance and self-liquidated in 1999.

69 LVA, fonds 1987, ser. 1, file 20293, p. 39.

70 For this reconstruction, I have used several sources: Voldemārs Beržinskis, "Atmiņas" [Memories]. Museum of the Occupation of Latvia (henceforth OMF), inv. no. 2514; Arturs Stradiņš, "Ērkšķainās gaitas" [Path of Thorns], OMF, inv. No. 3009; Romans Auzers, "Mēs vēl esam dzīvi. Mēs jums nepiedosim" [We Are Alive Still. We Will Not Forgive You, *Atmoda* 12 June 1990; Jānis Šneiders, "Uz dzīvības robežas" [On the Edge of Survival], *Literatūra un* Māksla 11 February 1989.

71 *Aizvestie* 560. The surnames of Jānis, Emilija and Ligita Dreifelds are to be found in *These Names Accuse. Nominal List of Latvians Deported to Soviet Russia in 1940–1941* (Stockholm: LNF, 1982) 94, which was compiled by Latvians who had found refuge abroad and who did not have the possibility to confirm the accuracy of the data in the archives. It was the first monumental reminder for the world of the tragedy of the Latvian nation.

72 Šneiders.

73 Ibid.

74 Bambals 140.

75 A detailed account of these circumstances is written up in the inspection report dated 20 January 1939. It is doubtful whether the situation had improved by 1941. It is more likely that it had deteriorated. See Viktor Berdinsky, *Vyatlag* (Kirov: Kirovskaja oblastnaja tipografija, 1998) 22. Cp. also Anne Applebaum's *GULAG: A History* (New York: Doubleday, 2003), esp. Chapter 19, "The War Begins" 411–19.

76 Berdinsky 24.

77 Ibid. 26.

78 Ibid. 25–26. The statistics that are accessible today regarding the death rate of the prisoners in Vyatlag confirm the horrific waste of life during the first year 1941–42. On 15 July – that is, after the arrival of the train from Latvia – it was estimated that 17,890 prisoners were in Vyatlag, on 1 January 1944 their number had decreased to 11,979. In the interim the number of prisoners had also been expanded by more than 3000 Germans from the former German Soviet republic of Volga. In comparison to the pre-war period, Group "C" weaklings had increased from 7% up to nearly 30%, while in the first group ("A") now there were only 15% of the prisoners. Applebaum 414, quotes an officially stated GULAG death rate of 25% in 1942 and 20% in 1943, "almost certainly an underestimate."

79 Māra Grīnberga and Anita Brauna, "Nomocīto sarakstus dabū neoficiāli" [Lists of Tortured Obtained Unofficially], *Diena* 14 June 2000.

80 Berdinsky 26.

81 Ibid.

82 Šneiders.

83 Dr. Silvestrs Čamanis' narration in the film *Ekspedīcija Vjatlags – Usoļlags* '95 [Expedition Vyatlag–Usollag '95], director Ingvars Leitis.

84 Shortly after the publication of this book in Latvia, in the summer of 2003, Alfreds Puškevics, who had been imprisoned in Vyatlag, brought me the Jānis Dreifelds'case file No. 41468 from the Kirov Region. In it I found my grandfather's request written on 22 November 1941, in which he asks the prison camp authorities to inform him of the fate of Emilija and Ligita. Across the request is scrawled: Respond that NKVD organs do not deal with searches for relatives.

85 Feliks Dzerzinsky (1877–1926), Bolshevik leader, head of the first Soviet secret police, the All-Russian Extraordinary Commission for Combating Counterrevolution and Sabotage (Cheka). He had a reputation as an incorruptible, ruthless, and fanatical communist.

War in Latvia

86 According to War Museum statistics, approximately 50,000 people retreated from Latvia together with the Red Army.

87 In fonds 1986 of the Latvian National Archive there is information about 7292 persons (excluding the deportees on June 14), who were arrested during the period from June 17, 1940, to July, 1941. See Rudīte Vīksne, "Represijas pret Latvijas iedzīvotājiem 1940.–1941. un 1944.–1945.gadā: kopējais un atšķirīgais" [Repressions against Residents of Latvia 1940–1941 and 1944–1945: Similarities and Differences]," *Latvija Otrajā pasaules karā* [Latvia in World War II]. ed. Daina Bleiere and Iveta Šķiņķe (Rīga: Latvijas vēstures institūta apgāds, 2000) 288.

88 During the early days of the German Occupation, Latvian politicians gathered in a united front in the Latvian Organisation Centre and started to create a state administration apparatus, but on the 17th of July Hitler established a special ministry for the administration of the Eastern territories and appointed as the minister the Baltic German Alfred Rosenberg. The newly administered unit was called *Reichskommissariat Ostland*, and Hinrich Lohse was designated as the Reich Commissioner (*Reichskommissar*). Otto Heinrich Drechsler became the *Generalkommissar* of the *Generalkommissariat Lettland*. The interests of the local population were ostensibly represented by Self-Administration of the Land (*Landesselbstverwaltung*), which did not have any authority and which primarily executed the orders of the German General Commissioner. The Self-Administration consisted of General Directorates, whose directors were Latvians. See *Latvju enciklopēdija 1962–1982* [Latvian Encyclopaedia], ed. Edgars Andersons, vol. 3 (Rockville, MD: ALA Latvian Institute, 1987): 303.

89 Arturs Žvinklis, "Latviešu prese nacistiskās Vācijas okupācijas laikā" [Latvian Press During the Occupation by Nazi Germany], *Latvija Otrajā pasaules karā* 353.

90 Arnolds Aizsilnieks, *Latvijas saimniecības vēsture 1914–1945* [Economic History of Latvia] (Stockholm: Daugava, 1968) 885.

91 Heinrihs Strods, *Latvijas lauksaimniecības vēsture* [Agricultural History of Latvia] (Rīga: Zvaigzne, 1992) 189.

92 Aizsilnieks 909, 933.

93 Andrievs Ezergailis, *Holokausts vācu okupētajā Latvijā 1941.–1944.* [The Holocaust in German-Occupied Latvia] (Rīga: Latvijas vēstures institūta apgāds, 1999) 69, 139, 142–44.

94 The Rumbula operation was implemented by about 1700 men, whose degree of responsibility and involvement varied. About 700 men were from the German SS units. Approximately 1000 of these could have been Latvians, who primarily were responsible for guard duties: 350–400 Latvian SD men, 80–100 Latvian ghetto guards, and about 450 precinct police. The operation was planned and worked out in detail by the German SD under the leadership of General Friedrich Jeckeln. When the operation started in the Rīga Ghetto, the Jews refused to submit and a massacre began, in which, according to approximate estimates, up to 1000 persons were killed. German policemen (*Schutzpolizei*) were supplemented by an indeterminate number of men from the notorious Arājs Commando, a Latvian SD unit. In the court proceedings against Jeckeln it was determined that Latvians had not participated in the shootings at Rumbula. This was done by 12 men specially selected by the General, who with a bullet in the back of the head killed each of the Jews lying in the pit. During the court proceedings against Friedrich Jahnke in Hamburg, it was determined that until the evening of

November 29 the substance of the operation was known only to the immediate subordinates of Jeckeln. Mid-level German officers, as well as Latvian officers only found out about the operation in the prior evening, but its full extent only in the Rumbula woods. See Ezergailis 278–85.

95 The Lāčplesis Order is a Latvian national citation awarded to those who had distinguished themselves in action during the liberation of Latvia between 1915 and 1925. The order was first introduced on November 11, 1919. It was awarded until 1928. In total 2116 military personnel were given the citation, among whom were also some Lithuanians, Estonians, Poles, French, Finns and other nationalities that had participated in the struggle for the independence of Latvia.

96 Ezergailis 298, 307, 415.

97 Ibid. 91. The regime of President Kārlis Ulmanis limited the freedom of expression, but it was not anti-Semitic, and Jews enjoyed the same rights as other ethnic groups in Latvia. Even up to the Soviet occupation in 1940, Ulmanis kept the borders open for Jewish refugees from Germany and Austria, when other European countries had ceased to do so.

98 Jānis Martinsons, "Cīņa pret žīdismu" [The Struggle against Jewry], *Tēvija* 1 December 1941.

99 German information sources kept silent about the fact that among the Soviets subjected to repression there were 1771 Jews, proportionally being the group that had suffered the most of all the inhabitants of Latvia. Latest statistics indicate that 1.93% of Latvia's Jews were deported as compared to 0.85% of ethnic Latvians. See Riekstiņš 703 and Indulis Zālīte and Sindija Eglīte, "1941. gada 14. jūnija deportācijas struktūranalīze" [Structural Analysis of the 14 June 1941 Deportation], *Aizvestie* 688. In researching the composition of the brigades who did the deporting, there is no basis for the opinion that Jews dominated these. Also Russians and Latvians collaborated. The group that deported my mother's family is a typical example: two Russians – Bogorad and Sozonov; two Latvians – Briedis and Dembergs; and one Jew – Šteinbaums.

100 The most characteristic examples: J. Silabriedis and B. Arklans, *"Political Refugees" Unmasked* (Rīga: Latvian State Publ. House, 1965) 225; J. Dzirkalis, *Kāpēc viņi bēga. Patiesība par latviešu nacionālo fondu Zviedrijā* [Why Did They Flee? The Truth About the Latvian National Foundation in Sweden] (Rīga: Zvaigzne, 1965) 87; E. Avotiņš, J. Dzirkalis and V. Pētersons, *Kas ir Daugavas vanagi* [Daugavas Vanagi: Who Are They?] (Rīga: LVI, 1962) 125; M. Birznieks, *No SS and SD to…* [From SS to SD to…] (Rīga: Zvaigzne, 1979) 175. Hiding behind the pseudonyms was for the most part Pauls Ducmanis, who had served already well in the Nazi propaganda apparatus. See Andrew Ezergailis, *Nazi/Soviet Disinformation about the Holocaust in Nazi-Occupied Latvia. Daugavas Vanagi: Who Are They – Revisited* (Rīga: OMF, 2005).

101 In the Jumprava manor at the beginning of December a primitive prison camp was installed, where at the beginning of 1942, 2500 Western European Jews were incarcerated. The majority of them were killed in March 1942 in Biķernieki forest. See Ezergailis, *Holokausts* 421.

102 Thirty-five Latvian citizens have received the honour of "The Righteous among the Nations" from the State of Israel. The most distinguished among these is Žanis Lipke, who saved the lives of 56 Jews. In total 400 people and more than a thousand and a half of their family members have taken part in saving Jews in Latvia. See: Marģers Vestermanis, "Retter im Lande der Handlanger. Zur Geschichte der Hilfe für Juden in Lettland während der "Endlösung"" [Saviours in the Country of Henchmen. Concerning the History of Assistance to Jews in Latvia during the "Final Solution"], *Solidarität und Hilfe für Juden während der*

NS-Zeit [Solidarity and Assistance for Jews during Nazi Rule] (Berlin: Metropol, 1998) 231–73; Leo Dribins, *Ebreji Latvijā.* [Jews in Latvia] (Rīga, 1996) 29; Frank Gordon, *Latvians and Jews between Germany and Russia* (Stockholm: Memento, 2001) 84–93.

103 At the end of July, 1941 there were about a hundred men in Arājs' unit. In November there were no more than 300. This shooting squad in total killed 26,000 people: 14,000 Latvian Jews, 8000 foreign Jews, 2000 Gypsies and mentally ill individuals and 2000 Communists from Latvia. In total the number of Latvians who were directly involved with the shooting, are no more than 500 men. Approximately 1500 men could have been involved in doing guard duty for the executions. See Ezergailis, *Holocaust* 39, 218.

104 From 19 to 30 October 1943 the Conference of Foreign Ministers of Great Britain, USA and USSR took place in Moscow in preparation for the 28 November–1 December 1943 Teheran Conference, in which Roosevelt, Stalin and Churchill agreed to the creation of a second front. It is during the Teheran Conference that Roosevelt and Stalin had an informal meeting, during which they agreed about the fate of the Baltic States after the war. This agreement was ratified at the Yalta Conference of 4–11 February 1945.

105 *Mūsu atbilde Maskavai ir cīņa* [Our Response to Moscow Is to Fight], *Tēvija* 14 November 1943.

106 "Boļševiki slepkavo latviešu strādājošos" [The Bolsheviks Are Murdering Latvian Workers], *Tēvija* 14 November 1943.

107 Jānis Dzintars, "Komjaunieši Rīgas antifašistiskajā pagrīdē" [Young Communists in the Anti-Fascist Underground of Rīga], *LPSR ZA Vēstis* 10 (1968): 21.

108 Aizsilnieks 896.

109 Discussions regarding the granting of greater autonomy to Latvia and Estonia began in Berlin at the beginning of 1942. Two opposing points of view clashed on this issue in the government ranks – to win the war at any price would accomplish the preliminary work for the Germanisation of the Baltics. The people who represented the first faction were for autonomy and the proclamation of independence, thus providing for the mobilisation of 250,000 more soldiers from Ostland. The second faction blocked these plans, intending to flood Latvian and Estonian territories with 100,000 German colonists. In total five projects were worked out, of which the fifth, dated 17 February 1943, was approved by Hitler, delaying the final decision regarding increased autonomy until after the war. Starting November 1942 there were widespread rumours about imminent positive reforms. The spreading of these rumours was encouraged by German officials to enforce a positive public attitude in Latvia to the formation of the Legion. See: Heinrihs Strods, "Vācijas projekti Igaunijas un Latvijas autonomijai1942.–1944. gadā [German Plans for Autonomy of Estonia and Latvia in 1942–1944], *Latvijas Vēstures Institūta Žurnāls* 1 (1992): 102–08.

110 Even though the Legion was formed within the framework of the *Waffen SS*, its soldiers had nothing in common with the political SS elite guard. The Latvian Self-Administration clearly formulated its position – it must be granted greater independence and the Legion was not to fight in the West. The legionnaires were soldiers of fighting units at the front, whose goal was to fight against Bolshevism. They first fought at the Volkhov front near Leningrad and never turned their weapons against the Western Allies nor took part in operations against civilians or Jews. The last battles for the 15th division were at the lower reaches of the Oder River in 1945 where at the order of the German High Command the division was disarmed. The majority of the soldiers in the division voluntarily surrendered to the Americans. In compliance with the decision by a commission of the UNRRA (United

Nations Relief and Rehabilitation Administration), they were granted the status of displaced persons, because the "Baltic armed SS units in terms of their objective, ideology, action and structure in terms of their classification are to be considered as separate from and different than the German SS units." The 19th Division took part in the battles in the Kurzeme stronghold. On May 9 they capitulated, and Latvian soldiers were taken prisoner. They were deported to Siberia, were many died. The ones who survived were granted amnesty in 1955. See Andrew Ezergailis, ed., *The Latvian Legion. Heroes, Nazis or Victims. A Collection of Documents from OSS War Crimes Investigation Files 1945–1950* (Rīga: The Historical Institute of Latvia, 1997) 31–34, 38–40 The total number of Latvians in German military formations has been variously estimated between 80,000 and 165,000. Recent research suggests that the number, though still an estimate, may be closer to 110–15,000. See Kārlis Kangeris, Nacionālsociālistiskās Vācijas militārajos formējumos iesaistītie Latvijas iedzīvotāji: skaita problēma"[Inhabitants of Latvia in Nazi-German Military Formations: Numerical Problem], *Latvijas Kara muzeja gadagrāmata* [Yearbook of the War Museum of Latvia] (Rīga: Latvijas kara muzejs, 2000) 139.

111 In total, approximately one million soldiers from the occupied territories fought in the German military formations. In this number there were 488,000 soldiers that were mobilised from the USSR occupied territories. The majority of the soldiers viewed as their objective the struggle against Bolshevism, which Greater Germany deftly manipulated, to its benefit. See Heinrihs Strods, *Zem melnbrūnā zobena: Vācijas politika Latvijā* [Under the Black-and-Brown Sword: German Policies in Latvia, 1939–1945] (Rīga, 1994) 94. See also Inesis Feldmanis, "Waffen-SS Units of Latvians and Other Non-Germanic Peoples in World War II: Methods of Formation, Ideology and Goals," *The Hidden and Forbidden History of Latvia under Soviet and Nazi Occupations 1940–1991*, Symposium of the Commission of the Historians of Latvia 14, eds. Valters Nollendorfs and Erwin Oberländer, (Rīga: Historical Institute of Latvia, 2005) 334–351.

112 The cynicism of both occupation regimes is evidenced by the fact that in Kurzeme Soviets sent the 130th Latvian Red Riflemen Corps in battle against the 19th Division of the Latvian Legion fighting on German side. In total, about 100,000 Latvian soldiers fought in the Soviet armed forces. Half of these were Latvians from Russia and residents of Latvia who had retreated together with the Soviet armed forces in the summer of 1941. The other half was from the mobilisation in the Vidzeme and Latgale regions at the end of 1944 and beginning of 1945 after the second Soviet occupation.

113 As the end of the war neared, the German command with increasing frequency employed political promises to motivate the legionnaires. In the 1 January 1945 order of the Commander of the 15th Latvian Division, Obwurtzer, it is stated: "You are fighting for the renewal of an independent Latvia!" In January 1945, Commander Krieger of the 6th Corps said: " There will be a Latvia, and it will be the result of the heroic battles of its own soldiers..." See Uldis Neiburgs, "Latviešu karavīri Vācijas un PSSR armijās: galvenās problēmas" [Latvian Soldiers in the German and USSR Armies: Main Problems], *Latvija Otrajā pasaules karā* 201.

114 On 3 March 1944, the Ostland Military Command established the Baltic Evacuation Headquarters, whose task was to work out a plan on how to evacuate 3 million people. But amongst the Reich leadership there was no unanimity about the evacuation, and in July the faction that believed that the Baltic countries must be defended at any cost gained upper hand. Evacuation was prohibited, and on 9 July 1944 Himmler granted Friedrich Jeckeln

emergency powers to hunt down local residents, to put them in work and military service for the defence of the Baltic. Because of the fast advance of the Soviet Army, evacuation was restarted on 15 August. Up to January 1945, 180,000 people left Latvia. Kārlis Kangeris, "Die Baltischen Völker und die deutschen Pläne für die Räumung des Baltikums 1944" [The Baltic Nations and German Plans for the Evacuation of the Baltic], *Baltisches Jahrbuch 1988*: 177–92 estimates the number of evacuees at 180,000. Mirdza Kate Baltais, "Piespiedu iesaukšana darbam Vācijā, militāram dienestam un evakuācija uz Vāciju" [Forced Labour, Military Service and Evacuation to Germany], *Okupācijas varu nodarītie postījumi Latvijā 1940–1990*, ed. Tadeušs Puisāns (Stockholm: Memento, 2000) 198, estimates the total number of Latvians in German territory during the war at 217,000, including forced labourers, military personnel and refugees

115 Up to December 1943, in total 16,800 people were herded from Latvia to work in Germany. By the end of the war this number had increased. See Baltais 193–99.

116 "What d'you think, will I trudge to Berlin?" Translated from the Russian.

117 In seven month long battles, approximately 3500 soldiers of the 19th Division died in Kurzeme. 14,000 surrendered to become prisoners of war after the capitulation. See: Osvalds Freivalds, *Kurzemes cietoksnis* [The Kurzeme Stronghold], part 1 (Copenhagen: Imanta, 1954) 178.

"I beg you – shoot me or exonerate me"

118 Immediately after capitulation, about 4000 people went into the woods in Kurzeme. According to Soviet documentation, in the post war period from 1944 to 1956, approximately 20,000 people had been involved in national resistance. See Heinrihs Strods, *Latvijas nacionālo partizānu karš 1944–1956* [The War of Latvian National Partisans] (Rīga: Preses nams, 1996) 158.

119 By a 15 August 1941 order, all residents had to register at the Labour Administration. The instituted census system allowed control that no local resident would evade work. See Aizsilnieks 938.

120 According to the statistics about persons mobilised during 1943–44, about 18% of the men called into the army tried to evade mobilisation. On 15 July 1944, General Jeckeln proclaimed total mobilisation across the Ostland territory, calling in 50% of men aged from 16 to 55. During this period evasion of mobilisation considerably increased. See Neiburgs 197–204.

121 Strods, *Latvijas nacionālo partizāņu karš* 129.

122 Rīga and most of Latvia was occupied in October 1944. By 1 December 1944, the People's Commissariat of the Interior had arrested 4914 people; the army counter-espionage unit had detained 2127 individuals. On 16 October, the first two prison camps for arrested persons was established in Latvia – No. 291 near the city of Rēzekne and No. 292 near the city of Daugavpils. Subsequently their number increased by another three. The existing prisons also were overfilled. The arrests were so massive, that some of the party functionaries started to complain to the administration about the lack of workers in schools and hospitals. See Strods, *Latvijas nacionālo partizānu karš* 124–27.

123 Precise statistics about the number of Latvian refugees during World War II do not exist. The numbers vary in various sources. It is generally agreed, however, that at least 200,000 Latvians

were outside Latvia in the West, primarily in Germany and German-occupied areas in the latter part of 1944 and until the end of the war. After the war, up to 120,000 remained in the West, primarily in refugee camps in British, US and French occupation zones of Germany. These included refugees, forced labourers and military personnel. Many were overtaken by the Red Army during its 1945 offensives and either sent back or to the so-called "filtration," prisoner of war and GULAG camps. See *Latvju enciklopēdija*, "Bēgļu laiki" [Refugees] 235–36 and "DP nometnes Vācijā" [DP Camps in Germany] 507. Cf. also Baltais 198.

124 "Come out, bandit! I'll shoot!" Translated from the Russian.

125 LVA, fonds 1986, ser. 1, file 17170, vol. 8, pp. 117–52 (Property taken away at the time of arrest of Aleksandrs Kalnietis).

126 Letter of Aleksandrs Kalnietis to Milda Kalniete, 2 November 1950.

127 Fricis Sirsniņš, who was arrested on 2 October 1945 and was at the Cheka at approximately the same time as Aleksandrs Kalnietis, has described in striking detail his interrogation, life in prison and the stages in his deportation. See Fricis Sirsniņš, "Atmiņas" [Memories], *Pretestības kustība okupācijas varām Latvijā* [Resistance Movement against Occupation Regimes in Latvia] (Rīga: SolVita, 1997) 62–67. Cf. also Anne Applebaum's chapters on "Arrest" (121–145), "Prison" (146–158) and "Transport, Arrival, Selection" (159–182).

128 LVA, fonds 1986, ser. 1, file 17170 ("Latvijas nacionālo partizānu organizācijas sakaru schema" [Communication Structure of the National Partisan Organisation of Latvia]).

129 LVA, fonds 1986, ser. 1, file 17170, vol. 2, p. 69. Article 19 of the Criminal Code of the Russian Federal Soviet Socialist Republic (RFSSR) makes a person accountable for the preparation of a criminal act and creation of favourable circumstances for a criminal act. Article 58 and its 12 sections deals with counterrevolutionary crimes. In the case of Aleksandrs Kalnietis: being a traitor to the Soviet Fatherland; collaboration with the enemy; the performance of terror acts; destruction of state and public property; appeal to overthrow the Soviet regime; participation in the organisation of the above-mentioned crimes. See *RFSSR Criminal Code* (Moscow, 1944) 9, 20–23.

130 LVA, fonds 1986, ser. 1, file 17170, vol. 7, p. 313.

131 In the tight security prison camps the prisoners were permitted to write to their relatives twice a year, however the prison camp administration often arbitrarily decided to permit or prohibit correspondence. See Jacques Rossi 47, 77. See also Applebaum 247–52.

132 Letter of Aleksandrs Kalnietis to Aivars Kalnietis 5 May 1950

133 Ustyvimlag was created on 16 August 1937. It was operative until January 1, 1960. See *Sistema iapraviteļno-trudovih lagerei v SSSR*.. 1923–1960 (Moscow: *Zvenya*, 1998) 275.

134 Pechorlag was created on 24 July 1950. It was closed on5 August1959. Ibid. 275.

135 Letter of Aleksandrs Kalnietis to Milda Kalniete 22 August 1950.

136 Letter of Aleksandrs Kalnietis to Milda Kalniete 27 April 1951.

137 The infamous Latvian KGB officer Jānis Vēveris was a member of the Commission. Under his leadership an expeditionary group of investigators of the People's Commissariat for State Security (PCSS) in 1941 invented criminal cases in Vyatlag and Usollag, recommending death sentences for government officials and public organisation leaders deported in 1941. LVA, fonds 1986, ser. 1, file 17170, vol. 7, p. 374. Vēveris' signature is also on the case materials of my grandfather Jānis Dreifelds.

138 Ibid. p. 459.

Forced Settlement and Starvation

139 The deportation of farmers in parallel with the collectivisation process in the USSR took place according to plan. Thus in accordance with "The 30 January 1930 decision of the Politburo of the All Union Communist Party (Bolsheviks) Central Committee regarding "Expropriation of 'Kulaks'" instructions were given for the following four-month period (February–May), based on approximate estimates, to send to concentration camps 60,000 and deport to distant regions 150,000 kulaks. "To deport 70 thous. families to the regions of the Northern Territory; 50 thous. families to Siberia; 20–25 thousand families to the Urals; 20–25 thous. families to Kazakhstan. Places of deportation shall be uninhabited or sparsely populated areas, in order to employ the deportees in agricultural works or forestry operations, fishery and other works." *Policy of Occupation Powers in Latvia* 28–30

140 Rūta Upīte, *Vēl tā gribējās dzīvot. Pārdzīvojumu stāsts* (New York: *Grāmatu Draugs*, 1978) 26. Rūta Upīte, *Dear God, I Wanted to Live* (New York: Grāmatu Draugs, 1982) 26.

141 On 6 January 1957, when the notice came about Ligita Dreifelde's removal from the administrative forced settlement list, the sixteenth registration form had been started at the Commandant's Office. In total Ligita Dreifelde spent 164 months in Siberia. In the interim she was allowed to spend 16 months in Latvia.

142 *Pod glasnim nadzorom*. – In Russian.

143 Official report by the Head of the of Forced Settlement Work and Specialized Forced Settlement Division of the Chief Administration of Correction Work Prison Camps and Colonies of the People's Commissariat of the Interior (PCI), M. Kondrotov, to the Deputy Head of the PCI, V. Chernishov, about the settlement and employment of the deported forced settlers. See: *Aizvestie* 80.

144 Ibid 83. Report of the Head of the Chief Administration of Reconstruction Work Prison Camps and Colonies of the USSR PCI, V. Nasedkin, to the Deputy Head of the, V. Chernishov, regarding the transfer of supervision of the deported forced settlers to the USSR PCI to the Special Relocation Section.

145 The oldest sister Rūta Upīte, after returning to Latvia in 1947, wrote down her recollections of what she had experienced in Siberia. After her death, the manuscript was taken abroad in 1967, and it was published anonymously in 1977, in order to protect her father and her sister Dzidra, who had survived the repression. In reading the book for the first time, I did not know that the Mrs. D. and L. mentioned in the book were my grandmother and mother. See Upīte, *Dear God, I Wanted to Live* 141 .

146 Upīte, *Dear God* 77.

147 It is probable that the decision to settle 300 people on the uninhabited island is connected with the report of the PCI Novosibirsk region administration chief, A. Vorobyov, of 22 August 1941 to the USSR PCI Deputy Chief,V. Chernishov: "Due to the great distances, the persons who 2–3 times per month must come to register at the PCI Regional Divisions, will not be able to comply with these requirements. For the same reason, the administrative supervision of the contingent is extraordinarily difficult [...] Therefore, in order to enforce the regimen in places organized for employment of the settlers [...] taking in account this period of war, I consider it necessary: 1. To apply the regimen to the settlers that has been specified in the Regulation Regarding Special Villages approved by the USSR PCI Decision No. 2122–617– ps of 29 December 1939 [...]." Bilina was precisely such a "special village." *Aizvestie* 18.

148 The "comrades-in-arms" of Bilina who are alive today and living in Latvia are Aina Baginska, née Zālīte and Māra Kramiņa. The mother of the latter, Vera Kramiņa, died in 1941. Aina's mother Jūlija Zālīte died the day after she returned from Bilina on 3 March 1944, while Aina's cousin Juris Kolbergs died a month after his return on 6 April 1944. Olita Siliņa married a deported Moldavian during the 1950s and after being freed went with her husband to live in Moldavia. She has now died. Vitauts Siliņš returned to Latvia and died in a car accident. The mother of both the Siliņš died in Siberia during the 1950s.

149 1 pood = 16.38 kg.

Changes

150 Due to lack of paper, during the first years in exile the deportees wrote letters on birch bark. Such letters are in the collection of the Museum of the Occupation of Latvia. See *Latvijas Okupācijas muzejs: Latvija zem Padomju Savienības un nacionālsociālistiskās Vācijas varas 1940–1991 Latvia under the Rule of the Soviet Union and National Socialist Germany: Museum of the Occupation of Latvia*, ed. Valters Nollendorfs (Rīga: OMF, 2002) 146.

151 In the memoirs of the deportees there is mention of receiving the first letters in the spring of 1945. These were letters that were written from that part of Latvia, which in October 1944 was occupied by the Soviet army. Communication with the people living in the Kurzeme cul-de-sac became possible only in May 1945.

152 During the Yalta Conference 4–11 February 1945, the Allies agreed on the repatriation of USSR citizens. The residents of the annexed USSR territories were saved by the unclear formulation of the agreement that classified USSR territory as having the boundaries defined on 1 September 1939. Nonetheless, as a result of this USSR decision, in the period from 1943 to 1947, the Allies in total handed over to the Soviet Union approximately 2,272,000 Soviet citizens, including refugees who had left Russia after the 1917 Bolshevik revolution and had never taken out USSR citizenship. In January 1946, the government of Sweden, ignoring protests from the public, handed over 130 Latvians, 7 Estonians and 9 Lithuanians to the USSR. See Nikolai Tolstoy, *Victims of Yalta* (n.p.: Corgi Book, 1990) 468, 481, 515.

153 In the Soviet Zone of Germany 36,000 Latvian soldiers were taken prisoner on Victory Day. See: Uldis Neiburgs, "Karagūstekņu traģēdija" [The Tragedy of Prisoners of War], *Lauku Avīze* 8 May 2001.

154 Letter of Ligita Dreifelde to Viktors Dreifelds. 16 May 1947.

155 Precise data on how many refugees responded to Soviet propaganda is not available. According to estimates made by historians, their number is no more than 3% of all refugees (*Latvju enciklopēdija* 237). It is known that in 1945/46 3650 Latvian soldiers voluntarily were repatriated to the Soviet Union. See Neiburgs, "Karagūstekņu traģēdija."

156 Letter of Anna Dumpe and Jānis Dumpis to Viktors Dreifelds. 7July 1947.

157 In the Visa Section of the USSR Ministry of the Interior the following documents were required to be handed in: a personal invitation confirmed by a USSR Embassy; a receipt that the state fee had been paid; a recommendation from the place of employment approved by the Party Committee; a written confirmation that the wife or husband did not object to the trip abroad; an autobiography, wherein all relatives living abroad were to be listed; a certificate confirming registration of the place of residence; a form, in which precise information about all dead and living first generation relatives; four photos.

158 Alfrēds Staris, *1941. gadā okupantu izsūtīto Latvijas iedzīvotāju bērnu ērkšķainais atceļš uz dzimteni* [The Thorny Return Path to Their Native Land by the Children of Latvian Residents Deported by the Occupiers in 1941], *Latvijas Vēsture* 1 (1995): 37–44.

159 Ibid. – According to the provisory lists created in Latvia, about 600 children were to be re-evacuated. For this purpose, 180 thousand roubles were put aside in total.

160 Ibid.

161 "Mahle is from Africa. Mahle is not pretty." Translation from the German.

162 *Dzeguze* means cuckoo in Latvian. A literal translation from Russian, because a cuckoo is a *kukushka* in Russian

My Grandmother Emilija

163 In Siberia women were often called by their husband's name. "Jānis' wife thus became "Janovna."

164 "For ten years in a high security prison camp without a right to written communication" was a standard explanation that was given to relatives in instances when a death sentence had been carried out for a prisoner or he or she had died. The KGB considered that hiding the information about a death created the possibility to fabricate new cases and to reveal the collaborators of the sentenced person, with the dead person's "testimony" serving as proof of guilt.

165 A perspective on how expensive prices were can be seen in wholesale prices: 1 kg butter – 45 to 65 roubles; 1 kg cod fillets – 13 roubles; a wool dress – 313 to 557 roubles; men's short boots – 313 roubles. See *Informacionnyii spravochnik sprosa i predlozhenia tovarov*. 1949. *Ministerstvo torgvlii Soyuza SSR*.

166 Letter of Emilija Dreifelde to Ligita Dreifelde. 17 July 1949.

167 A kilogram of bread cost 14 roubles; a pail of potatoes – 10 roubles in the summer and 5 roubles after the new crop was gathered.

168 Letter of Emilija Dreifelde to Ligita Dreifelde. September, 1949.

169 Letter of Emilija Dreifelde to Ligita Dreifelde. August, 1948.

170 Ibid.

171 The Soviet authorities fluctuated between two positions regarding the property of persons deported on 14 June 1941: to view the property as ownerless property or as a nationalized property. In March 1949, the Supreme Council of the LSSR adopted a decree that "the property of those persons who are administratively sentenced to be deported outside the boundaries of Latvian SSR during 1940–41 for hostile actions against the Soviet regime, is subject to nationalisation and incorporated into the State Property Fund." See Jānis Riekstiņš, "Aizvesto manta" [Property of the Deportees], *Labrīt* 14 June 1994.

172 The assignment of living space was regulated by the Latvian SSR Council of Ministers and the Republican Trade Union Council Decision No. 81 "On the Procedures for Distribution of Living Space in LSSR." There were different minimum living area norms established in the deputy council territory of each city or country region that gave the right to apply for improved living conditions or the acceptance on a waiting list for a flat. In Rīga the minimum living area size per person was 4.5 square meters, or 48.5 square feet. See: *Pilsoņu dzīvokļu tiesības* [Citizen Rights to Living Space] (Rīga: Liesma, 1969) 31.

173 In 1964 a bookkeeper's salary was 60 roubles per month and for an engineer – 120 roubles per month. General consumer product prices were: rye bread – 0.40 roubles; beef – 4 rou-

bles/kg; butter – 3.50 roubles/kg; a winter coat – 150 roubles; a good pair of women's shoes – 40 roubles; men's shirt – 10 roubles; a good pair of men's shoes – 30–80 roubles. The data has been taken from: Andrivs Namsons, "Lebensbedingungen und Lebensstandard der Landbevölkerung in Sowjetlettland" [Living Conditions and Living Standards of Rural Population in Soviet Latvia], *Acta Baltica*. Liber Annalis Instituti Baltici 4 (1964): 65–91.

174 Letter of Emilija Dreifelde to Ligita Dreifelde. May 1949.

175 Letter of Emilija Dreifelde to Ligita Dreifelde. 21 July 1949.

176 Letter of Emilija Dreifelde Ligita Dreifelde. 17 February 1949.

177 Letter of Emilija Dreifelde Ligita Dreifelde. 20 March 1949.

178 Letter of Emilija Dreifelde Ligita Dreifelde. 24 January 1949.

179 Letter of Emilija Dreifelde Ligita Dreifelde. 2 September 1949.

180 Letter of Emilija Dreifelde Ligita Dreifelde July 1949.

181 Letter of Emilija Dreifelde Ligita Dreifelde. 19 March 1949.

182 Letter of Emilija Dreifelde Ligita Dreifelde. May 1949.

183 Letter of Emilija Dreifelde to Ligita Dreifelde. July 1949.

184 Letter of Frida Dzene to Anna Dumpe. 29 April 1950.

Family Members of a Bandit

185 Up to 1953, in addition to the victims of deportation of 25 March 1949, another 76,000 people suffered repression. A further 91,034 persons were imprisoned in so-called filtration camps after the war. See Indulis Zālīte, "Okupācijas režīmu upuri Latvijā 1940.–1991. g." [Victims of Occupation Regimes in Latvia 1940–1991], a paper presented at the conference "The Latvian Legion in Latvia's History in the Context of Soviet and German Occupations," Rīga, 10 June 2000.

186 "Paraugnoteikumi par iekšējo darba iekārtu valsts, kooperatīvo un sabiedrisko uzņēmumu un iestāžu strādniekiem un kalpotājiem" [Model Regulations Regarding Internal Work Organisation for Lower and Upper Grade Employees of State, Co-operative and Public Enterprises and Institutions] adopted by the USSR Council of People's Commissars on 18 January 1941 specified criminal liability for missing work. In accordance with these regulations persons guilty of a socially dangerous action or non-action directed against the established order of the Soviet state shall be sentenced by court judgment: "[...] for missing work without a valid reason, lower and upper grade employees of state, co-operative and public enterprises and institutions shall be brought before the court and with a judgment by the peoples' court sentenced to rehabilitative labour in their workplace for a period up to six months, with up to 25% reduction of their salary. (USSR Supreme Council Presidium's Decree of 26 June 1940, Article 5, Part 2) [...] The principal factor that qualifies missed work as a crime is the absence of a valid reason for not arriving at work, being late or leaving work early." See *Darba likumdošana. PSSR darba likumdošana un KPFSR darba likumu kodeksa komentāri*. [Labour Legislation. USSR Labour Legislation and RSFSR Labour Code Commentary] (Rīga: LVL, 1950) 78–81.

187 Aivars Kalnietis, "Tumšie gadi: atmiņas par izsūtījumu. 1990. gada rudens" [The Dark Years: Recollections about the Deportation. Fall 1990] 2. Family archive.

188 Ibid.

189 In the 29 January 1949 Decision No. 390–138 of the USSR Council of Ministers it is specified that the following "categories" of inhabitants have to be deported from Latvia, Lithuania

and Estonia: kulaks and their families; family members of bandits and nationalists; family members of executed and convicted bandits; former bandits and their family members who have resumed anti-Soviet activities; family members of people who are supporting bandits. See *Policy of Occupation Powers in Latvia* 294.

190 Order No. 0068 of 28 February 1949 by the USSR State Security Minister regarding USSR State Security Ministry's top-secret operation "Coastal Surf" ("*Priboi*") for deporting inhabitants of the Baltic States. See Heinrihs Strods and Matthew Kott, "The File on Operation 'Priboi': A Reassessment of the Mass Deportations of 1949" *Journal of Baltic Studies* 33.1 (2002): 1–31.

191 *Policy of Occupation Powers in Latvia* 298

192 In total 76,212 persons were involved in carrying out the operation "Coastal Surf" in Latvia, Estonia and Lithuania; of these 28,404 persons were members of the Communist Party or the Young Communist League; 18,387 were paramilitaries (special battalions that were formed from among armed volunteers of Communist Party and Young Communist League activists, ex-front-line fighters and partisans, and citizens who had returned from Eastern regions of the USSR); the other persons were soldiers from various special army units. See Strods and Kott 24.

193 Zālīte, "Okupācijas režīmu upuri Latvijā."

194 In the March 1949 deportations, 20,713 persons were deported from Estonia and 31,917 persons from Lithuania. See Strods and Kott 20.

195 Heinrihs Strods, "Latvijas cilvēku izvedēji 1949. gada 25. martā" [Deporters of Latvians on 25 March 1949], *Latvijas Vēsture* 1 (1999): 72.

196 LVA, fonds 1894, ser. 1, file 463, p. 39 (dossier on the family of bandit sympathiser Aleksandrs Kalnietis) and fonds 1986, ser. 1, file 17170, vols. 1–9 (criminal case of Aleksandrs Kalnietis and other persons).

197 Ibid., p. 32.

198 Ibid., p. 9.

199 Ibid, p. 7.

200 Ibid., p. 17.

201 Jānis Riekstiņš, "Genocīds: 1949. gada 25 marta deportācijas akcija Latvijā" [Genocide: 25 March 1949 Deportation in Latvia], *Latvijas Vēsture* 3 (1991): 27.

202 No precise data exist regarding the number of reviewed cases and persons that were allowed to return from deportation.

203 An entry on the issuance of the 16 December 1949 secret regulation of the Latvian SSR Council of Ministers can be found in the log of the Latvian SSR Council of Ministers (LVA, fonds 270, ser. 10, file 12), but the document itself cannot be found in the archive materials of the Latvian SSR Council of Ministers (LVA, fonds 270, ser. 2, file 980). A facsimile of the regulation is in the personal archive of Sandra Kalniete.

204 Kalnietis 5.

205 In accordance with the 12 March 1949 order of the USSR Minister of the Interior S. Kruglov "On the deportation of 'kulaks' and their families, the families of 'bandits and nationalists': "Deportees are allowed to take with them their own personal valuables, household implements (clothes, plates and dishes, petty agricultural, trade or housekeeping inventory) and the food reserve of the total weight to 1500 kilograms per family." The short time frame for executing the operation "Coastal Surf" and the detainees' state of shock rendered this provision meaningless. Even the "amenities" of the cattle cars, with 50 to 60 people per wagon,

did not leave room for transporting such baggage. Deportees managed to take along only the bare necessities. *Policy of Occupation Powers in Latvia* 272; *Latvijas Vēstnesis*, 4 March 1999.

206 Kalnietis 3.

207 A train consisted of 55 to 60 wagons, with up to 60 persons in each wagon. See Zenons Indrikovs, "Sāpju ceļš uz Austrumiem" [The Torturous Road to the East], *Kaujas Postenī* 26 April 1990 [Newspaper of the Ministry of the Interior]. The persons who were settled in the camp were primarily from Rīga and the environs (6 wagons).

208 Jānis Riekstiņš, Lauksaimniecības kolektivizācija un "kulaku" deportācija Latvijā. 1949. gads" [Collectivisation of Agriculture and Deportation of 'Kulaks' from Latvia 1949], *Latvijas ZA Vēstis*, Part A 1/2 (2000): 59–60 [Journal of the Latvian Academy of Sciences].

209 Kalnietis 5.

210 Jurģi – St. George's Day, 23 April, the traditional moving day for farmhands who changed their employers. Now a familiar Latvian term for "moving day.."

211 Kalnietis 5

212 The 1932 regulation of the Central Executive Committee and the Council of Peoples' Commissars "On the Introduction of Passport System and Mandatory Registration" was first instituted in the cities. Farmers did not receive passports; therefore they were denied freedom of movement. See *Sovetskoye obshchestvo: vozniknoveniye, razvitiye, istorichesky final. T. 2. Apogei i strah stalinizma* [The Origin, Development and Final Disintegration of Soviet Society, vol. 2, Apogee and the Fear of Stalinism] (Moscow: RGGU, 1997) 675.

213 The workday is a measure of work accomplished, which is used to calculate the wage in kind for collective farm workers.

214 "Fascist, you've murdered my sons!" Translated from the Russian

215 Letter of Matilde Kaimiņa to Milda Kalniete. 10 July 1949.

216 Letter of Matilde Kaimiņa to Milda Kalniete. 30 October 1949.

217 Letter of Matilde Kaimiņa to Milda Kalniete. 6 January 1951.

218 Letter of Voldemārs Kaimiņš to Milda Kalniete. 12 September 1949.

219 Letter of Arnis Kalnietis to Milda Kalniete. 31 March 1950.

220 Letter of Arnis Kalnietis to Milda Kalniete. 9 January 1951.

221 Kalnietis 11.

222 Ibid. 12.

223 Ibid. 13.

224 Ibid.

225 "Who are you? Show me your papers!" Translation from Russian.

226 "A fine radio." Translation from the Russian.

"My mother will wash my hair in rainwater"

227 LVA, fonds 1987, ser. 1, file 20293, p. 19.

228 Because of sloppy completion of the documents in Jānis Dreifeld's family dossier, the data regarding Ligita Dreifelde in the book *Aizvestie* are incorrect. Ligita Dreifelde's registration card, on which the last entry was made on 15 April 1948, is in the family archive. In the book it is stated that she tried to escape on 15 April 1947, when in fact she was in Togura. See *Aizvestie* 560.

229 LVA, fonds 1987, ser. 1, file 20293, p. 20.

230 Ibid. 17.

231 Ibid.

232 Māra Vidnere has researched the influence of the deportation on deportees' personalities. She sought to discover the sources of strength that helped people to survive under extreme conditions; however, this research does not delve into the post-traumatic manifestations in the subsequent life of the deportees. See Māra Vidnere, *Ar asarām tas nav pierādams*…[Tears Alone Are Not Proof Enough…] (Rīga: University of Latvia, 1997) 312.

233 "You probably had a hut and a cow?" Translated from the Russian.

234 "I had a piano." Translated from the Russian.

235 International Women's Day was an official holiday in Soviet Union, celebrated on March 8, in keeping with proclamation of the International Conference of Socialist Women, Aug. 25–27, 1910.

236 "Halt!" Translated from the Russian.

"We won't give birth to any more slaves"

237 With a December 1947 decision of the Central Committee of the CPSU and the Council of Ministers, the USSR abolished the ration card system and implemented money reform. See *Latvijas PSR vēsture* [History of the Latvian SSR], vol. 2 (Rīga: Zinātne, 1986): 248.

238 "*Posiltorg*" was a mail order system. The buyer ordered the goods by making a money transfer in payment for them. The goods were delivered by mail.

239 "In the name of the Union of Soviet Socialist Republics, I pronounce you man and wife." Translated from the Russian.

240 Because of starvation experienced by deported girls during their teen years, their pelvic bones, ovaries and uterus often did not fully develop, resulting in infertility. This subject is so painful that it is rarely mentioned in the recollections of deported women.

The Long Way Home

241 In Moscow the wake started at 10:00 am. There is a time difference of four hours between Moscow and the Tomsk region.

242 In the USSR, Y. Levitan's thundering voice was associated with events of historic importance. He was the one who, on 22 June 1941, announced on the radio Germany's attack on the Soviet Union. He was entrusted to read on the radio the most important announcements made by Stalin or the CPSU Central Committee.

243 There are no precise data on the number of the dead and wounded. The information ranges from several hundred to several thousand. See Edvard Radzinsky's book *Stalin* (Moscow: Vagrius, 1997) 622.

244 The "doctors' case" was the last large campaign of repression begun during Stalin's lifetime. Several doctors and their family members were accused of spying and terrorism. By the 3 April 1953 decision of the Presidium of the CPSU Central Committee the case was terminated and 37 people were exonerated.

245 The arrest of Lavrenty Beria on 26 June 1953 was not announced in the media. News of the arrest was learned from a press release issued about the Plenary Session of the CPSU Central

Committee held on 2–7 July, after which the media started a campaign of criticism in the traditional aggressive Stalinist style. After a six-month investigative process, the court pronounced a death sentence for Beria, who was executed on 24 December 1953. The "Beria case" allowed Malenkov and Khrushchev to dispose of their most dangerous rival for power and to put all the blame for the repressions on Beria and a few of his collaborators, while temporarily protecting Stalin from culpability.

246 On 27 March 1953, the Presidium of USSR Supreme Council passed a Decree of Amnesty, according to which persons who had been sentenced to five years in prison were released and living conditions for other categories of prisoners were improved. See *Sbornik zakonov SSSR i ukazov Prezidiuma Verkhovnogo Soveta SSSR. 1938–1975* [Collection of Laws of the USSR and Decrees of the Presidium of the Supreme Soviet of the USSR. 1938–1975], vol. 3 (Moscow: Izvestiya, 1976): 409.

247 In accordance with the USSR Council of Ministers decision of 5 July 1954, children up to the age of sixteen were removed from the special settlement registration list. See Riekstiņš, "Deportation in Latvia …" 709.

248 The 13 July 1954 decision of the USSR Supreme Council Presidium revoked the USSR Supreme Council Presidium decision of 26 November 1948 ordering deportation for life. See *Sbornik zakonodatelnykh i normativnykh aktov o repressiyakh i reabilitatsiy zhertv politicheskikh represii* [Collection of Legislative and Normative Acts on Repression and on the Exoneration of Victims of Political Repression] (Moscow: Izvestiya, 1976) 125.

249 LVA, fonds 1987, ser. 1, file 20293, p. 25.

250 My father also wrote appeals in 1951 and 1953, but they are not in the archive files. See LVA, fonds 1984, ser. 1, file 463, p. 30.

251 LVA, fonds 1987, ser. 1, file 20293, p. 30.

252 Ibid. p. 34.

253 In accordance with paragraph 6 of the 20 July 1954 decision No. 13 by the USSR Prosecutor General, a regulation was issued "… to increase political instruction of deportees by involving them in social and political activities. The deportees must be invited to join labour unions and the Young Communist League, their accomplishments in work should be encouraged and rewarded, and their employment must be commensurate with their education and specialisation." See *Sbornik zakonodatelnykh i normativnykh aktov o repressiyakh i reabilitatsiy zhertv politicheskikh represii* 127.

254 Mariya Zezina, "Shokovaya terapiya: ot 1953 k 1956 godu" [Shock Therapy: From 1953 to 1956]. *Otechestvennaya Istoriya* 2 (1995): 133.

255 Letter of Ligita Kalniete to Viktors Drefelds. 5 November 1955.

256 Nikita Khrushchev's report to the 20th Congress of the CPSU was read on 25 February in a closed session, which was also attended by Communist Party leaders from abroad. It is obvious that one of them had leaked the text of the speech to the press, and in the beginning of June it appeared in the press in the United States, France and England. See Dmitrii Volkogonov, *Triumph i tragediya. Politicheskiy portret I. V. Stalina. Kn. 2 Ch. 2* [Triumph and Tragedy: Political Portrait of J.V. Stalin. Book 2, Part 2] (Moscow: Agentstva pechati novosti, 1989): 230. In the USSR the complete text of Khrushchev's speech was published in the journal *Izvestiya CK KPSS* 3 (1989): 128–70.

257 The CPSU Central Committee approved the resolution "On Becoming Familiar with the Report by N.S. Khrushchev to the 20th Congress of the CPSU 'On the Personality Cult and Its Consequences'" With this resolution the report's "top secret" classification was removed,

but its publication in the press was still prohibited. See "O kulte lichnosti i yego posledstviyakh: doklad Pervogo sekretarya CK KPSS tov. Khrushcheva N.S. XX syezdu Kommunisticheskoy partii Sovetskogo Soyuza 25 fevralya 1956 goda" [On the Cult of Personality and Its Consequences: Report by N.S. Khrushchev, the 1st Secretary of the CPSU Central Committee, at the 20th Congress of the CPSU, 25 February 1956], *Izvestiya CK KPSS* 3 (1989): 166.

258 Ibid. 151.

259 Ibid. 152.

260 Otto J. Pohl, *The Stalinist Penal System: A Statistical History of Soviet Repression and Terror, 1930–1953* (Jefferson, NC.: MacFarland, 1997) 43.; Nikolai Bugai, "40.–50. godi: posledstviya deportatsii narodov" [The 1940s and 1950s: Consequences of the Deportation of People], *Istoriya SSSR* 1 (1992): 132; Applebaum 506–07.

261 Yurii Zhukov, "Borba za vlast v partiyno–gosudarstvennykh verkhakh SSSR vesnoy 1953 goda" [The Struggle for Power between the Party and State Leadership of the USSR in the Spring of 1953], *Voprosy Istoriy* 5/6 (1996): 50.

262 Ibid. 55; Vladimir Naumov, "N.S. Khrushchev i reabilitatsiya zhertv massovykh politicheskikh repressii" [N.S. Khrushchev and the Exoneration of Victims of Mass-Scale Political Repression], *Voprosy Istoriy* 4 (1997): 24.

263 "O kulte lichnosti i yego posledstviyakh" [On the Cult of Personality and Its Consequences], *Pravda* 2 July 1956.

264 On 19 December 1956 the CPSU Central Committee sent a letter to party organizations "On Intensifying Political Work among Party Organizations and the Masses, in order to Avert Anti-Soviet Activities by Hostile Elements"; after its dissemination the arrests began. See Naumov 30.

265 Naumov 31.

266 On 24 March 1956 the USSR Supreme Council Presidium adopted the resolution "On Reviewing the Cases of Persons Who are Serving Sentences for Political, Service or Economic Crimes"; this was followed by several orders of the USSR Prosecutor General that clarified the review and release procedures for various categories of specially settled persons. See *Sbornik zakonodatelnih i normativnih aktov o repressiyah i reabilitatsii zhertv politicheskih represii* 125.

267 LVA, fonds 1894, ser. 1, file 20293, p. 37.

268 Ibid,. 34.

269 LVA, fonds 1987, ser. 1, file 20293, p. 37.

270 Letter of Ligita Kalniete to Viktors Dreifelds. 3 October 1956.

271 Letter of Aivars Kalnietis to Viktors Dreifelds. 25 December 1956.

272 Notice of the removal from the special settlement registation list is kept in the family archive.

273 Letter of Ligita Kalniete to Voldemārs Dreifelds. 28–30 December 1956.

Time spent in deportation
by Kalnietis family members who survived Siberia

Ligita Kalniete

Year	Jan	Feb	Mar	Apr	May	June	July	Aug	Sept	Oct	Nov	Dec
1941						14.06	×	×	×	×	×	×
1942	×	×	×	×	×	×	×	×	×	×	×	×
1943	×	×	×	×	×	×	×	×	×	×	×	×
1944	×	×	×	×	×	×	×	×	×	×	×	×
1945	×	×	×	×	×	×	×	×	×	×	×	×
1946	×	×	×	×	×	×	×	×	×	×	×	×
1947	×	×	×	×	×	×	×	×	×	×	×	×
1948	×	×	×	×	×	×						
1949												07.12
1950	×	×	×	×	×	×	×	×	×	×	×	×
1951	×	×	×	×	×	×	×	×	×	×	×	×
1952	×	×	×	×	×	×	×	×	×	×	×	×
1953	×	×	×	×	×	×	×	×	×	×	×	×
1954	×	×	×	×	×	×	×	×	×	×	×	×
1955	×	×	×	×	×	×	×	×	×	×	×	×
1956	×	×	×	×	×	×	×	×	×	×	×	×
1957	×	×	×	×	30.05							

Aivars Kalnietis

Year	Jan	Feb	Mar	Apr	May	June	July	Aug	Sept	Oct	Nov	Dec
1949			23.03	×	×	×	×	×	×	×	×	×
1950	×	×	×	×	×	×	×	×	×	×	×	×
1951	×	×	×	×	×	×	×	×	×	×	×	×
1952	×	×	×	×	×	×	×	×	×	×	×	×
1953	×	×	×	×	×	×	×	×	×	×	×	×
1954	×	×	×	×	×	×	×	×	×	×	×	×
1955	×	×	×	×	×	×	×	×	×	×	×	×
1956	×	×	×	×	×	×	×	×	×	×	×	×
1957	×	×	×	×	×	×	11.07					

Milda Kalniete

Year	Jan	Feb	Mar	Apr	May	June	July	Aug	Sept	Oct	Nov	Dec
1949			23.03	×	×	×	×	×	×	×	×	×
1950	×	×	×	×	×	×	×	×	×	×	×	×
1951	×	×	×	×	×	×	×	×	×	×	×	×
1952	×	×	×	×	×	×	×	×	×	×	×	×
1953	×	×	×	×	×	×	×	×	×	×	×	×
1954	×	×	×	×	×	×	×	×	×	×	×	×
1955	×	×	×	×	×	×	×	×	×	×	×	×
1956	×	×	×	×	×	×	×	×	×	×	×	×
1957	×	×	×	×	30.05							

Sandra Kalniete

Year	Jan	Feb	Mar	Apr	May	June	July	Aug	Sept	Oct	Nov	Dec
1952												22.12
1953	×	×	×	×	×	×	×	×	×	×	×	×
1954	×	×	×	×	×	×	×	×	×	×	×	×
1955	×	×	×	×	×	×	×	×	×	×	×	×
1956	×	×	×	×	×	×	×	×	×	×	×	×
1957	×	×	×	×	×	30.05						

Chronology of Events

As much as possible, the cited figures and facts reflect findings and conclusions of latest historical research.

Year	Family Events	Historical Political Events
January 6, 1878	Jānis Dreifelds born to Kristaps and Paulīne Dreifelds	
January 14, 1891	Ilze Emilija Gāliņa born to Indriķis and Lība Galiņš	
March 5, 1907	Aleksandrs Kalnietis born.	
May 7, 1908	Milda Hermīne Kaimiņa born to Pēteris and Milda Kaimiņš	
November 10, 1912	Marriage of Jānis Dreifelds and Ilze Emilija Gāliņa. The newlyweds leave for Russia after the wedding.	
August 1, 1914		WW I starts. 850,000 Latvian inhabitants become refugees in Russia. As a result of military action 30,000 Latvian Riflemen and civilians are killed.
November 1, 1914	Son Voldemārs born to Jānis and Emilija Dreifelds.	
February 25, 1917		Russian Czar Nicholas II is dethroned and a democratic republic is established in Russia.

November 18, 1918		Proclamation of Independence of the Republic of Latvia.
June 8, 1919.	Son Viktors born to Jānis and Emilija Dreifelds.	
End of 1919	The Dreifelds family returns from Russia to Latvia.	
February 1920		Latvian territory is freed of Soviet and German intervention.
1920	The Kaimiņš family returns from Russia to Latvia.	
August 11, 1920		A "Peace Accord between Latvia and Russia" is signed, in which Russia "gives up in perpetuity any rights to the nation and territory of Latvia."
January 26, 1921		A conference of the Allies in Paris approves a resolution regarding recognition of the Republic of Latvia de jure.
December 9, 1926	Daughter Ligita born to Jānis and Emilija Dreifelds.	
May 10, 1931	Son Aivars born to Milda Kaimiņa.	
1937	It is thought that Jānis Dreifelds' sister Aleksandrīna Vilnīte is killed during the Stalinist repressions in the USSR.	
December 18, 1937	Marriage of Aleksandrs Kalnietis and Milda Kaimiņa.	

June 22, 1938	A son Arnis is born to Aleksandrs and Milda Kaimiņš.	
August 23, 1939		The Soviet Union and Germany sign a reciprocal non–aggression agreement, with secret protocols appended, in which both countries agree to divide East Europe into spheres of influence.
September 1, 1939		Germany invades Poland. WW II starts.
October 5, 1939		Latvia is forced to agree to a Mutual Assistance pact with the Soviet Union. 21,000 Soviet soldiers are stationed in Soviet garrisons across Latvia.
October 11, 1939		The People's Deputy Commissar of USSR State Security I. Serov issues Order No. 001223 "Regarding Anti–Soviet Element Deportation Procedures for Lithuania, Latvia and Estonia."
October 30, 1939		Latvia and Germany sign an "Agreement Regarding Relocation of German origin Latvian Citizens to Germany." Within a few months 45,000 persons leave Latvia.

June 16, 1940		Charging breaches of the Mutual Assistance treaty, the USSR government issues an ultimatum to the government of Latvia demanding free entry for Soviet armed forces into Latvia and installment of a new government. The government of Latvia accepts the provisions of the ultimatum.
June 17, 1940		USSR armed forces occupy Latvia.
June 14 and 15, 1940		Undemocratic Saeima (Parliament) elections, where only candidates from the "Working People's Block" list are allowed to run for election.
July 21, 1940		Saeima approves a Declaration requesting admission to the USSR.
August 5, 1940		Latvia is incorporated into the USSR.
June 9, 1941	Captain S. Shustin of the People's Commissariat of State Security signs a decision regarding the arrest of Jānis, Viktors, Emilija and Ligita Dreifelds.	
June 14, 1941	Jānis, Emilija and Ligita Dreifelds are arrested and sent to Siberia.	15,424 persons are deported from Latvia. In total in the"Year of Terror" 34,250 inhabitants suffer repression.

June 20, 1941	Jānis Dreifelds is separated from Emilija and Ligita at the Babinino railway station.	
June 22, 1941	Jānis Dreifelds is imprisoned in Yukhnovo prison camp.	Germany invades USSR.
End of June, 1941	Jānis Dreifelds is moved from Yukhnovo prison camp to Vyatlag.	Approximately 8000 persons from Latvia are imprisoned in Yukhnovo. About 1000 arrested past officers from Latvia, Lithuania and Estonia are placed in a separate fenced-off area.
July 1, 1941		German armed forces enter Rīga. The second occupation of Latvia begins.
July 10, 1941	Jānis Dreifelds is imprisoned in Vyatlag 7 prison camp. In total, 3281 inhabitants from Latvia are imprisoned in Vyatlag.	
July 10, 1941	Emilija and Ligita are settled in the "Great Chigas" kolkhoz in the Parabel district, Novosibirsk region.	
July 17, 1941		Hitler creates the Ostland Ministry to administer the occupied eastern regions. He appoints Alfred Rosenberg as *Reichsminister*. 25,000 German officials arrive to administer the new territory.

November 30 and December 8, 1941	Matilde Kaimiņa is an eyewitness to Jews being convoyed to be executed in the Rumbula forest. In two days 25,000 Jews are exterminated there.	By a German order, by January 1942, 70,000 Latvian Jews are exterminated in the territory of Latvia. In addition, 20,000 Jews from Western Europe are exterminated .
December 31, 1941	Jānis Dreifelds dies in Vyatlag.	From July 1941 to July 1942, 2337 inhabitants of Latvia die in Vyatlag.
February 10, 1943		Hitler issues an order to form a Latvian Volunteer Legion. On March 9 the first "volunteers" are mobilised.
June 1943	Emilija and Ligita are settled on the death island of Bilina, where they remain until March 1944.	
March 26, 1944	Aleksandrs Kalnietis is mobilised into the Latvian Legion.	About 110-115,000 Latvians, mostly conscripts, fight in various German military formations. Close to 100,000 are drafted into the Soviet army. The casualty rate is very high. About 25,000 Latvian soldiers surrender to the Western Allies. Latvian soldiers in German ranks are subjected to imprisonment in Soviet camps.
October 13, 1944		The Soviet army takes Rīga. The third occupation of Latvia begins.

Spring 1945	Voldemārs, Arnolds and Viktors Dreifelds and their families become refugees heading via different routes to Germany.	After the war there are about 200,000 Latvian refugees located in Germany.
May 8, 1945		Admiral Doenitz signs Germany's unconditional surrender.
May 9, 1945	Aleksandrs Kalnietis begins his partisan days in the Kurzeme forests.	After the surrender of the German contingent in Kurzeme, about 4000 Latvian soldiers join the partisan movement. An estimated 20,000 Latvians fight in the partisan war 1944–1956.
October 30, 1945	Aleksandrs Kalnietis returns to his family in Rīga.	
November 13, 1945	The operative group of the People's Commissariat of State Security arrests Aleksandrs Kalnietis.	
Winter 1946	Emilija Drefelde is lost for three days in a forest in Siberia, suffering frostbite and becoming seriously ill.	
Spring 1946	Emilija and Ligita receive the first package from Latvia.	
May 6, 1946	A Soviet War Tribunal sentences Aleksandrs Kalnietis to ten years in a high security prison camp plus five years in forced settlement.	

October 26, 1946	The GULAG medical commission finds Aleksandrs Kalnietis incapable to work.	
May, 1947	Emilija and Ligita Dreifelde find out that Voldemārs, Arnolds and Viktors Dreifelds are in the West.	In total, the number of Latvians finding refuge in various countries abroad reaches 120,000.
Spring 1947	Emilija and Ligita Dreifelde are transferred to the village of Togur.	
April 1948.	Ligita Dreifelde receives a permit to return to Latvia.	
June 1948	Ligita Dreifelde returns to Latvia.	
January 29, 1949		A top-secret decision regarding the deportation of various “categories” of inhabitants of Latvia, Lithuania and Estonia is made by the USSR Council of Ministers.
March 25, 1949.	Milda and Aivars Kalnietis are arrested and sent to Siberia.	The top–secret USSR MIA operation “Coastal Surf” (“*Priboi*”) is implemented in Latvia, during which 43,000 persons or 2.28% of the total population of Latvia are deported to Siberia.
April 20, 1949	Milda and Aivars Kalnietis are imprisoned in the Tomsk city transfer camp, where they are informed that they have been deported for life.	

May 1949	Milda and Aivars Kalnietis are settled in the Sokhta village in the Kolpashevo district, Tomsk region.
May 10, 1949	The administration of the Tomsk Region Internal Affairs Division initiates an All Union search for Ligita Dreifelde.
July 1949	Milda and Aivars Kalnietis receive their first letter from Latvia.
December 7, 1949	Ligita Dreifelde is arrested in Tukums and moved through various prisons back to her previous place of forced settlement in the village of Togur in Kolpashevo District, Tomsk region.
February 5, 1950	Emilija Ilze Dreifelde dies in Togur.
May 1950	Ligita Dreifelde reaches Kolpashevo and is released from the prison convoy.
August 1950	Ligita Dreifelde and Aivars Kalnietis meet.
May 25, 1951	Wedding of Aivars Kalnietis and Ligita Dreifelde.
Summer 1952	Matilde Kaimiņa dies in Latvia. Arnis Kalnietis is left without any family.
December 22, 1952	Daughter Sandra is born to Aivars and Ligita Kalnietis.

February 18, 1953	Aleksandrs Kalnietis dies in Pechorlag AA–274 prison camp.	
March 5, 1953		Death of CPSU CC General Secretary Joseph Stalin
March 27, 1953		The USSR Supreme Council Presidium approves a Decree "Regarding Amnesty," followed by improvement in the living conditions of some categories of persons imprisoned or settled in the GULAG.
June 2, 1954	Ligita Kalniete writes a petition to the USSR Supreme Council Presidium Chairman K. Voroshilov requesting to be freed from special settlement. The petition is refused.	
July 5, 1954		USSR Council of Ministers decision "Regarding Revocation of Some Limitations in the Legal Status of Specially Settled Persons"
August 1954	Sandra Kalniete is removed from the special settlement registration list. Ligita, Aivars and Milda Kalnietis are permitted free movement rights throughout the Tomsk region, and their twice-monthly registration at the Commandant's Office is revoked.	

November 3, 1955	After a seven-year hiatus, Ligita Kalniete's contact with her brothers abroad is renewed.	
February 25, 1956		Nikita Khrushchev reads a Report "Regarding the Personality Cult and Eradication of its Consequences" at the CPSU 20th Congress, in which Stalinist repressions are unmasked.
March 24, 1956		USSR Supreme Council Presidium approves the decree "Regarding Review of Case Files of Persons Who Are Serving Sentences for Political, Service and Social Crimes." This decision opens the door for freeing specially settled persons.
August 1956	Aivars Kalnietis enrolls in the Tomsk Polytechnic Institute in the Mining Industry Electrical Engineering Faculty.	
December 30, 1956	Milda and Aivars Kalnietis are removed from the special settlement registration list.	
April 20, 1957	The Kalnietis family starts their journey back to Latvia.	
November 5, 1975	Death of Milda Kalniete in Rīga.	

June 8, 1989		LSSR Supreme Council Presidium adopts the decree "Regarding Rehabilitation of Citizens Deported from Latvia SSR Territory during the 40s and 50s."
December 24, 1989		The USSR People's Congress of Deputies adopts the resolution "Regarding the Political and Legal Evaluation of the Non-Aggression Pact of 1939 between the USSR and Germany," as a result of which the secret protocols appended to the Ribbentrop–Molotov Pact are found to have no legal basis and to be invalid from the day of the signing of the Pact.
April 5, 1990	The criminal case No. 20 293 begun against Jānis Dreifelds is terminated, and he is rehabilitated.	
April 21, 1990	The Unjustly Repressed Citizen Rehabilitation Division of the Ministry of Internal Affairs of the Latvian SSR finds the deportation of Ligita Kalniete to forced settlement illegal, and she is rehabilitated.	

May 4, 1990		The Supreme Council of Latvian SSR approves the Declaration "Regarding the Renewal of Independence of Latvia."
August 3, 1990		The Supreme Council of the Republic of Latvia adopts the Law "Regarding the Rehabilitation of Illegally Repressed Persons."
February 28, 1991	The Unjustly Repressed Citizen Rehabilitation Division of the Ministry of Internal Affairs of Latvian SSR finds the deportation of Aivars Kalnietis to forced settlement illegal, and he is rehabilitated.	
September 6, 1991		The USSR Supreme Council accepts the resolution "Regarding Recognition of the Independence of the Republic of Latvia"
September 26, 1994	The criminal case of Aleksandrs Kalnietis is reviewed and, based on the Republic of Latvia Law "Regarding the Rehabilitation of Illegally Repressed Persons" it is found that he merits rehabilitation.	

Bibliography

Latvian State Archive (LVA)

LVA, fonds 1986, ser. 1, file 17170, vols. 1–9. "Latvijas PSR VDK par sevišķi bīstamiem pretvalstiskiem noziegumiem apsūdzētu personu krimināllietas (1940–1985)" [Latvian SSR KGB Regarding Criminal Cases of Persons Accused of Particulary Dangerous Anti-State Crimes (1940–1985)]. Source for the Criminal Cases of Aivars Kalnietis and other persons.

LVA, fonds 1987, ser. 1, file 20293. "1941. gada 14. jūnijā no Latvijas izsūtīto iedzīvotāju personu lietas" [Individual Case Files of Inhabitants of Latvia Deported on June 14, 1941]. Source of Jānis Dreifelds deportation case file.

LVA, fonds 1894, ser. 1, file 463. "1949. gada 25. martā no Latvijas izsūtīto iedzīvotāju personu lietas" [Individual Case Files of Inhabitants of Latvia Deported on March 25, 1949]. Source of the registration case file of the "bandit supporter" Aleksandrs Kalnietis family.

Books and Articles in Latvian

Aizsilnieks, Arnolds. *Latvijas saimniecības vēsture. 1914–1945* [Economic History of Latvia. 1914–1945]. Stockholm: Daugava, 1968.

Aizvestie. 1941. gada 14. jūnijs [Deportees. June 14, 1941]. Ed. Elmārs Pelkaus. Rīga: Latvijas Valsts arhīvs/Nordik, 2001.

Alks, Dzintris. *Latvijas mediķi politisko represiju dzirnās, 1940. –1953.g.* [Latvian Physicians Caught between the Grindstones of Political Repression 1940–1953]. Rīga: Rīgas starptaut. med. zin. un farm. Centrs/Latvijas ebreju nacionālā kult. biedrība, 1993.

Andersons, Edgars. *Latvijas vēsture. 1920–1940. Ārpolītika* [History of Latvia. 1920–1940. Foreign Policy]. Volume 2. Stockholm: Daugava, 1984.

Avotiņš, E.; Dzirkalis J.; Pētersons V. *Kas ir Daugavas vanagi?* [Daugavas Vanagi: Who Are They?]. Rīga: LVI, 1962.

Baltais, Mirdza Kate. "Piespiedu iesaukšana darbam Vācijā, militārajam dienestam un evakuācija uz Vāciju." *Okupācijas varu nodarītie postījumi Latvijā: rakstu krājums 1940–1990.* [Mobilisation of Forced Labour to Germany, Military Service and Evacuation to Germany. Destruction Wrought by Occupation Regimes in Latvia: Collection of Essays. 1940–1990]. Stockholm: Memento; Toronto: Daugavas Vanagi, 2000: 193–99.

Bambals, Ainars. "1940./41. gadā represēto latviešu virsnieku piemiņai. Virsnieku Golgātas ceļš un liktenis gulaga nometnēs (1941–1959) / In Memory of the Latvian Officers Repressed in 1940–1941. Their Road to Golgotha and Fate in the Stalinist GULAG camps. 1941–1959." *Latvijas Okupācijas muzeja gadagrāmata 1999. Genocīda politika un prakse / Yearbook of the Occupation Museum of Latvia 1999. Policies and Practices of Genocide*. Rīga: Latvijas 50 gadu okupācijas muzeja fonds [OMF], 2000: 92–158.

Beika, Aivars. "Latvieši Padomju Savienībā – komunistiskā genocīda upuri (1929–1939) / Latvians in the Soviet Union: The Victims of Communist Terror. 1929–1939." *Latvijas Okupācijas muzeja gadagrāmata 1999. Genocīda politika un prakse / Yearbook of the Occupation Museum of Latvia 1999. Policies and Practices of Genocide*. Rīga: Latvijas 50 gadu okupācijas muzeja fonds [OMF], 2000: 43–91.

Bērziņš, Alfrēds. *Labie gadi. Pirms un pēc 15. Maija* [The Good Years. Before and After May 15]. New York: Grāmatu Draugs, 1963.

Bērziņš, Valdis; Bambals, Ainars. *Latvijas armija* [Latvian Army]. Rīga: Zinātne, 1991.

Birznieks, M. *No SS un SD līdz...* [From SS and SD to...]. Rīga: Zvaigzne, 1979.

Brancis, Māris. "Latviešu bēgļu gaitas Vācijā 1944.–1949. gadā" [Latvian Refugees in Germany 1944–1949]. *Latvijas Arhīvi* 4 (2000): 175–78.

Darba likumdošana. PSRS darba likumdošanas un KPFSR darba likumu kodeka komentāri [Labour Legislation. Commentary on USSR Labour Legislation and RSFSR Labour Law Code]. Rīga: LVI, 1950.

Dribins, Leo. *Ebreji Latvijā* [Jews in Latvia]. Rīga: Latvijas ZA Filoz. un sociol. inst. Etnisko pētījumu centrs, 1996.

Dunsdorfs, Edgars. *Kārļa Ulmaņa dzīve. Ceļinieks. Politiķis. Diktators. Moceklis* [The Life of Kārlis Ulmanis. Pathfinder. Politician. Dictator. Martyr]. Stockholm: Daugava, 1978.

Dzintars, Jānis. "Komjaunieši Rīgas antifašistiskajā pagrīdē" [The Young Communists in the Anti-Fascist Underground of Rīga]. *LPSR ZA Vēstis* 10 (1968): 10–21.

Dzirkalis, J. *Kāpēc viņi bēga. Patiesība par latviešu nacionālo fondu Zviedrijā* [Why Did They Flee. The Truth About the Latvian National Foundation in Sweden]. Rīga: Zvaigzne, 1965.

Es sapni par dzimteni pagalvī likšu: atmiņu un dokumentu krājums [I'll Keep My Dream of My Homeland Under My Pillow: Recollections and Documents]. Compiled by Gunārs Freimanis. Volumes 1–3. Rīga: Liesma, 1993–1996.

Ezergailis, Andrievs. *Holokausts vācu okupētajā Latvijā. 1941–1944* [The Holocaust in German Occupied Latvia. 1941–1944]. Rīga: Latvijas Vēstures institūta apgāds, 1999.

Feldmanis, Inesis; Stranga, Aivars; Virsis, Mārtiņš. *Latvijas ārpolitika un starptautiskais stāvoklis. 30. gadu otrā puse* [Latvian Foreign Policy and International Situation. Second Half of the 1930s]. Rīga: Latvijas Ārpolitikas institūts, 1993.

Freivalds, Osvalds. *Kurzemes cietoksnis: dokumenti, liecības un atmiņas par latviešu tautas likteņiem 1944/1945.g.* [The Stronghold of Kurzeme: Eyewitness Accounts and Recollections of the Fate of the Latvian People 1944/1945]. Part I. Copenhagen: Imanta, 1954.

Freivalds, Osvalds. *Lielā sāpju draudze: latviešu tautas posta, ciešanu un sāpju asinsliecinieki, Kristus ceļa gājēji – mocekļi* [The Large Congregation of Sorrow: Blood Witnesses of Destruction, Suffering, and Pain, Christ's Companions – Martyrs]. Copenhagen: Imanta, 1954.

Gordons, Franks. *Latvieši un žīdi. Spīlēs starp Vāciju un Krieviju* [Latvians and Jews. Caught in a Vise between Germany and Russia]. Stockholm: Memento, 1994.

Gore, Ilga; Stranga, Aivars. *Latvija: neatkarības mijkrēslis. Okupācija: 1939. g. septembris–1940. g. jūnijs* [Latvia: the Twilight of Independence. Occupation: September 1939–June 1940]. Rīga: Izglītība, 1992.

Gūtmanis, Olafs. *Dzīves grāmata: atmiņu attēlojumi* [Book of Life: Memory Portraits]. Rīga: Liesma, 1992.

Kalme, Alberts. *Totālais terors: genocīds Baltijā* [Total Terror: Genocide in the Baltic]. Translated from the English by Mārtiņš Zelmenis. Rīga: Kabata, 1993.

Komunistiskā totalitārisma un genocīda prakse Latvijā [The Practice of Communist Totalitarianism and Genocide in Latvia]. Compiled by Irēne Šneidere. Rīga: Zinātne, 1992.

KPFSR kriminālkodekss: ar pārgroz. līdz 1944.g. 15. apr. [RSFSR Criminal Code: with Ammendments to April 15, 1944]. LPSR Tieslietu tautas komisariāts. Maskava [Moscow]: PSRS TTK Jurid. izd., 1944.

Latviešu karavīrs Otrā pasaules kara laikā: dokumentu un atmiņu krājums [The Latvian Soldier in World War II: A Collection of Reminiscences and Documents] Volumes 1–7. Minstere: Daugavas Vanagu centrālā valde, 1970–1979.

1: *No 1939. gada septembra līdz 1941 . gada jūnijam* [From September 1939 to June 1941]. Chief ed. Osvalds Freivalds; Military ed. Oskars Caunītis. 1970.

5: *Kaujas Vidzemē, Zemgalē un Kurzemē* [Battles in Vidzeme, Zemgale and Kurzeme]. Compiled by Rūdolfs Kociņš. 1977.

7: *Latviešu aviācija. Latviešu karavīru papildus un palīgvienības. Karavīru aprūpe. Latviešu leģiona ģenerālinspekcija. Otrā pasaules kara noslēgums* [Latvian Aviation. Auxiliary and Support Units of Latvian Armed Forces. Purveyance of the Troops. General Inspection of the Latvian Legion. End of WW II]. Ed. Vilis Hāzners, Alfrēds Jānis Bērziņš. 1979.

Latvija citu valstu saimē. Kulturāli saimniecisks apskats [Latvia Among a Community of Nations. A Cultural and Economic Overview]. Rīga: MLAF, 1939.

Latvija Otrajā pasaules karā [Latvia in World War II]. Starptautiskās konferences materiāli 1999.g. 14.–15. jūnijs, Rīga. Latvijas Vēsturnieku komisijas raksti 1 / Symposium of the Commission of the Historians of Latvia 1. Rīga: Latvijas Vēstures institūta apgāds, 2000.

Latvijas brīvības cīņas. 1918–1920 [Latvian Freedom Battles. 1918–1920]. Enciklopēdija. Rīga: Preses nams, 1999.

Latvijas Okupācijas muzeja gadagrāmata 1999. Genocīda politika un prakse / Yearbook of the Occupation Museum of Latvia 1999. Policies and Practices of Genocide. Rīga: Latvijas 50 gadu okupācijas muzeja fonds [OMF], 2000.

Latvijas PSR vēsture. No vissenākiem laikiem līdz mūsu dienām [History of Latvian SSR. From Prehistoric Times to the Present]. LPSR ZA Vēstures inst. Ed. Aleksandrs Drīzulis. Volume 2. Rīga: Zinātne, 1986.

Latvijas PSR vēsture [History of Latvian SSR]. LPSR ZA Vēstures un materiālās kultūras inst. Chief ed. Kārlis Strazdiņš. Volume 3. *No 1917. gada līdz 1950. gadam* [From 1917 to 1950]. Rīga: LPSR ZA, 1959.

Latvijas valsts pasludināšana 1918. gada 18. novembrī [Proclamation of the Statehood of Latvia on November 18, 1918]. Rīga: Madris, 1998.

Latvju enciklopēdija [Latvian Encyclopedia]. Ed. Arveds Švābe. Volume 1. Stockholm: Trīs zvaigznes, 1950.

Latvju enciklopēdija. 1962–1982 [Latvian Encyclopedia. 1962–1982]. Ed. Edgars Andersons. Volume 3. Rockville: ALA Latviešu institūts, 1987.

Lismanis, Jānis. *1915–1920. Kauju un kritušo karavīru piemiņai* [1915–1920. Remembering the Battles and the Fallen Soldiers]. Rīga: NIMS, 1999.

Neiburgs, Uldis. "Latviešu karavīri Vācijas un PSRS armijās: galvenās problēmas" [Latvian soldiers in German and USSR Armed Forces: Main Problems]. *Latvija Otrajā pasaules karā / Latvia in World War II.* Latvijas Vēsturnieku komisijas raksti 1 / Symposium of the Commission of the Historians of Latvia 1. Rīga: Latvijas Vēstures institūta apgāds, 2000: 197–207.

Ozoliņš, Juris. *Mani sāpju ceļi* [My Via Dolorosa]. Rīga: Latonija, 1991.

Pāri jūrai 1944./45.g. 130 liecinieku atmiņas [Across the Sea in 1944/45. 130 Eyewitness Accounts]. Compiled by Valentīne Lasmane. Stockholm: Memento, 1993.

Pilsoņu dzīvokļu tiesības [Citizen Rights to Residential Space]. Rīga: Liesma, 1969.

Pretestības kustība okupācijas varām Latvijā: atmiņās un dokumentos no 1941. līdz 1956. gadam [Resistance Movement against Occupation Regimes in Latvia: Recollections and Documents from 1941 to 1956]. Rīga: SolVita, 1997.

Riekstiņš, Jānis. *Bāra bērni* [Orphans]. Rīga: Avots, 1992.

Riekstiņš, Jānis. *Ekspropriācija (1940–1959)* [Expropriation (1940–1959)]. Rīga: Ievanda, 1998.

Riekstiņš, Jānis. "Genocīds: 1949. gada 25. marta deportācijas akcija Latvijā" [Genocide: the March 25, 1949 Deportation Campaign in Latvia]. *Latvijas Vēsture* 2 (1991): 24–39; 3 (1991): 24–29.

Riekstiņš, Jānis. *"Kulaki" Latvijā (1940 –1953. gads): kā varasvīri Latvijā "kulakus" taisīja un kādas sekas tas radīja. Dokumenti un fakti* ["Kulaks" in Latvia (1940–1953): How the Authorities Created "Kulaks" and What Were the Consequences. Documents and Facts]. Latvijas Valsts arhīvs. Rīga: Ievanda, 1997.

Riekstiņš, Jānis. "Lauksaimniecības kolektivizācija un 'kulaku' deportācija Latvijā. 1949. gads" [Collectivization of Agriculture and "Kulak" Deportation from Latvia. The Year 1949]. *LZA Vēstis. A daļa.* 1/2 (2000): 59–69.

Sociālistiskās revolūcijas uzvara Latvijā 1940. gadā. Dokumenti un materiāli [Victory of the Socialist Revolution in Latvia in 1940. Documents and Materials]. LPSR ZA Vēstures institūts ; LPSR CVA. Rīga: LPSR ZA, 1963.

Staris, Alfrēds. "1941. gadā okupantu izsūtīto bērnu ērkšķainais atceļš uz dzimteni" [The Thorny Return to Their Homeland of the Children Deported in 1941 by the Occupants]. *Latvijas Vēsture* 1 (1995): 37–44.

Stradiņš, Arturs. *Ērkšķainās gaitas* [Path of Thorns]. Rēzekne: Latgales Kultūras centra izd., 2001.

Stradiņš, Jānis. "Atmiņai, atskārsmei un cerībai: latvju tautas martirologu apcerot" [To Remember, Be Aware and Hope: Reflections on the Martyrs of the Latvian People/Nation]. *Via Dolorosa: staļinisma upuru liecības* [Via Dolorosa: Testimony of Victims of Stalinism]. Volume 1. Rīga: Liesma, 1990: 8–19.

Strods, Heinrihs. *Latvijas lauksaimniecības vēsture. No vissenākiem laikiem līdz XX gs. 90.g.* [Agricultural History of Latvia. From Prehistoric Times to the 1990s of the 20th Century]. Rīga: Zvaigzne, 1992.

Strods, Heinrihs. "Latvijas cilvēku izvedēji 1949. gada 25. martā" [Deporters of People from Latvia on March 25, 1949]. *Latvijas Vēsture* 1 (1999): 68–73.

Strods, Heinrihs. *Latvijas nacionālo partizāņu karš. 1944–1956* [Latvian National Partisan War. 1944–1956]. Rīga: Preses nams, 1996.

Strods, Heinrihs. "PSRS valsts drošības ministrijas pilnīgi slepenā Baltijas valstu iedzīvotāju izsūtīšanas operācija 'Krasta banga' ('Priboy') (1949. gada 25. februāris–23. augusts)" [USSR State Security Ministry top secret deportation of inhabitants of the Baltic States in the operation 'Coastal Surf'('*Priboy*') (February 25 to August 23, 1949)]. *Latvijas Vēsture* 2 (1998): 39–47.

Strods, Heinrihs. "Vācijas projekti Igaunijas un Latvijas autonomijai 1942.–1944. gadā" [German Plans for Autonomy of Estonia and Latvia during 1942–1944]. *Latvijas Vēstures Institūta Žurnāls* 1 (1992): 102–18.

Strods, Heinrihs. *Zem melnbrūnā zobena: Vācijas politika Latvijā, 1939–1945* [Under the Black-Brown Sword: German Policies in Latvia, 1939–1945]. Rīga: Zvaigzne, 1994.

Šilde, Ādolfs. *Pa deportēto pēdām. Latvieši padomju vergu darbā* [In the Footsteps of the Deportees. Latvians Doing Slave Labour for the Soviets]. New York: Grāmatu Draugs, 1956.

Šilde, Ādolfs. *Pasaules revolūcijas vārdā* [In the Name of World Revolution]. New York: Grāmatu Draugs, 1983.

Unāms, Žanis. *Karogs vējā. Kara laika atmiņas divos sējumos* [A Flag in the Wind. Recollections of the War in Two Volumes]. Waverly, IA.: Latvju grāmata: 1969.

Upīte, Rūta. *Vēl tā gribējās dzīvot. Pārdzīvojumu stāsts* [Dear God, I So Wanted to Live. A Story of Experiences]. New York: Grāmatu Draugs, 1979.

Valters, Miķelis. *Mana sarakste ar Kārli Ulmani un Vilhelmu Munteru Latvijas traģiskajos gados* [My Correspondence with Kārlis Ulmanis and Vilhelms Munters during Latvia's Most Tragic Years]. Stockholm: Jaunā Latvija, 1957.

Vanaga, Melānija. *Dvēseļu pulcēšana* [Gathering of Souls]. Rīga: Karogs, 1999.

Veigners, Ilmārs. *Latvieši ārzemēs* [Latvians Abroad]. Rīga: Latvijas enciklopēdija, 1993.

Via Dolorosa: staļinisma upuru liecības [Via Dolorosa: Testimony of Victims of Stalinism]. Compiled by Anda Līce. Volumes 1–4. Rīga: Liesma; Preses Nams, 1990–1995.

Vidnere, Māra. *Ar asarām tas nav pierādāms...(represēto cilvēku pārdzīvojumu pieredze)* [Tears are not Proof Enough...(Emotional Experiences of People who Suffered Repression)]. Rīga: LU, 1997.

Vīksne, Rudīte. "Represijas pret Latvijas iedzīvotājiem 1940–1941. un 1944–1945. gadā: kopējais un atšķirīgais" [Repressions of the Inhabitants of Latvia 1940–1941 and 1944–1945, Common Factors and Differences]. *Latvija Otrajā pasaules karā / Latvia in World War II.* Latvijas Vēsturnieku komisijas raksti 1 / Symposium of the Commission of the Historians of Latvia 1. Rīga: Latvijas Vēstures institūta apgāds, 2000: 288–94.

Zālīte, Indulis; Dimante, Sindija. "Četrdesmito gadu deportācijas. Struktūranalīze" [Deportations of the 1940s. A Structural Analysis]. *Latvijas Vēsture* 2 (1998): 73–82.

Žvinklis, Arturs. "Latviešu prese nacistiskās Vācijas okupācijas laikā" [Latvian Press During Occupation by Nazi Germany]. *Latvija Otrajā pasaules karā / Latvia in World War II.* Latvijas Vēsturnieku komisijas raksti 1 / Symposium of the Commission of the Historians of Latvia 1. Rīga: Latvijas Vēstures institūta apgāds, 2000: 353–59.

Foreign Language Books and Articles

Applebaum, Anne. *Gulag: A History*. New York: Doubleday, 2003.

Berdinskiy, Viktor. *Vyatlag* [Vyatka Regional Administration of Forced-Labor Camps]. Kirov: Kirovskaya oblastnaya tipografiya, 1998.

Bugai, Nikolai. "40.–50. godi: posledstviya deportatsii narodov" [The 1940s and 1950s: Consequences of the Deportation of People]. *Istoriya SSSR* 1 (1992): 122–43.

Champonnois, Suzanne; Labriole, Francois de. *La Lettonie: de la servitude a la liberté* [Latvia: from Slavery to Freedom]. Paris: Editions Karthala, 1999.

Eksteins, Modris. *Walking Since Daybreak: A Story of Eastern Europe, World War II and the Heart of the Twentieth Century*. Boston: Peter Davison Book, 1999.

Ezergailis, Andrew. *The Latvian Legion. Heroes, Nazis or Victims? A Collection of Documents from OSS War-Crimes Investigations Files 1945–1950*. Rīga: The Historical Institute of Latvia, 1997.

Ezergailis, Andrew. *Nazi/Soviet Disinformation about the Holocaust in Nazi-Occupied Latvia. Daugavas Vanagi: Who Are They? – Revisited.* Rīga: OMF, 2005.

The Hidden and Forbidden History of Latvia under Soviet and Nazi Occupations 1940–1991. Symposium of the Commission of the Historians of Latvia 14. Eds. Valters Nollendorfs and Erwin Oberländer. Rīga: The Historical Institute of Latvia, 2005.

Informatsionnyi spravochnik sprosa i predlozheniya tovarov. 1949 [Informative Directory on the Demand and Supply of Goods. 1949]. *Ministerstvo torgovli Soyuza SSR.*

Lettonie–Russie. Traités et documents de base in extenso [Latvia–Russia. Dissertations and Foundation Documents in Extenso]. Compiled by Ansis Reinhards. Rīga: Collection "Fontes" Bibliothèque Nationale de Lettonie, 1998.

Latvijas Okupācijas Muzejs: Latvija zem Padomju Savienības un nacionālsociālistiskās Vācijas varas 1940–1991 Latvia under the Rule of the Soviet Union and National Socialist Germany: Museum of the Occupation of Latvia. Ed. Valters Nollendorfs (Rīga: OMF, 2002). [Bilingual edition.]

Le livre noir du communisme [The Black Book of Communism]. Stephane Courtois, Nicolas Werth, Jean-Louis Panné. Paris: Robert Laffont, 1997.

Namsons, Andrievs. "Lebensbedingungen und Lebensstandard der Landbevölkerung in Sowjetlettland" [Living Conditions and Standards of the Rural Population in Soviet Latvia]. *Acta Baltica. Liber Annalis Instituti Baltici.* 4 (1964): 65–91.

Naumov, V. "N.S. Khrushchev i reabilitatsiya zhertv massovykh politicheskikh repressii" [N.S. Khrushchev and the Exoneration of Victims of Mass-Scale Political Repression]. *Voprosy Istoriy* 4 (1997): 19–35.

"O kulte lichnosti i yego posledstviyakh": doklad Pervogo sekretarya CK KPSS tov. Khrushcheva N.S. XX syezdu Kommunisticheskoy partii Sovetskogo Soyuza 25 fevralya 1956 goda [On the Cult of Personality and Its Consequences: Report by N.S. Khrushchev, the 1st Secretary of the CPSU Central Committee, at the 20th Congress of the CPSU, 25 February 1956]. *Izvestiya CK KPSS* 3 (1989): 128–70.

Pohl, Otto J. *The Stalinist Penal System. A Statistical History of Soviet Repression and Terror, 1930–1953.* Jefferson, NC; London: McFarland & Co., 1997.

Policy of Occupation Powers in Latvia. 1939–1991: A Collection of Documents. State Archive of Latvia. Ed. Elmārs Pelkaus. Rīga: Nordik, 1999.

Radzinskiy, Eduard. *Stalin.* Moscow: Vagrius Publishers, 1997.

Rossi, Jacques. *Le Manuel du GOULAG* [The GULAG Manual]. Paris: Cherche Midi Editeur, 1997.

Sbornik zakonodatelnykh i normativnykh aktov o repressiyakh i reabilitatsiy zhertv politicheskikh repressii [Collection of Legislative and Normative Acts on Repression and on the Exoneration of Victims of Political Repression]. Moscow, 1993.

Sbornik zakonov SSSR i ukazov Prezidiuma Verkhovnogo Soveta SSSR. 1938–1975 [Collection of Laws of the USSR and Decrees of the Presidium of the Supreme Soviet of the USSR. 1938–1975]. Volume 3. Moscow: Izvestiya Publishers, 1976.

Shifrin, Abram. *The First Guide Book to Prisons and Concentration Camps of the Soviet Union.* [Switzerland]: Stephanus Edition, 1980.

Silabriedis, J., Arklans B. *"Political refugees" Unmasked.* Rīga: Latvian State Publishers, 1965.

Sistema ispravitelno – trudovykh lagerey v SSSR 1923–1960: spravochnik [Guide Book: The System of Forced-Labor Camps in the USSR. 1923–1960]. Memorial, GARF. Moscow: Zvenya Publishers, 1998.

Sovetskoye obshchestvo: vozniknoveniye, razvitiye, istoricheskiy final. T. 2. Apogei i strakh stalinizma [The Origin, Development and Disintegration of Soviet Society. Volume 2. Apogee and the Fear of Stalinism]. Moscow: RGGU, 1997.

Strods, Heinrihs and Matthew Kott, "The File on Operation 'Priboi': A Reassessment of the Mass Deportations of 1949." *Journal of Baltic Studies* 33.1 (2002): 1–31.

Taylor, Telford. *Munich: The Price of Peace.* New York: Vintage Books, 1980.

These Names Accuse. Nominal list of Latvians Deported to Soviet Russia in 1940–41: Second Edition with Supplementary List. Stockholm: LNF, 1982.

Tolstoy, Nikolai. *Victims of Yalta*. London: Corgi Book, 1990.

Upite, Ruta. *Dear God, I Wanted to Live*. Translated from Latvian by R. Liepa. New York: Grāmatu Draugs, 1983.

Vestermanis, Marģers. "Retter im Lande der Handlanger. Zur Geschichte der Hilfe für Juden in Lettland während der 'Endlösung'" [Rescuers in the Land of Accomplices. Historical Notes Concerning Aid for Jews in Latvia during the "Final Solution"]. *Solidarität und Hilfe für Juden während der NS–Zeit*. Berlin: Metropol, 1998.

Volkogonov, Dmitrii. *Triumph i tragediya. Politicheskiy portret J. V. Stalina. Kn. 2 Ch. 2* [Triumph and Tragedy: Political Portrait of J.V. Stalin. Book 2, Part 2]. Moscow: Agentstva pechati novosti, 1989.

We Sang Through Tears: Stories of Survival in Siberia. Rīga: Jānis Roze Publishing House, 1999.

Zezina, Mariya. "Shokovaya terapiya: ot 1953 k 1956 godu" [Shock Therapy: From 1953 to 1956]. *Otechestvennaya Istoriya* 2 (1995): 121–34.

Zhukov, Yurii. "Borba za vlast v partiyno–gosudarstvennykh verkhakh SSSR vesnoy 1953 goda" [The Struggle for Power between the Party and State Leadership of the USSR in the Spring of 1953]. *Voprosy Istoriy* 5/6 (1996): 39–57.

Periodicals

Atpūta. 5 January 1940–20 December 1940; 3 January 1941–20 June 1941.

Cīņa. 26 June 1940–31 December 1940; 1 January 1941–27 June 1941.

Daugavas Vanagi. Latviešu karavīru frontes laikraksts [Latvian soldier newspaper from the front]. 27 March 1942–24 December 1944.

Jaunākās Ziņas. 2 January 1939–30 December 1939; 2 January 1940–9 August 1940.

Latvijas Arhīvi. Pielikums. Represēto saraksti. 1949 [Latvian State Archives. Supplement. Lists of the Repressed. 1949]. 3 (1995). Limbažu apriņķis – Tukuma apriņķis [Limbaži District – Tukums District].

Latvijas Vēsture. 1 (1991); 4 (2000).

Likumu un Valdības rīkojumu krājums. 18 September 1920.

Rīgas Jūrmalas Vēstnesis. 14 May 1938; 31 December 1938; 6 January 1939; 7 October 1939.

The Museum of the Occupation of Latvia

Beržinskis, Voldemārs. "Atmiņas" [Recollections]. OMF, Inv. No. 2514.

Stradiņš, Arturs. "Ērkšķainās gaitas" [Path of Thorns]. OMF, Inv. No. 3009.

Conference Materials

Zālīte, Indulis. "Okupācijas režīmu upuri Latvijā 1940–1991.g." A paper presented at the conference " Latviešu leģions Latvijas vēsturē padomju un vācu okupācijas kontekstā" [Latvian Legion Within the Historic Context of Latvia Under the Soviet and German Occupation] on June 10, 2000 in Rīga.

Family Archive

Aivars Kalnietis. "Tumšie gadi: atmiņas par izsūtījumu. 1990. gada rudens" [The Dark Years: Recollections about Deportation. 1990. Autumn].
Aleksandrs Kalnietis' letters to Milda Kalnietis. 5 May 1950; 27 April 1951.
Arnis Kalnietis' letters to Milda Kalnietis. 9 January 1951; 20 July 1952.
Emilija Dreifelde's letters to Ligita Dreifelde. 5 July 1948; 2 September 1949.
Frīda Dzene's letters to Anna Dumpe. 29 April 1950.
Jānis Dumpe's and Anna Dumpe's letters to Viktors Dreifelds. 7 July 1947; 22 January 1956; 19 October 1959.
Ligita Kalniete's diary. 9 January 1950–8 March 1950.
Ligita Kalniete's letters to Viktors Dreifelds. 1947–1957.
Ligita Kalniete's letters to Voldemārs Dreifelds. 1956–1957.
Matilde Kaimiņa's letters to Milda Kalniete. 10 July 1949–19 July 1952.

Acronyms and Abbreviations Used in the Book

AUCP(B) – All Union Communist Party (Bolsheviks)
ALA – American Latvian Association
ASSR – Autonomous Soviet Socialist Republic
CC – Central Committee
CM – Council of Ministers
CPSU – Communist Party of the Soviet Union
CSHA – Central State History Archives
GULAG – *Glavnoye Upraleniye Lagerei* – Central Camp Administration
KGB – *Komitet Gosudarstvennoi Bezopasnosti SSSR* (USSR State Security Committee)
LA – Latvian Army
LPF – Latvian Popular Front
LSSR – Latvian Soviet Socialist Republic
LVA – *Latvijas Valsts arhīvs* (Latvian State Archive)
MIA – Ministry of Internal Affairs
OMF – Occupation Museum Foundation
PCI – People's Commissariat of the Interior
PCJ – People's Commissariat of Justice
PCSS – Peoples Commissariat of State Security
RFSSR – Russian Federation of Soviet Socialist Republics
SARF – State Archives of the Russian Federation
SC – Supreme Council
SD – *Sicherheitsdienst* (Security Service – German WW2)*
SS – *Schutzstaffel* (Protection Staff – German WW2)*
SSM – State Security Ministry
SSR – Soviet Socialist Republic
USSR – Union of Soviet Socialist Republics
TASS – *Telegrafnoye agentstvo Sovetskovo Soyuza* (Soviet Union Telegraph Agency)
TTT – Tram and Trolleybus Trust
UL – University of Latvia

* SS (German *Schutzstaffel*, Protection Staff) was an organisation of the National Socialist German Workers' Party (NSDAP). It was formed in 1925 to protect Hitler and other high functionaries of the party. From 1929 on it was under the leadership of the SS *Reichsführer* Heinrich Himmler. As the purest embodiment of NSDAP ideals, the SS laid claim to being the Nazi elite. The *Waffen-SS* in a more restricted sense were combat units, which were formed from 1939 on and were subordinated to the leadership of the SS but fought under the army military command. SD (German *Sicherheitsdienst*, Security Service) was NSDAP secret service, which was involved in fighting political enemies and internal party opposition. From 1939 on it worked together with Gestapo (German *Geheime Staatspolizei*, Secret State Police) as part of the Central Office of State Security.

USA – United States of America
VEF – *Valsts elektrotehnikas fabrika* (State Electrotechnical Factory)
ZA – *Zinātņu Akadēmija* (Academy of Sciences)

Pronunciation of Latvian

The Latvian language orthography with few exceptions reflects the phonetic structure. However, not all Latvian sounds have exact equivalents in English. The following table designates approximations as such. The stress in Latvian is always on the first syllable.

a	**u**p, b**u**t (approx.)
ā	f**a**ther, c**a**r
ai	**I**, m**i**ne
au	**ou**t, cl**ou**t (approx.)
b	**b**ut, **b**a**b**y
c	**ts**unami (with t pronounced as in ca**ts**)
č	**ch**oice, **ch**erry
d	**d**oor, **d**og
dž	**J**ohn, **j**u**dg**e
e	b**e**d or m**a**t (both short sounds)
ē	M**a**ry, pr**a**irie (approx.)
ei	**ei**ght, w**ay**
f	**f**ive, bu**ff**
g	**g**o, e**gg**
ģ	Na**di**a (approx.)
h	**h**at, be**h**ave
i	t**i**p, **i**n
ī	**ea**gle, d**ee**d
ie	M**ia** (approx.)
j	**y**ou, **y**east
k	**c**an, la**ck**
ķ	Ka**tj**a (approx.)
l	**l**ike, be**ll** (tongue higher)
ļ	gui**ll**otine (approx.)
m	**m**i**m**e, gu**m**
n	**n**o**n**e, ba**n**
ņ	**n**ews, ca**ny**on (approx.)
o	**O**ct**o**ber (both short and long "o" - in foreign words) **wa**nder, **wa**s (approx. – in Latvian words)
p	**p**et, o**p**en
r	**r**ed, bea**r**ing (approx. – pronounced with tip of the tongue)
s	**s**it, le**ss**
š	**sh**oe, ma**ch**ine
t	**t**wo, be**t**
u	p**u**t, w**oo**d
ū	r**u**le, l**oo**t
v	**v**i**v**id, lo**v**e
z	**z**one, prai**s**e
ž	vi**s**ion, plea**s**ure

Нарым
Камчатка
Пугосвая
Кр.Яр
Коганька
Рыбный
оз.Медведь
Алтаево
Каленан
Пиго
КЕТЬ
Русановка
ПАРАБЕЛЬ
Кедровый Мыс
Южный
Белорыбный
Чевага
Школьный
Высокий Яр
Белка 2-я
ОБЬ
Кандин Бор
Караси
Ласкино
Лапин Бор
Некрасова
8
ПАРАБЕЛЬ
Сухушина
Толмачево
Нельман
М.Бугры
Б.Бугры
Кучи
Б.Нестерово
Польджа
Мумышево
Басмасово
Копыловка
Новосельцево
Смольный
Щукино
Белка
Сочь-Ига
Болотный
Ключи
Кириловка
М.Пашня
Б.Пашня
Чигара
Невальцево
Сагандукова
4
Былина
Покровка
Заречка
Б.Чигас
М.Чигас
Петкуль
Аргун
Голубец
Карза
Ровный
Павловка
6
Березовка
Пасека
Инкино
Мысовая
5
Чигас
Вяловка
оз.Ижет
Карза
Ельцовка
Плотбище 2-е
Плотбище 1-е
Каршан
Сохта
7
Каршан
Шуделька
Красная
оз.Карбинское
Тайжо
Б.Каршан
М.Каршан
оз.Б.Андреевское
оз.Сапыревское
Именевка
2-е Тайжо
Деминский
1-е Тайжо
Андреевка
Яковлевка
Степной
Покосный
Шуделька